ANTHROPOLOGICAL PAPERS

MUSEUM OF ANTHROPOLOGY, UNIVERSITY OF MICHIGAN

No. 10

The Culture and Acculturation Of The Delaware Indians

by

WILLIAM W. NEWCOMB, JR.

ANN ARBOR
UNIVERSITY OF MICHIGAN, 1956

ISBN (print): 978-1-949098-33-4
ISBN (ebook): 978-1-951519-57-5

Browse all of our books at
sites.lsa.umich.edu/archaeology-books.

Order our books from the University of Michigan
Press at www.press.umich.edu.

For permissions, questions, or manuscript queries,
contact Museum publications by email at umma-
pubs@umich.edu or visit the Museum website at
lsa.umich.edu/ummaa.

PREFACE

Any group of people who have been able to preserve even some of the beliefs and customs of their ancestors of three and a half centuries ago in the face of intense, largely continuous pressure to abandon them merits the interest and attention of the social scientist. The Delaware Indians of Oklahoma are such a people — a people who only today are finally relinquishing a cultural tradition old in the time of John Smith and Henry Hudson.

Despite the wealth of documentary material dealing with Delaware culture, no comprehensive description of its early form has been written. Herman has recently reconstructed the early historic culture from documentary sources; her study, however, is not comprehensive.[1] Kinietz has attempted "to assemble and analyze data on the culture. . . from the earliest white contact to the present, with a view to determining what changes have taken place in their culture, when, and why."[2] Unfortunately, this analysis was only partly successful.[3] Several aspects of Delaware culture have received adequate treatment. The religious beliefs and practices, particularly of later times, have been described at length.[4] Delaware language has been described and analyzed,[5] and the Walam Olum or Red Score has been discussed extensively.[6] Apart from Kinietz' preliminary effort, there has been no attempt to describe or analyze Delaware acculturation. Likewise, no consideration has ever been given to the final phases of Delaware acculturation, or assimilation, particularly the part which the Delawares are playing in what has been termed the Pan-Indian society. The aims of this study are, then, to reconstruct the early historic culture of the Delawares, to describe how it changed under the impact of Euro-American civilization, and to explain, at least in broad terms, why the changes took place.

This study was originally prepared under the direction of the Department of Anthropology, University of Michigan, in partial fulfillment of the requirements of the Doctor of Philosophy degree. New data have altered the original dissertation to some extent, although the organization and conclusions remain essentially the same. Two chapters were deleted and included in others, and a map has been added.

During the summer months of 1951 and 1952 an ethnographic study was made of the Delaware Indians in Oklahoma. The cost of this field work was borne in part by funds provided by the Ford Foundation and administered by the Department of Anthropology, University of Michigan. I gratefully acknowledge this assistance. I particularly want to thank

[1] Herman, 1950, pp. 45-77.

[2] Kinietz, 1946, p. 15.

[3] Speck, 1948, pp. 723-24.

[4] Speck, 1931; Harrington, 1921.

[5] C. F. Voegelin, 1946; C. F. and E. W. Voegelin, 1946.

[6] Brinton, 1885; Lilly, 1944, pp. 33-40; E. W. Voegelin, 1940, pp. 28-31; Lilly, *et al.*, 1954. See Griffin, 1955, for a review of the preceding volume; Newcomb, 1955, pp. 57-63.

Dr. Leslie A. White for making this grant possible and for his guidance throughout the study. I also want to express my appreciation for the assistance given by the other members of my doctoral committee, Professors David F. Aberle, Richard K. Beardsley, James B. Griffin, and Volney H. Jones. John Witthoft has also read the manuscript and it has benefited from his many corrections and additions. For any shortcomings or errors which this study may contain I assume full responsibility.

The greater part of the field work was done in Washington County, Oklahoma. I am indebted to many Delawares in this county for valuable information and for their patience and co-operation. I particularly wish to thank Ollie Beaver Anderson, Lenora Dean, Jim Thompson, Reuben Wilson, and Fred Washington. Approximately one month was spent in Anadarko, in southwestern Oklahoma, where Mary Bob was a perceptive and kindly informant. I also wish to thank her granddaughter, Mrs. Charley Caddo, for her excellent interpretation of the Delaware language. Lastly, I wish to thank my wife, Gleny, for her invaluable assistance and constant encouragement both in the field and with the manuscript.

Texas Memorial Museum

CONTENTS

Page

Part I. Early Historic Delaware Culture

I. Delaware Origins and Affiliations 1
Delaware Prehistory: a Summary 1
Traditional Origins 4
The Location and Divisions of the Early Historic Delawares 5
Linguistic Affiliations 9
Population in the Seventeenth Century 10

II. The Reconstruction of Delaware Culture 12
Introduction 12
Delaware Technology 13
Delaware Economics 20
Material Culture 24

III. Delaware Sociology 31
Life Cycle 31
Kin Groups 43
Social Control 51
War 54

IV. Delaware Ideology 59
Religion and Magic 59
Folklore 71

Summary of Delaware Culture 77

Part II. Delaware Culture Change

V. Delaware Acculturation 79
The Contact Period (1524-1690) 80
The Period of Consolidation (1690-1750) 84
Nativistic Period (1750-1814) 87
Decadent Period (1814-1867) 97

VI. Delaware Assimilation 106
Settlement Pattern 106
Technological Assimilation 106
Sociological Assimilation 108
Religious Assimilation 109
Linguistic Assimilation 115
Pan-Indianism 117

Summary and Analysis of Delaware Acculturation 123

Appendix 129

Literature Cited 132

ILLUSTRATIONS IN THE TEXT

Page

FIGURES

1. Delaware kinship terminology, consanguineal. 45
2. Delaware kinship terminology, affinal. 46
3. Modern Delaware kinship terminology 47
4. The relationship between language and age among the Cherokee-Delawares 116

MAP

1. The Delawaran peoples, early seventeenth century 6

PART I. EARLY HISTORIC DELAWARE CULTURE

I. DELAWARE ORIGINS AND AFFILIATIONS

At the opening of the seventeenth century all of the Atlantic coastal peoples north of North Carolina and extending to the Maritime Provinces and the St. Lawrence were culturally similar to one another. Kroeber, however, distinguished two cultural provinces within the Algonkian area, a North Atlantic Slope and a Middle Atlantic Slope.[1] On the basis of an analysis of cultural traits Flannery divided this coastal area into three divisions, or subareas: Northern New England, Central, and Virginia-Maryland.[2] Kroeber's Middle Atlantic Slope is roughly equivalent to Flannery's Central area. The aborigines who were to become known as Delawares in the eighteenth century inhabited this Central or Middle Atlantic Slope area. They did not comprise, as the name Delaware implies, a single social, political, or linguistic entity. They did, however, inhabit a continuous area extending from Delaware Bay on the south, through Manhattan Island, and up the west side of the Hudson River to the Catskills on the north. Inland, they occupied the banks of the Delaware River and its tributaries northeast to the Hudson. This territory included part of the present state of Delaware, all of New Jersey, eastern Pennsylvania, and part of southern New York (Map 1).

The Delawaran peoples were centrally located within the Middle Atlantic Slope area. To the north were the Mahican, on the east bank of the Hudson lived the Wappinger division of the Mahican, and on Long Island were the Montauk, another Mahican group. To the south, in Maryland and part of Delaware, lived the Conoy, Nanticoke, Choptank, and associated peoples.[3] The other peoples of this area are little known apart from the notes in Captain John Smith's memoirs.[4] All of these peoples were similar to one another in culture and language, and remnants from most, if not all, of these tribes in later times became incorporated with the Delaware tribe. To the west, in eastern Pennsylvania, lived the Conestoga (or Susquehannock), an Iroquoian people.[5] To the northwest and north, in what is now New York State, were their Iroquoian relatives, the Five and later Six Nations.

Delaware Prehistory: a Summary

It is a difficult task to identify archaeological sites in the Middle Atlantic Slope area with historic tribes. This difficulty stems from two factors. First, soon after contact the coastal peoples emigrated, were dispersed, or died, with the result that it is impossible to find many coastal sites which contain contact materials. Second, since much

[1]Kroeber, 1947, p. 93.

[2]Flannery, 1939, p. 192.

[3]Kroeber, 1947, Map 1*a*, p. 93; Weslager, 1943, pp. 42-43.

[4]Smith, 1884, pp. 55, 351.

[5]Kroeber, 1947, Map 1*a*, p. 93.

of the area has been heavily urbanized, many sites have been destroyed.[6] Despite these difficulties the early historic Delawaran peoples have been partly identified with archaeological complexes of the area. The East River Aspect is a case in point. Smith said:

> The East River aspect represents the culture of the Algonkian-speaking peoples who inhabited the area in historic times. Specifically, the Wappinger, western Metoac, and some groups of Delaware appear to have carried the culture designated as the East River aspect.[7]

This Aspect takes in the area around the mouth of the Hudson River including western Long Island. At present it encompasses four foci: Massapeag, Clasons Point, Rosenkrans Ferry, and Bowmans Brook.[8] Smith, estimating that this culture made its appearance about A.D. 1000, said:

> Its advent represents a cultural discontinuity, for the underlying culture is the Clearview focus, an early stage in the development of Windsor. The different character of the artifacts in the East River culture and the survival of the Windsor culture elsewhere militate against attributing the change to diffusion. It seems to represent an invasion by new groups of people with a different cultural tradition.[9]

The East River Aspect apparently came into the area from New Jersey. Witthoft has said that the East River ceramic tradition developed from the poorly known ceramic style found on Abbott's Farm at Trenton, New Jersey. The upper levels of the Overpeck and Diehl sites, both located near Easton, Pennsylvania, and dug by MacNeish and Witthoft, also are connected with the early historic natives of the area.[10] The Overpeck ceramic series was also derived from Abbott's Farm, specifically from a ceramic type which Witthoft has termed Abbott Zoned pottery.[11]

The East River Aspect should probably be enlarged to include the Red Valley Focus of New Jersey. Cross used this term in preference to the "Early" Focus which was previously used by Ritchie for the Coastal Aspect.[12] Cross used Red Valley because ". . . in light of the homogeneity of the New Jersey culture, the temporal implications of 'Early' and 'Late' as applied to foci do not seem justifiable."[13] Sites in northern New Jersey are "more closely affiliated with the Rosenkrans Ferry or 'Late' Focus."[14] The conjectures which have derived the New York foci of the East River Aspect from New Jersey by migration, and by implication from the Red Valley Focus, would seem to indicate a closer affiliation with Delawaran peoples than was given by Smith. In short, about A.D. 1000 people who were probably Delawares extended their range to coastal New York.

Smith stated that the East River Aspect "may be connected with the

---

[6]Ritchie, 1938, p. 94.
[7]Smith, 1950, p. 116.
[8]*Ibid.*, p. 116.
[9]*Ibid.*, p. 108.
[10]MacNeish, 1952, p. 52.
[11]Personal communication from John Witthoft; Cross, 1953.
[12]Cross, 1941, p. 210; Ritchie, 1938, pp. 103-6.
[13]Cross, 1941, p. 211.
[14]*Ibid.*

Northeastern phase"[15] of the Woodland pattern. The pottery "suggests" Owasco and Iroquois "in many of its traits."[16] Although the East River Aspect is intrusive at the mouth of the Hudson and cannot be derived from the Clearview Focus of the Windsor Aspect, it evidently is closely related to, and possibly derived from, the Owasco Aspect of the Northeastern Phase.[17] The suggestion made by Smith received support from Ritchie's thesis that the Castle Creek Focus (probably the latest stage of Owasco) is partly Delaware "on the grounds of territorial overlapping"[18] The masklike faces which are frequent on Castle Creek pipe bowls and the "conventionalized human effigies" which are present on one Castle Creek pot also are said to suggest the magico-religious mask cult of the historic Delawares.[19]

Another group of Delawares, the Munsi, has been definitely associated with an archaeological complex. The principal village of the peoples who were to become the historic Munsi was on Minisink Island. Heye and Pepper excavated this site, and in 1947 Ritchie conducted further excavations.[20] Ritchie summed up this work by saying:

> Basically, then, the Munsee culture as it first appeared on the Bell-Philhower Site, is identifiable with . . . the Castle Creek Focus of the Owasco Aspect, and there can be little doubt that it represents an importation from upriver in New York state. In its New Jersey milieu it underwent progressive changes as the result of acculturation through contacts with neighboring groups, chief of which was probably the Unami with whom the Munsee confederated and for whom they served as a buffer stage against the Iroquois.[21]

The historic Delaware culture may then be derived from "Late Prehistoric period"[22] cultures of the New York-New Jersey area. These cultures were in turn partial outgrowths of earlier cultures of the Intermediate period. Agriculture and shellfish collection, at least along the coast, were important during this interval. Pottery was common, bone and antler artifacts were present, and there was a preoccupation with burial in some places.[23] According to Ritchie, the Intermediate period in New York "represents successive diffusions over several centuries from the Great Lakes area, mainly Ohio, via the Alleghany Valley and south shore of Lake Erie. . . ."[24] The Archaic period, which underlies the Intermediate, is said to have lasted to about 1000 B.C. and was characterized as a wild food economy, including shellfish collection. Chipped stone projectile points were more abundant than in the subsequent period, but bone and antler artifacts were rare or absent. Ceramics, horticulture, and smoking pipes were also absent.[25]

The course of Delaware prehistory, then, was not that of a pure, internally developing system. Ritchie has expressed this point of view, stating that a knowledge of this area "recognizes the probability of

[15]Smith, 1950, p. 108.
[16]*Ibid.*, p. 117.
[17]Ritchie, 1944, p. 5, Pl. 1.
[18]*Ibid.*, p. 56.
[19]*Ibid.*, p. 57.
[20]Heye and Pepper, 1915; Ritchie, 1949; Philhower, 1953.
[21]Ritchie, 1949, p. 195.
[22]Ritchie, 1944, p. 7, Pl. 2.
[23]Smith, 1950, p. 106; Ritchie, 1944, p. 324.
[24]Ritchie, 1944, p. 324.
[25]Smith, 1950, p. 106; Ritchie, 1944, p. 321; Ritchie, 1951; Smith, 1955.

infusions of new complexes, probably in many cases associated with population movements which have acted to alter decidedly the tones and values of the cultural picture."[26] This does not mean, however, that there were extensive migrations into the area in recent times; the peoples of Delaware culture, on the contrary, had deep roots in the immediate vicinity. Migrations and the diffusion of cultural traits were important, but were not on the scale suggested by the Walam Olum or the oral traditions.

Traditional Origins

Some investigators, on the basis of the Walam Olum or other Delaware traditions, have suggested that the Delawares were recent immigrants from other areas.[27] The archaeological and the linguistic evidence does not seem to warrant, however, the postulation of any extensive recent eastward or southward migration of Delawaran peoples. It appears that the traditional western origin cited by many investigators is based upon the accounts found in Heckewelder and Zeisberger.[28] To summarize these accounts, the Delawares hundreds of years ago lived on the western side of the Mississippi and for unknown reasons they slowly migrated east. The "Mengwe" (Iroquois) also took part in this eastward migration and united with the Delawares to fight the "Talligewi" or "Alligewi," who held the land east of the river. The invaders ultimately triumphed, but after living for some time in the east these two allies fell out and warred upon each other. The Iroquoian tribes, on the losing side in these battles, were forced to confederate during the fifteenth and sixteenth centuries. A military stalemate followed until European contact was established, when the Dutch aided the Iroquois in making "women" of the Delawares.

The migration legend found in the Walam Olum (pictographic bark record of the Delawares) is similar to the one obtained by Zeisberger and Heckewelder. I have suggested elsewhere that the migration account of the Walam Olum was derived from the traditional legends, but that it was altered to suit the political circumstances of nineteenth-century Delaware life.[29] According to Brinton's translation of the Walam Olum, the origin of the Delawares was in the far northeast, "probably at Labrador." This legend recounts:

> [They] journeyed south and west, till they reached a broad water, full of islands and abounding in fish, perhaps the St. Lawrence about the Thousand Isles. They crossed and dwelt for some generations in the pine and hemlock regions of New York, fighting more or less with the Snake people, and the Talega, agricultural nations, living in stationary villages to the southeast of them, in the area of Ohio and Indiana. They drove out the former, but the latter remained on the upper Ohio and its branches. The Lenape, now settled on the streams in Indiana, wished to remove to the East to join the Mohegans and other

[26]Ritchie, 1944, p. 320.

[27]Kroeber, 1947, p. 93; Lilly, 1944, pp. 33-40; Lilly, *et al.*, 1954, pp. 273-85.

[28]Heckewelder, 1881, pp. 47-70; Zeisberger, 1871, pp. 32-36.

[29]Newcomb, 1955, pp. 57-63.

of their kin who had moved there directly from northern New York. They, therefore, united with the Hurons (Talamatans) to drive out the Talega (Tsalaki, Cherokees) from the upper Ohio. This they only succeeded in accomplishing finally in the historic period. But they did clear the road and reached the Delaware valley, though neither forgetting nor giving up their claims to their western territories.[30]

It is not my purpose to go into the authenticity of the Walam Olum or the accuracy of its migration account. Suffice it to say that the Walam Olum was probably a product of the Delawares during their phase of revivalistic nativism and that it seems "to be an account, by a despairing person unable to gain his customary satisfactions from a life that no longer existed, of a Golden Age which never was. . . . Indeed the Walam Olum plainly appears to be the mirror image of a nativistically oriented people, rather than an authentic account of their history."[31]

The Location and Divisions of the Early Historic Delawares

It is impossible, for the following reasons, to know precisely the name, location, and affiliations of all the peoples who at the end of the seventeenth century joined forces and became known as the Delawares. First, the Delawaran peoples were aboriginally and during most of the seventeenth century unorganized politically and composed of a large number of subdivisions. Second, three different European nations were in contact with Delawaran peoples during this century. Their names for various groups often differed, and their interest in the relationships and locations of the various divisions was often slight. Third, these natives were soon displaced geographically and much reduced in numbers. Lastly, an unknown number of non-Delawaran peoples were incorporated into the Delaware tribe at the end of the seventeenth century. I have not undertaken the prodigious task of locating the Delawaran peoples by investigating all of the primary sources, although such a study is sorely needed; instead, a synthesis of previous investigations and two seventeenth-century maps is presented. This discussion is, therefore, liable to inaccuracies of various kinds.

For convenience the Delawares at the opening of historic times may be described as being composed of three geographical groups, traditionally called the Munsi, Unami, and Unalachtigo. The people who were to become the core of the tribe composed the division which became known in the mid-eighteenth century as the Unami. According to Brinton, the term Unami means "people down the river."[33] Zeisberger used the term

[30]Brinton, 1885, pp. 165-66.

[31]Newcomb, 1955, p. 63.

[32]The following discussion and Map 1 are based on Ruttenber, 1872, pp. 89-93; Hrdlicka, 1902, pp. 33-37; Skinner, 1909, pp. 30-32; Bolton, 1920, pp. 226-86; Swanton, 1952, pp. 48-55; Van der Donck's map of New Netherland, 1656, opposite p. 294 in Jameson, 1909; and N. J. Visscher's Map of New Netherland, New England... about 1655, opposite p. 170 in Myers, 1912.

[33]Brinton, 1885, p. 36.

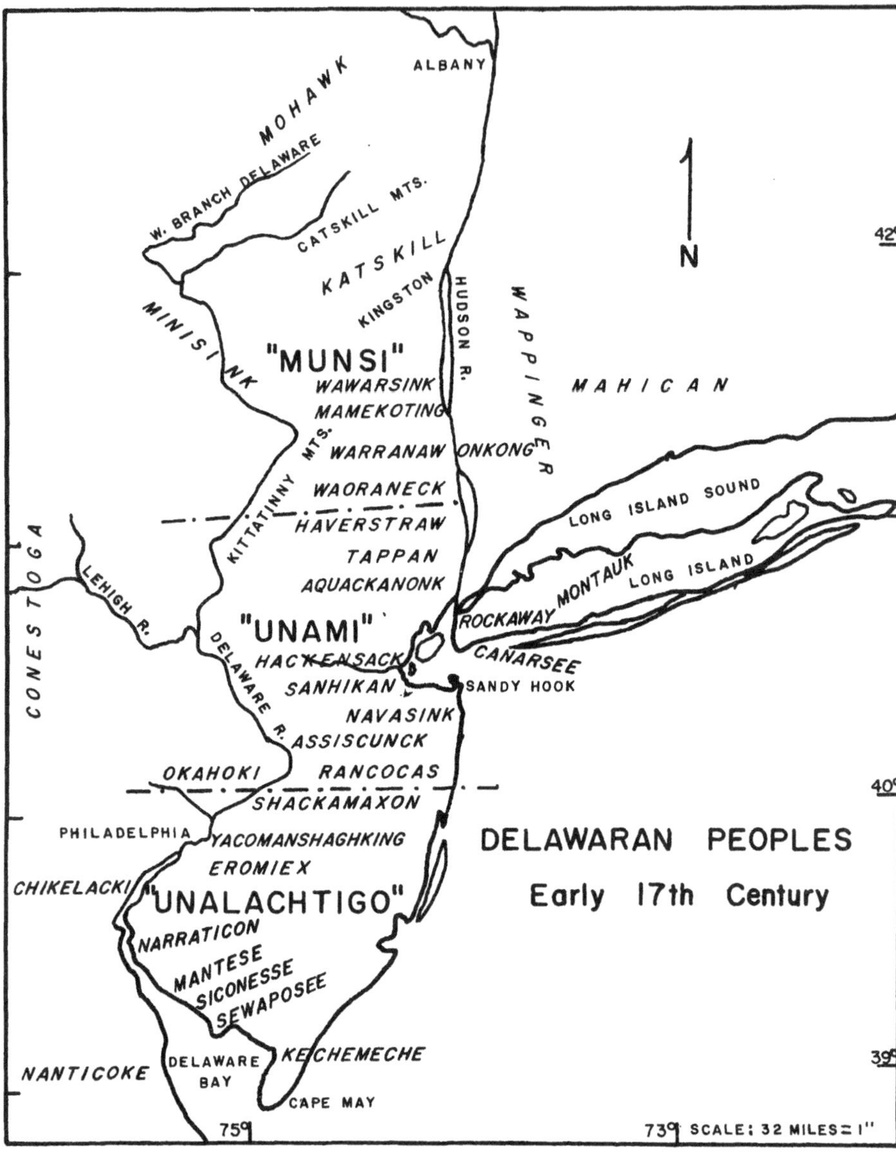
DELAWARAN PEOPLES
Early 17th Century
ALBANY
MOHAWK
W. BRANCH DELAWARE
CATSKILL MTS.
KATSKILL
KINGSTON
HUDSON R.
WAPPINGER
MAHICAN
MINISINK
"MUNSI"
WAWARSINK
MAMEKOTING
WARRANAW
ONKONG
WAORANECK
KITTATINNY MTS.
HAVERSTRAW
TAPPAN
AQUACKANONK
LONG ISLAND SOUND
LONG ISLAND
MONTAUK
ROCKAWAY
CANARSEE
CONESTOGA
LEHIGH R.
"UNAMI"
DELAWARE R.
HACKENSACK
SANHIKAN
SANDY HOOK
NAVASINK
ASSISCUNCK
OKAHOKI
RANCOCAS
SHACKAMAXON
PHILADELPHIA
YACOMANSHAGHKING
EROMIEX
CHIKELACKI
"UNALACHTIGO"
NARRATICON
MANTESE
SICONESSE
SEWAPOSEE
KECHEMECHE
NANTICOKE
DELAWARE BAY
CAPE MAY
N
42°
40°
39°
75°
73°
SCALE: 32 MILES = 1"

Map 1

to refer to that group of Delawares who "lived nearest to the sea."[34] The term seems to be of Munsi origin and was applied by them to the main body. The name first appeared in 1757 and was in use until the final removal to Oklahoma, but it is not remembered today.[35] The Unami occupied the middle reaches of the Delaware River including much of the Schuylkill River Valley. Besides territory in what is now Pennsylvania, they occupied a large part of New Jersey, as well as some territory on the lower Hudson.[36] The Unami were composed of the following subdivisions. The Navisink (or Neversinck, Navasink) "inhabited the Highlands south of Sandy Hook," the Sanhikan (also called Raritan) "were divided, it is said, in two sachemdoms and about twenty chieftaincies."[37] They occupied the Raritan Valley in northeast-central New Jersey, and probably the southern end of Staten Island. The third division was known as the Hackinsack (or Hackensack), and their territory included the valleys of the Hackinsack and Passaic rivers in northeastern New Jersey. The fourth division was the Aquackanonk; their territory included what is now Paterson, New Jersey, and they were "also described as occupying a considerable portion of the centre of New Jersey."[38] The fifth division, the Tappan (or Tapant), extended from the Hackinsack River to the highlands. They also seem to have had some land on the Hudson.[39] Wassenaer in 1624 associated a group called the Mechkentowoon with the Tappan; they may have been a separate group or a subdivision of the Tappan.[40] Swanton has termed them a Mahican subdivision.[41] The sixth division of the Unami was known as the Haverstraw; they lived north of the Tappan with undefined western boundaries and with Stony Point as their northern limit, according to Ruttenber. The Assiscunck and the Rancocas lived in the vicinity of Burlington, New Jersey, and Rancocas Creek to the south. Skinner gave the Okahoki as another division dwelling opposite the Rancocas on the west side of the Delaware. He also said that the Shackamaxon lived near and to the north of Philadelphia. These last two subdivisions Swanton assigned to the Unalachtigo. Some authorities list a number of other subdivisions in central New Jersey; these include Assunpink, Axion, Calcefar, Gashwechnagechga, Meletecunk, Mosilian, and Pompton. They may or may not have been independent Unami subdivisions. There is no assurance that the Unami groups were equal to one another in size or importance; they seem to have shared a common culture, but they were not unified politically.

On western Long Island two Montauk subdivisions, the Canarsee and the Rockaway, had close ties with the Unami and in part merged with the Delaware tribe in later times.[42] It is perhaps significant to recall that the East River Aspect also includes western Long Island. The Sanhikan, Hackensack, and Canarsee jointly occupied Staten Island, a

[34] Zeisberger, 1910, p. 114.

[35] Speck, 1931, p. 14; Hunter, 1951, p. 2; Hayes, 1954, p. 65.

[36] Mooney, 1911, p. 330.

[37] Ruttenber, 1872, p. 89.

[38] *Ibid.*, p. 91.

[39] Bolton, 1920, p. 281.

[40] Wassenaer, 1909, p. 67.

[41] Swanton, 1952, p. 41.

[42] Bolton, 1920, p. 271.

fact which is probably indicative of their close cultural affiliations. On the southern end of Manhattan Island were a people known as the Reckgawawanc. Bolton said they had close relationships with the Tappan, and in 1669 "they were driven away to a refuge among the Tappan by the warparties of the Mohawk."[43] To the north of the Reckgawawanc was a group known as the Weckquaesgeek, a Wappinger subdivision. They also seem to have been closely related to the peoples on the west side of the Hudson.

The second traditional division of the Delawares is known as the Munsi (or Munsee, Monsey, Minsi, Monthey, Minisink). This word means "people of the stony country" or perhaps "mountaineers."[44] The label is apt, for the Munsi inhabited the more mountainous area along the headwaters and tributaries of the Delaware River. The Munsi were a distinct group culturally and until the last century were often considered a separate tribe. Cherokee-Delawares are still able to point out members of this group, and the Munsi have persisted as a distinct group in Canada. The term Munsi does not appear in the literature until the eighteenth century, and Wallace contends that they were a coalescence of peoples around the Minisink community.[45]

The Waoraneck, who originally lived on the Hudson in Orange County, near Stony Point, were one of the peoples who probably became Munsi. They seem to have been one of the five or six "tribes" of the Esopus country. The Warranawonkong formed the second division, and their territory "embraced the waters of the Shawangunk, the Wallkill and the Esopus rivers."[46] The Mamekoting, the third division of the Munsi, lived in the Makating Valley. "Their history is so intimately blended with that of the Esopus Indians that identification is impossible further than by title."[47] The little-known Wawarsink were the fourth group of Esopus Indians. The Katskill, another group, lived north of the Saugerties and formed the eastern watershed of the Catskill Mountains.[48] The principal group of Munsi, inhabiting the headwaters of the Delaware River, was termed the Minisink.

The third and southernmost group of Delawares is not well known, since they seem to have merged with the Unami at an early date. Their name is usually given as Unalachtigo[49] (sometimes Unalachto) and signifies "people who live near the ocean."[50] Speck has suggested that they were really Naraticon of southern New Jersey "under the guise of a dialectic name."[51] Brinton, on the other hand, felt that they might be Nanticoke (Unechtigo).[52] Wallace said that since the term is found only "in the pages of Zeisberger, Heckewelder, and their copyists" there was no group so named.[53] He proposed, however, that the word Unalachtigo might refer "to any Indians — Delawares or otherwise — who lived in southern New Jersey along the shore."[54] Philhower said that the

[43] Bolton, 1920, p. 244.
[44] Brinton, 1885, p. 36.
[45] Wallace, 1949, p. 11.
[46] Ruttenber, 1872, p. 93.
[47] *Ibid.*, p. 95.
[48] *Ibid.*
[49] Harrington, 1913, p. 208.
[50] Brinton, 1885, p. 36.
[51] Speck, 1931, p. 15.
[52] Brinton, 1885, p. 36.
[53] Wallace, 1949, p. 12.
[54] *Ibid.*

Unalachtigo and Nanticoke were closely related in culture and had a common origin.[55] For convenience the term Unalachtigo is used for the natives of southern New Jersey who in later times became part of the Delaware tribe.

The southern tip of Cape May was inhabited by a people known as the Kechemeche, and in the same area Swanton located a group he termed the Tirans.[56] In the valleys of the rivers and creeks emptying into Delaware Bay were many small groups of Delawares. On Maurice Creek were the Sewaposee (or Sewapois), and above them on Cohansey Creek the Siconesse (or Sikonesses). The Mantese (or Manta, Mante) inhabited the vicinity of Salem Creek, and north of them on Raccoon Creek were the Narraticon (or Naraticon). A group termed Asomoche has also been mentioned for this vicinity. To the north of the Narraticon in New Jersey, in the neighborhood of Pensaukin Creek, were found the Eromiex (or Ermonex, Eriwonec, Eriwoneck, Armewaxes). Near Camden was a group called the Yacomanshaghking, and extending up the east bank of the Delaware River to Burlington were several poorly known bands. Opposite the Narraticon in the vicinity of Wilmington, Delaware, were the Chikelacki (Chikohoki?), as well as the Amimenipaty, Hopokohacking, Memankitonna, and Passayank.

In sum, the people who were to comprise the Delaware tribe of the eighteenth century were drawn from a large number of small, dispersed, and essentially autonomous groups. At the dawn of historic times they were not a tribe in the political sense, and since they differed somewhat from one another in other aspects of culture, it is perhaps unwise to think of them as a tribe. It was not until these groups had become consolidated in the early decades of the eighteenth century that the term Delaware is properly applicable to them. The English name Delaware was given to these people because they were concentrated near the Delaware River in the late seventeenth and early eighteenth centuries. Modern Delawares sometimes say that the term is derived from a Delaware expression meaning "I said" or "I meant." There is a phonetic similarity between this Delaware expression and the English name, but it is probably a rationalization.[57] The Delawares' term for themselves is "Lenape" which means "people."[58] They also occasionally refer to themselves as the "lenni lenape" which means the "real" or the "original people,"[59] or something similar to "we, the people."[60]

Linguistic Affiliations

The term Delaware has been used to refer to a language of the Central type of Eastern-Central Algonkin.[61] Eastern-Central Algonkin

[55]Philhower, 1931, p. 4. Weslager, 1950, pp. 48-54, 57-58, presents strong evidence against this identification, however.

[56]Swanton, 1952, p. 50.

[57]Zeisberger, 1910, p. 114, agrees on this point.

[58]Brinton, 1885, p. 34.

[59]Wallace, 1949, p. 7.

[60]Wissler, 1941, pp. 70-71.

[61]Michelson, 1912, pp. 221-90; Bloomfield, 1946, p. 85.

includes, among others, Mahican, Wappinger, and Pequot. Delawaran peoples spoke at least two mutually intelligible dialects termed Munsi and Lenape.[62] There are indications, however, that Munsi was more like Mahican than Lenape. Zeisberger said:

> The Unami and the Wunalachtico (Unalachtigo)... languages differ very little. That of the Monsys... is very different from these, so that had they not dwelt nearer together and been in constant contact in recent times they would hardly understand each other. Yet the speech of each of these peoples is but a dialect of one and the same language. The language of the Mahikanders (Mahican) bears much resemblance to that of the Monsys.[63]

Zeisberger and Heckewelder[64] have also pointed out that the Nanticoke language was very similar to Delaware. Unfortunately, both Mahican and Nanticoke are extinct languages and cannot be examined by modern linguistic techniques. Suffice it to say that there was considerable dialectic diversity among the people who became the historic Delawares. Michelson has ventured the opinion that Delaware "as Zeisberger has presented it is not a single dialect but a composite," and Trowbridge concurred in this conclusion.[65] In sum, the linguistic evidence suggests a lack of unity among the people who became the Delawares, which reinforces my conclusion that at the dawn of historic times Delawaran peoples were not a cohesive or homogeneous cultural unit.

Population in the Seventeenth Century

Ignorance of the composition and location of all the subdivisions which were to make up the Delaware tribe, and lack of information concerning introduced diseases, which at an early date may have decimated their ranks, are enough to make population estimates of the early seventeenth-century Delawaran peoples hazardous. Mooney in 1911 estimated the Delawares and Munsis as numbering "close to 12,000 souls" in 1600, but he reduced this figure to 8,000 by 1928.[66] Kroeber has followed Mooney in using the latter figure.[67]

The number of Delawaran peoples, whatever it may have been in 1600, was greatly reduced in the first century of contact with Europeans. In the literature of the seventeenth century the many allusions to this depopulation are unanimous in attributing it to disease, war, and demoralization. Alcoholism was a factor, but it was a greater contributor to depopulation in later times, although by the end of the seventeenth century the Delawares were described as loving drunkenness.[68] In the early part of the century the Munsis and Unamis suffered heavily in the Esopus wars with the Dutch,[69] and the Susquehannocks inflicted heavy casualties on the Unamis and Unalachtigos. In 1633, for example, the

[62]C. F. and E. W. Voegelin, 1946, pp. 188-89; C. F. Voegelin, 1946, pp. 130-57.

[63]Zeisberger, 1910, pp. 141-42.

[64]Heckewelder, 1881, p. 122; Zeisberger, 1910, p. 141.

[65]Michelson, 1912, p. 280; Trowbridge MS.

[66]Mooney, 1911, p. 333; 1928, p. 4.

[67]Kroeber, 1947, Table 7, p. 140.

[68]Pastorius, 1912, p. 433.

[69]Mooney, 1928, pp. 3-4.

Susquehannock burned a Delaware town and killed "ninety men" as well as women and children.[70] Lindestrom in 1654 mentioned that both the Delawares and the Swedes were suffering from illness and that the natives were blaming the Swedes for sickness and death.[71] Mooney said:

> As early as 1677 the Delawares accused the whites of having brought the smallpox among them, and in a council at Burlington, New Jersey, their speaker stated that it had already ravaged the tribe three times — in his grandfather's time, in his father's time, and in his own time. One of these visitations was probably that of 1637-1638, which swept all the region from the Chesapeake Bay to Lake Huron. Another was probably the same noted as ravaging the Conestoga in 1661-1663.[72]

Pastorius in a letter written in 1694 said:

> A great many of these savages have died, even since I came here, so that there are hardly more than a fourth part of the number now existing that were to be seen when I came to the country ten years ago.[73]

Denton as early as 1670 was able to say of the results of Indian contact with Europeans:

> . . . it is to be admired how strangely they [i.e., Indians] have decreast by the Hand of God since the English first settling of these parts; for since my time, when there were six towns, they are reduced to two small villages, & it has been generally observed that where the English come to settle, a Divine Hand makes way for them, by removing or cutting off the *Indians*, either by wars one with the other, or by some raging mortal disease.[74]

Kalm seems to have summed it up accurately when he remarked in the eighteenth century:

> . . . as the Europeans proceeded to cultivate the land, the Indians sold their land, and went further into the country. But in reality few of the Indians really left the country in this manner; most of them ended their days before, either by wars among themselves, or by the small-pox . . . it has killed incredible numbers of them . . . . But brandy is said to have killed most of the Indians.[75]

These scattered statements leave no room to doubt that the population decline of the Delawares in the seventeenth century was tremendous. There are two important factors to keep in mind concerning the early population and the subsequent depopulation. First, even if the estimates of the population in 1600 are grossly low, the population density in pre-Columbian times was surprisingly low considering the nature of the habitat and the capacity of the natives' technological system. The reasons for the low population density are discussed later. Second, the depopulation during the seventeenth century was a contributory factor in the ultimate appearance of the Delaware tribe. The emergence of the tribe is treated more fully under Acculturation.

---

[70]De Vries, 1857, p. 30.
[71]Lindestrom, 1925, pp. 127-28.
[72]Mooney, 1911, p. 333.
[73]Pastorius, 1912, p. 426.
[74]Denton, 1845, p. 6.
[75]Kalm, 1937, I: 258-59.

II. THE RECONSTRUCTION OF DELAWARE CULTURE

Introduction

The most recent reconstruction of early historic Delaware culture by Herman[1] failed to use the data made available by Kinietz[2] from the Trowbridge and Cass papers and minimized contemporary ethnographic data. Herman largely ignored modern ethnographic information because it "had combined material gained from different periods of time."[3] Kinietz used the previously unavailable Trowbridge and Cass data, but took little advantage of the other sources. His work also omitted a discussion of religion and some aspects of social organization. This study has utilized most of the source material of both of these investigators, as well as their results, and has in addition used other documentary materials. I have also used modern ethnographic data more extensively than have others. By using proper controls the ethnography of the Delawares can be made to cast valuable light on some of the less well-illuminated aspects of the early historic culture. The presence of a culture trait, whose existence could not be traced to white culture, to other Indian cultures, or to some sort of synthesis of these, was assumed to be of Delaware origin. It should be noted that some traits found in the field were considered Delaware on the basis of their absence among other groups; documentary materials later confirmed a Delaware provenance for many of these traits. Evidence from the field indicated, for example, that the Delawares possessed the trait of making a hole at the head of a coffin through which the soul could find its exit. Exit and reentrance were eased by the application of red ocher to this aperture. No evidence could be found which would indicate that this trait had been borrowed from other Indian cultures, nor was it derived from white culture, except that wooden coffins were used in place of bark receptacles. Later research substantiated the conclusion that this trait was of Delaware origin. In brief, by using a cautious and judicious approach it is possible to project ethnographic data back to early historic times with a fair degree of probability. Wherever this approach has been utilized, it is so noted in the text. I have also made a more serious effort to reconstruct the kinship terminology and general kinship structure of the early historic Delawares than has been attempted previously. This reconstruction is based mainly upon the recent suggestions of Murdock.[4]

The authorities for the data are given in chronological order, the seventeenth-century sources are given first, then the eighteenth-century, and so on down to the data recorded by myself in the field. When data secured from informants is used, the initials of the informant appear in the text or in a footnote with other references.[5] A discussion of the documentary sources is given in the Appendix.

---

[1] Herman, 1950, pp. 45-77.
[2] Kinietz, 1946.
[3] Herman, *op. cit.*, p. 48.
[4] Murdock, 1949, pp. 184-259, 323-52.
[5] Initials of informants are: O. A., Ollie Beaver Anderson; M. B., Mary Bob; N. D., Lenora Dean; J. T., Jim Thompson; F. W., Fred Washington; R. W., Reuben Wilson; L. F., Lillian Frenchman.

Delaware Technology

Subsistence

At the beginning of historic times all of the Middle Atlantic Slope cultures subsisted by means of hoe-gardening, fishing, and hunting. The relative importance of each of these subsistence methods has long been disputed for the area as a whole. Kroeber has maintained that agriculture was not basic to life in the Eastern Area, that "there is little to argue that the culture was leaning very fundamentally on agriculture."[6] He is almost certainly in error in minimizing agriculture and in the reasons he gives for its unimportance, at least so far as the Delawares were concerned. Among the more inland groups agriculture definitely was of paramount importance. In 1654 Lindestrom described a group on the Schuylkill who had ". . . . their dwellings side by side one another, wherefore this land is thereby being cleared and cultivated with great power."[7] Juet before 1610 described a group in the neighborhood of Sandy Hook as having a "great store of Maiz,"[8] and De Vries, De Laet, and William Penn all said that the principal food was maize.[9] Krieger in 1663, in an expedition against some New Jersey Delawares, cut down two hundred and fifteen acres of maize and burned over one hundred pits of corn and beans.[10] Wallace recently contended that agriculture was basic in the economy and added that the high status of women was a function of their basically important agricultural activities.[11] Hunting, gathering, and fishing were also important activities, and seasonally they may well have rivaled agricultural activity.

Gardening.—The principal crop plant was corn or maize (*Zea mays*), raised by the women.[12] They had several varieties ". . . .white, red, blue, flesh-colored, brown, yellow and spotted ears."[13] Holm in the early decades of the seventeenth century said the Delawares grew ". . . black maize of the colour of tar. . ."[14] Harrington in his field work among the Oklahoma Delawares noted six varieties that had been handed down from the early days and were still grown. There were "three soft and three hard" varieties.[15] The Delawares today remember or possess a white-flour corn used principally in bread;[16] red corn, a flint variety; Osage corn, a soft variety; blue corn; and Deer corn, a striped variety (J.T.). There is no assurance that these varieties have not been borrowed by the Delawares in recent times. The cultivated fields seem to have been rather small in extent. Kalm stated that an Indian's garden took up no more ground "than a farmer in our country takes to plant cabbage for his family. At least, a farmer's cabbage and turnip ground,

[6]Kroeber, 1947, p. 148.

[7]Lindestrom, 1925, p. 170.

[8]Juet, 1909, p. 18.

[9]De Vries, 1909, p. 218; De Laet, 1909, p. 57; Penn, 1912, p. 232.

[10]O'Callaghan, 1851, IV: 39.

[11]Wallace, 1947, pp. 9-10.

[12]De Laet, 1909, p. 49; Denton, 1845, p. 6; Van der Donck, 1909, p. 302; Thomas, 1912, p. 341; Penn, 1912, p. 232.

[13]Lindestrom, 1925, p. 179; see also De Rasieres, 1909, p. 107; Kalm, 1937, I: 74.

[14]Holm, 1834, p. 49.

[15]Harrington, 1913, p. 221.

[16]Lindestrom, 1925, p. 180, said bread was baked from white and yellow corn.

taken together, is always as extensive, if not more so, than all the corn fields and kitchen gardens of an Indian family."[17] Luckenbach, a Moravian missionary of the early nineteenth century, said that the fields were "limited to two or three acres of corn for each family."[18] The Delawares today term the gardens "squaw patches" and claim that they never exceeded five acres in size (M.B., O.A.).

Most Delaware archaeological sites are in creek or valley bottoms;[19] in the eighteenth century such bottom land was chosen for gardens, since it was easily worked and was generally fertile.[20] Zeisberger, in the eighteenth century, took pains to point out that land away from rivers, although suitable for tillage by Europeans, was not utilized at all for this purpose by Indians.[21] Garden plots were cleared by bruising or removing the bark of the trees, then burning the trees after they were dry.[22] The seventeenth-century Swedish writers stated that garden plots were moved after the soil was exhausted.[23] Van der Donck in the middle of the century and Loskiel in the next century denied the use of fertilizer.[24] New England Indians, however, fertilized the land with fish, and Wallace has suggested that this trait may have been present among the Delawares.[25]

Corn was planted in ". . . square hills (so far apart) that one can conveniently walk between the hills. . . . And in each hill 6 or 7 grains are set."[26] According to De Rasieres:

> They make heaps like molehills, each about two and a half feet from the others, which they sow or plant in April with maize, in each heap five or six grains; in the middle of May, when the maize is the height of a finger or more, they plant in each heap three or four Turkish beans . . . . It [corn] is a grain to which much labor must be given, with weeding and earthing-up, or it does not thrive; and to this the women must attend very closely.[27]

Squash, pumpkins, several varieties of beans, and tobacco were also grown.[28] According to M.B. tobacco was grown only by women past the menopause. The Delawares blended their tobacco with sumac, one third sumac to two thirds tobacco.[29]

Hunting.—Hunting was important to the Delaware economy, not only because it provided food, but also because pelts and hides provided most of the material for clothing. The main objects of the hunt were deer and bear, but virtually all of the other mammals of their habitat were hunted and utilized for clothing or for food. This list included fox, raccoon, skunk, porcupine, opossum, and squirrel.[30] The Delawares

[17]Kalm, 1937, I: 307.

[18]Luckenbach, 1938, pp. 598-99.

[19]Personal communication from John Witthoft.

[20]Zeisberger, 1910, p. 44.

[21]*Ibid.*, p. 36.

[22]Johnson, 1917, p. 279; Kalm, 1937, I: 230; Harrington, 1913, p. 221.

[23]Johnson, 1917, p. 279.

[24]Loskiel, 1794, p. 66.

[25]Flannery, 1939, p. 10; Wallace, 1947, p. 18.

[26]Lindestrom, 1925, p. 179.

[27]De Rasieres, 1909, p. 107; Johnson, 1917, p. 279; and Harrington, 1913, p. 221, contain similar accounts of their horticulture.

[28]Juet, 1909, p. 21; Johnson, 1917, p. 279; Kalm, 1937, I: 74; Lindestrom, 1925, pp. 180-81; Holm, 1834, p. 122.

[29]Speck, 1943, p. 324.

[30]Denton, 1845, p. 7; Van der Donck, 1909, p. 303; Zeisberger, 1910, pp. 37, 62-63.

traded to the Europeans and presumably they themselves utilized "otters, lynxes, fishes, minks, wild-cats, elk-hides. . .wolf skins, lion-hides, martins, and musk rat."[31] Neither the elk nor the bison formed an important part in Delaware subsistence in the eighteenth century, because their hides were "thick and heavy and of no value."[32] Neither animal was abundant in their habitat. Various birds formed a welcome addition to the diet and included "wild swans" (geese?), wild turkeys, wild pigeons, and partridges.[33] One seventeenth-century source described a method of pigeon hunting; trees which were favorite roosts for these birds were chopped nearly through, so that when a flock of pigeons settled down in the tree it would topple, killing a number of the birds.[34]

Individual hunting seems to have been confined primarily to the winter months; communal hunts, however, took place in the spring, summer, and fall.[35] One method of collective hunting, the "fire surround," was described by Lindestrom:

> When now the sachem wants to arrange his hunt, then he commands his people (to take a position) close together in a circle of 1/2, 1 or 2 miles, according to the number of people at his command... each one roots up the grass about 3 or 4 ells, so that the fire will not be able to run back, each one then beginning to set fire to the grass, which is mightily ignited, so that the fire travels away, in towards the center of the circle, which the Indians follow with great noise, and all the animals which are found within the circle, flee from the fire and the cries of the Indians.... When now the Indians have surrounded the center with a small circle, so that they mutually cannot do each other any harm, then they break loose with guns and bows on the animals.[36]

De Vries described a "surround" in which the game was driven into an enclosure and shot with a bow and arrow, and also a variant type in which the game was driven into a river and lassoed.[37] An informant told Kinietz that "four hunters were as many as ever hunted together," but this is contrary to what informants told me and surely did not hold true in early times.[38] Communal hunts were led by "the oldest or most expert, particularly if he be a member of the council."[39] Zeisberger related that there was a strictly formalized hunting etiquette:

> It is not considered good form for one to leave the party before the end of the hunt. If one has wounded a deer and another followed and killed it, the skin belongs to the first and either the half or the whole of the meat to the latter. If several take aim at once and they cannot determine which of them made the best shot, the skin is given to the oldest of the party, or, if he happened to be one of those taking aim, he is said to have killed the animal. Old men, therefore, no longer able to shoot well, generally get their share of the skins, if they only aim now and then with the others though they do not hit the mark.

---

[31] Lindestrom, 1925, p. 223.

[32] Zeisberger, 1910, p. 59; Loskiel, p. 79.

[33] Zeisberger, 1910, pp. 65-66.

[34] Lindestrom, 1925, p. 216.

[35] *Ibid.*, p. 213; De Vries, 1909, p. 220; Zeisberger, 1910, pp. 58, 91, 126; Loskiel, 1794, p. 79.

[36] Lindestrom, 1925, pp. 213-14.

[37] De Vries, 1909, p. 220; Brinton, 1890, p. 184.

[38] Kinietz, 1946, p. 64; J. T., M. B.

[39] Zeisberger, 1910, p. 91; Kinietz, 1946, p. 64.

Such old men, accompanying a hunting party, get both meat and skins, for the good hunters will not let them return empty-handed. They have, in general, and the Unami in particular, the custom that when a huntsman has shot a deer, and another Indian joins him or only looks on at a distance, he immediately gives him the whole animal and goes in pursuit of another.[40]

The blowgun was in use among the Munsi by 1824, but was apparently present earlier; it was never of any great economic importance.[41] "Calls" were made to attract deer and turkeys. The deer call or "bleat" was made of cedar and was used primarily during the spring and early summer before the fawns had been weaned.[42] Harrington mentioned that "the deadfall and the 'twitchup' snare seem to have been the most popular varieties of traps."[43] The Delawares were also reported to be excellent stalkers of game and pursued wounded animals until their prey dropped from exhaustion.[44] If a hunter could not at first get within range of a deer he would chase it until he could, this procedure perhaps consuming an entire day.[45] One eighteenth-century author mentioned that deer were hunted by torchlight at night.[46]

Fishing.—Van der Donck said that Delawaran peoples "use all kinds of fish, which they commonly cook without removing the entrails, and snakes, frogs and the like."[47] Specifically, they caught and ate rock fish, shad, yellow perch, trout, eels, catfish, sunfish, sturgeon, and undoubtedly others, from both fresh and salt water. In 1756 two harbor seals were shot and eaten, but this was an unusual incident.[48] Tortoises were caught, and shellfish in large quantities must have been taken, if Skinner was correct in attributing shell mounds of the area to the Delawares.[49] Juet stated that the natives brought out quantities of oysters to trade to the crew of Hudson's Half Moon.[50]

Methods of fishing varied somewhat; Lindestrom described a method in which a stream was dammed when the water was high, so that fish were stranded behind the dam when the water was low. The fish were caught with bare hands or shot with the bow and arrow.[51] De Rasieres said that the Indians around Manhattan caught fish with "a drag-net they themselves knit very neatly, of the wild hemp, from which the women and men spin the thread."[52] Brinton mentioned fishhooks of bone and dried claws of birds, and Pastorius reported the use of hooks.[53] Harrington mentioned several methods of fishing. These may not be aboriginal since they do not appear elsewhere. He stated that fish were stupefied by large quantities of crushed green walnuts thrown into ponds. He also noted spearing and shooting of fish at night by torchlight.[54] Fish

[40]Zeisberger, 1910, p. 91.

[41]Harrington, 1913, p. 221; Kinietz, 1946, p. 63; Ketchum, 1865, II: 190 (1796).

[42]Foreman, 1937, p. 107; J. T., F. W.

[43]Harrington, 1913, p. 222.

[44]Zeisberger, 1910, p. 23.

[45]*Ibid.*, p. 23.

[46]Brickell, 1842, p. 47.

[47]Van der Donck, 1909, p. 303.

[48]Holm, 1834, p. 48; De Rasieres, 1909, p. 105; Zeisberger, 1910, p. 37.

[49]Holm, 1834, p. 48; Denton, 1845, p. 7; Skinner, 1909, pp. 5-17, 45-46; J. T.

[50]Juet, 1909, p. 20.

[51]Lindestrom, 1925, p. 219; Berlin, 1887, pp. 167-69.

[52]De Rasieres, 1909, p. 105.

[53]Brinton, 1885, p. 52; Pastorius, 1912, p. 434.

[54]Harrington, 1913, p. 222.

were sometimes impounded by driving them with a brush roll, a technique widespread in the Southeast and among the Iroquois.[55]

Wild plant food.—The beans of the groundnut or wild bean, (*Apios americana*), were eaten, and its roots were boiled and eaten "instead of bread."[56] Kalm also said the Indians boiled, or roasted in ashes, a root which he called Katniss, apparently *Sagittaria latifolia* (Wapato, Water Nut, Swamp Potato). The roots of "Tawho," probably *Arisaema triphyllum* or jack-in-the-pulpit, were utilized "when bread and grain gave out."[57] They were placed in a pit, covered with earth, and baked by building a fire over the pit.[58] The dried and boiled seeds of the golden club (*Orontium aquaticum*) were eaten.[59]

From the eighteenth century on wild potatoes (*Ipomoea pandurata*) were frequently mentioned in the documents. They were baked into bread and were especially used in time of famine.[60] One informant (O.A.) also said that the wild potato, if boiled and mashed, was particularly useful as food for young children. Ginseng was gathered in the Ohio Valley during the eighteenth century and seems to have been sold to traders.[61] Other wild roots and tubers, utilized at least in later times, were wild onions, wild cabbage, "greens" (otherwise unidentified by O.A., M.B.), and water lily roots.[62] Zeisberger wrote of a time when his Christian Indians "industriously brought roots here from down the creek, of which they got many loads to town, which they cut thin, dry in the sun, pound and bake bread from, and this is now their principal food."[63] The Delawares utilized many varieties of wild fruits, including wild grapes, strawberries, gooseberries, blackberries, raspberries, wild plums, huckleberries, and cranberries.[64] The "Indians," probably including Delawares, ate the fruit of the May apple (*Podophyllum peltatum*).[65] They also made use of many nuts, chief among them being hickory (Skinner found them in archaeological deposits), hazelnut, and chestnut.[66] In Oklahoma the post-oak acorn (*Quercus stellata*) was eaten with hominy (J.T., O.A.).

The most important wild plant food of the eighteenth century was the sap of the sugar maple. Sugaring was not just an occasional pastime, for even in a bad year an individual made as much as one hundred pounds.[67] If a man owned several kettles, it was possible in good years to make several hundred pounds of sugar and some syrup.[68] This trait, however, was not mentioned by any of the seventeenth-century sources and was undoubtedly of less importance in pre-European times. As

[55]Zeisberger, 1776, p. 36; Fenton, 1942.

[56]Kalm, 1937, I: 259; De Vries, 1909, p. 219.

[57]Lindestrom, 1925, pp. 158-59.

[58]Kalm, 1937, I: 261; Zeisberger, 1887, p. 161, calls the Jack Maksaweek, "it causes purging," however.

[59]Kalm, 1937, I: 261.

[60]Zeisberger, 1910, p. 47; M. B., O. A.

[61]Zeisberger, 1885, II: 47.

[62]*Ibid.*, p. 109.

[63]*Ibid.*, pp. 109-10.

[64]Juet, 1909, p. 18; Kalm, 1937, I: 261; Zeisberger, 1910, p. 46; Heckewelder, 1881, p. 266; Loskiel, 1794, pp. 68-69; Skinner, 1909, p. 43; O. A., M. B., J. T.

[65]Zeisberger, 1910, p. 47.

[66]De Vries, 1909, p. 219; Brinton, 1890, p. 185; Skinner, 1909, p. 46.

[67]Zeisberger, 1885, II: 349.

[68]Zeisberger, 1910, pp. 50-51.

soon as European utensils became available (early in the seventeenth century), maple sugar rapidly became a more important food. Honey was considered a delicacy when it could be obtained, but it was not an early food source since honey bees were not indigenous to the Delaware habitat.[69]

Preparation of food.— Dried and green corn was prepared in a wide variety of ways. Most corn seems to have been dried, ground, and baked. Typically, "they make flat cakes of the meal mixed with water, as large again as a farthing cake in this country, and bake them in the ashes, first wrapping a vine-leaf or maize-leaf around them. When they are sufficiently baked in the ashes, they make good palatable bread."[70] William Penn said: "Their diet is Maze, or Indian Corn, divers ways prepared; sometimes Roasted in the Ashes, sometimes beaten and Boyled with Water, which they call *Homine*; they also make cakes, not unpleasant to eat."[71] Dried corn was placed in a wooden mortar made from a fire-hollowed log and ground with a wooden or stone pestle.[72] The meal was sifted through "a small basket, which they understand how to weave. . . ."[73] Harrington also mentioned the sifting of flour, saying that it was sifted "through sieve baskets of varying degrees of fineness."[74] The finest meal was used in the above-mentioned bread, and the coarser corn meal was used in porridge, or gruel.[75] The white-flour corn was usually utilized in the bread, but other varieties were used in hominy and gruel (M.B., O.A., J.T.). Berries were often added to the bread, and meat, berries, beans, nuts, and pumpkins were sometimes added to the gruel.[76] In later times "dumplings" were made by frying corn meal dough in grease, usually with added berries (O.A.). Hominy was prepared by boiling dried corn with ashes, which removed the husk. The hominy was washed repeatedly in a stream after it was cooked.[77]

"Those stalks [of corn] which are low and bear no ears, they pluck up in August, and suck out the sap, which is as sweet as if it were sugar-cane."[78] Green ears were roasted whole in ashes, grated and baked in the ashes, or boiled. The roots of water lily plants were peeled, cut into small chunks, and boiled (O.A.). Wild potatoes were prepared by boiling, skinning, and then mashing and were eaten with various kinds of "greens." The Delawares that live in the rural areas still gather and eat wild potatoes. An account of the preparation of maple sugar gives an ample description of this eighteenth-century trait:

> A number of small troughs are made for receiving the sap. Usually, the Indians make them of wood, cutting them out roughly with a hatchet. Some Indians are able to make twenty or thirty of them in a day. Some do not go to so

[69] Zeisberger, 1885, I: 310.

[70] De Vries, 1909, pp. 218-19; also see Pastorius, 1912, p. 426; Van der Donck, 1909, p. 303.

[71] Penn, 1912, p. 232.

[72] De Rasieres, 1909, p. 107; Lindestrom, 1925, p. 253.

[73] De Rasieres, 1909, p. 107; De Vries, 1909, p. 218.

[74] Harrington, 1913, p. 221.

[75] Luckenbach, 1938, p. 599.

[76] Lindestrom, 1925, p. 254; Luckenbach, 1938, p. 599.

[77] Penn, 1912, p. 232; O. A., M. B.

[78] De Rasieres, 1909, p. 107.

much trouble, but make dishes of the bark or bast of a tree, which serve quite as well.... Besides the smaller troughs and dishes, there must be several of larger size in which the sap is collected.... The sap, which is of a brownish color and becomes darker the longer it boils, is boiled until it gets to be of the consistency of molasses, is then poured off and kept. When a sufficient quantity of this consistency has been secured, it is boiled over a slow fire until it becomes sugar.... As the Indians lack the dishes and do not care to take the time to prepare it in this way, they usually form it into cakes, put it in a kettle or dish, or in default of these, on a stone and let it cool, when it becomes hard and may be easily preserved in baskets.[79]

Preservation of food. — Corn, beans, and other agricultural produce were stored in mat-lined pits.[80] De Rasieres said that the dried grain was placed in "baskets woven of rushes or wild hemp" and then buried.[81] The grain was buried after the harvest or stored in the house for use after the return from the winter hunt.[82] Pit storage seems to have disappeared after the seventeenth century, at least there is no mention of it in the later documents. Modern information casts more specific light on methods of food preservation, which are probably similar to those of early historic times. Informants (O.A., M.B., J.T.) claimed that virtually every type of food was preserved by drying; ears of corn were braided in strings and stored in a specially made crude shelter or in the house. Green corn was boiled, cut off the cob, dried, and stored away. Corn was not ordinarily ground until ready for use, but sometimes dry corn was grated, the meal cooked in ovens, then crumbled and further dried in the sun, and stored. Pumpkins were sliced in rings as thick as a finger, sticks were run through these rings, and they were then dried in the sun. After drying they were stored away in sacks for winter use. Beans were boiled for a few minutes and then dried. Fruits and berries were sun dried, the smaller berries being mashed before drying.

Meat was preserved by jerking, that is, the flesh was cut into thin strips and dried. Venison, which formed the bulk of jerked meat, was dried by placing it over poles in the hot sun or over a fire. When ready to eat, the jerked meat was boiled with corn or vegetables or was simply pounded and eaten raw. Bear lard was preserved by rendering the lard and pouring it into the stomach or intestine of a bear. This lard was used in cooking, as was the oil from hickory nuts. The latter was produced by roasting the nuts, pounding the kernels to a fine consistency, boiling them in water, then skimming off the oil which came to the surface.[83]

Holm was the only one who mentioned a type of ration for journeys in the seventeenth century. He said: ". . .they take with them a kind of bread, made of Indian corn and tobacco juice, which is very good to allay hunger and quench thirst...."[84] Zeisberger mentioned a ration for

[79] Zeisberger, 1910, pp. 48-50.

[80] De Vries, 1909, pp. 219-20; Lindestrom, 1925, p. 253; Jemison, 1918, p. 52.

[81] De Rasieres, 1909, p. 108.

[82] Johnson, 1917, p. 279; Harrington, 1913, p. 218.

[83] Zeisberger, 1910, p. 46.

[84] Holm, 1834, p. 121.

journeys in which corn was crushed into a meal, "or roasted in hot ashes, then crushed." To this maple sugar was added. This mixture could be stirred in water and boiled or could be eaten dry without cooking.[85] Adams, a Delaware and historian of his people, added that "they carried very simple food," parched corn pounded into a brown meal, sweetened with maple sugar, and mixed together with bear's lard.[86]

Water was the principal drink although various fruits and nuts were sometimes added. They "prepared a kind of liquor like milk by gathering a great number of hickory and black walnuts, dried and crushed them. Then they took out the kernels, pounded them as fine as flour, and mixed this with water so that it looked like milk and was almost as sweet."[87] Both Kinietz' and my informants (O.A., M.B.) held that their ancestors had regular meal times. Penn said that "they eat twice a day, Morning and Evening."[88] Men and women apparently ate together but children ate separately (O.A.). All of my informants stressed the fact that in the past an individual could eat anywhere in the village, and that everybody shared what food was available.

Food taboos. — It is unlikely that there were any general, culture-wide food taboos in early historic times. Certain foods may have been denied to an individual by his guardian spirit, but this is merely a supposition. Not even the animals symbolic of the phratries were taboo. Heckewelder, however, noted a taboo on the rabbit, identified with a culture-hero. He said that the Delawares, among other tribes, avoided the horse, dog, wildcat, ground hog, panther, fox, muskrat, and wolf;[89] De Laet, however, quoting Henry Hudson, described a "fat dog" which was butchered for a feast.[90] Rather than emphasize the few things that were not eaten by the Delawares, it would be more in keeping with the facts to state that the Delawares made relatively complete use of the edibles available to them, except rabbit and ground hog. Their tastes were catholic and were only slightly blunted by socioreligious proscriptions.

Delaware Economics

Although the methods by which and the persons by whom the need-serving goods were processed, distributed, and consumed are properly an aspect of social organization, it probably contributes more to an understanding of Delaware technology to discuss them under the heading of economics.

Division of Labor

The division of labor among the Delawares, as is true of cultures with analogous means of production, was predominantly sexual in

[85] Zeisberger, 1910, p. 22.
[86] Adams, 1905, p. 8.
[87] Kalm, 1937, I: 269.
[88] Penn, 1912, p. 233; Luckenbach, 1938, p. 599, agreed on this point.
[89] Heckewelder, 1881, pp. 251-52, 196; Zeisberger, 1910, pp. 132, 140.
[90] De Laet, 1909, p. 49.

character. Hunting was the primary occupation of men and gardening that of women. Although game did not form a preponderant part of the diet, it was extremely important in that wild animals provided clothing and other nonedible essentials.[91] The game which a man brought home was the property of his wife to do with as she saw fit; conversely, the woman's harvest of corn was "considered as belonging to the husband, who, if he has suffering friends, may give them as much of it as he pleases. . . ."[92] Men also built the dwellings, obtained or made the necessary axes, hoes, canoes, dishes, bowls, and other artifacts.[93] They were also supposed to keep in a constant state of readiness in case of attack, and they appear to have helped clear the land for gardens.[94] The women, in addition to planting, cultivating, harvesting, and storing the garden produce, bore the burden of all the household tasks. They cut and carried the firewood and made the carrying straps and bags, as well as the family clothing, and tanned the skins.[95] The women also carried the household goods when a family was on the trail.[96] De Vries said: ". . .the women are compelled to work like asses, and when they travel, to carry the baggage on their backs, together with their infants. . . ."[97] Mary Jemison said, however:

> Our labor was not severe; and that of one year was exactly similar, in almost every respect, to that of all others, without that endless variety [of white people]. Notwithstanding the Indian women have all the fuel and bread to procure, and the cooking to perform, their task is probably not harder than that of white women . . . .[98]

It should also be added that many of the tasks of the women were accomplished by a co-operative group of relatives, who lightened their labors with feasts and gaiety; the men, on the other hand, were frequently alone when hunting.[99] There were a few individuals who were part-time specialists; these were the wampum makers, other artisans, shamans, and sachems. All of these individuals took part in the basic subsistence activities of their sex.

Annual Round

Important to the understanding of the subsistence activities and the general economy of the Delawares is a discussion of the subsistence cycle or annual round. A. F. C. Wallace has recently investigated this phase of their culture and his conclusions correspond closely to mine, though based on slightly different evidence.[100] In the spring and summer

[91]Pastorius, 1912, p. 385; Van der Donck, 1909, p. 302; Heckewelder, 1881, pp. 155-57.

[92]Heckewelder, 1881, p. 158; Zeisberger, 1910, p. 16, agrees on this point.

[93]Van der Donck, 1909, p. 302; Heckewelder, 1881, pp. 155-57.

[94]Denton, 1845, p. 6; O. A., M. B.

[95]Van der Donck, 1909, p. 302; Brickell, 1842, p. 47; Zeisberger, 1910, p. 16; M. B.

[96]Heckewelder, 1881, p. 156; Zeisberger, 1910, p. 24.

[97]De Vries, 1909, p. 218.

[98]Jemison, 1918, pp. 46-47; Heckewelder, 1881, p. 156, echoed this point of view.

[99]Heckewelder, 1881, p. 156; M. B., J. T., O. A.

[100]Wallace, 1947, pp. 16-18.

the Indians congregated in their small villages, gardening and, if near the sea or a river, fishing. After they had planted the gardens they regularly visited the Europeans.[101] Following the harvest, and at least in later times after the socioreligious ceremonies climaxed by the Big House Ceremony, the villages were deserted as individual families scattered to their hunting territories. The first fall hunt was for deer and seems to have been communal, perhaps prior to the dispersal to individual hunting grounds. After the deer hunt bears and other game were sought by individual hunters.[102] The men hunted until February or March, depending upon the season. In later times the individual families then went to their sugaring grounds; there the women collected and boiled down the maple sap while the men continued to hunt.[103] In spring they again moved to their villages and planted their crops. Wallace has pointed out, however, that there were some exceptions to the hunting-gardening cycle;[104] different sorts of adjustment by different groups were necessary in the relatively diverse habitat of the Delawares.

Property Concept and Hunting Territories

The concept of private ownership of personal equipment, tools, and the like was well developed among the Delawares. Heckewelder, who had a good grasp of this subject, said:

> There is nothing in an Indian's house or family without its particular owner. Every individual knows what belongs to him, from the horse or cow down to the dog, cat, kitten and little chicken. Parents make presents to their children, and they in return to their parents. A father will sometimes ask his wife or one of his children for the loan of his horse to go out a hunting. For a litter of kittens or brood of chickens, there are often as many different owners as there are individual animals. In purchasing a hen with her brood, one frequently has to deal for it with several children. Thus, while the principle of community of goods prevails in the state, the rights of property are acknowledged among the members of a family. This is attended with a very good effect; for by this means every living creature is properly taken care of. It also promotes liberality among the children, which becomes a habit with them by the time they are grown up.[105]

Although most of Heckewelder's examples were items introduced by Europeans, there seems to be no reason why this sort of property concept was not an early one. This type of ownership is akin to our own concept of property; the "ownership" of other kinds of property was quite distinct from our own.

W. C. MacLeod,[106] utilizing Speck's[107] investigation, has presented a well-documented case for the family ownership of hunting grounds. The purpose of his paper was obviously to support the contentions of

[101]Denton, 1845, p. 7; Holm, 1834, p. 123; De Rasieres, 1909, pp. 107-8.

[102]De Vries, 1909, p. 222; Zeisberger, 1910, pp. 12-13; Loskiel, 1794, p. 78.

[103]Zeisberger, 1910, p. 13.

[104]Wallace, 1947, p. 17.

[105]Heckewelder, 1881, pp. 158-59.

[106]MacLeod, 1922, pp. 448-63.

[107]Speck, 1915, pp. 289-305.

R. H. Lowie[108] and others who at this time (*ca.* 1920) were attempting to demonstrate that private ownership was the rule and not the exception in primitive society. I do not deny that the Delawares shared in the Eastern Algonkian trait of family-held hunting grounds. I do deny, however, that the early historic concept of land ownership was analogous to the European one. Wallace, who has made the most penetrating study of early Delaware land tenure, summed up their concept by saying:

> To the Delaware Indian, land was an element, a medium of existence, like the air and the sunlight and the rivers. To him, "ownership" of land meant, not exclusive personal title to the soil itself, but occupation of a certain position of responsibility in the social unit which exploited the soil. The "sale" of land (to use the white man's term) might, to the Delaware, be almost any mutually satisfactory change in the relationship of two groups of persons subsisting on the land. In the earliest sales, the Indians seem to have intended only to give the whites freedom to use the land in conjunction with the native population.[109]

MacLeod in a footnote tacitly agreed with this point of view, saying: "The selling of land of course was a notion foreign, so far as we know, to native ideas or practice."[110]

There are no seventeenth-century sources which, to my knowledge, described directly and in straightforward fashion the hunting territories. On the basis of the records of early land transactions, however, both MacLeod and Wallace have reconstructed the system which must have existed. The smallest unit of land was a named "hunting territory covering up to two hundred square miles of land."[111] Their boundaries were often vague, and territories overlapped, although natural landmarks were used as boundaries. "Such territories are often associated in European documents with the names of individual Indians, who are called 'owners.'"[112] Most of these territories were, however, sold by groups of Indians. In short, the so-called "owners" were simply representatives of the social units who used this land.[113] It also appears that disposition of these territories did not rest solely in the hands of these individuals, but was the privilege of the community.[114] Wallace has demonstrated that a number of individual hunting territories made up a larger unit which he terms "communal territories" of "up to 1500 square miles."[115]

Inheritance of hunting territory right is but vaguely understood. MacLeod has suggested that the inheritance of hunting territory was through the paternal line, since it was used primarily by males. If this was true it would suggest either that matrilineal reckoning of kinship was a historic accretion to Delaware culture, or that the two systems existed side by side.[116] Wallace has concluded, as have I, that the maternal lineage was the social unit that "owned" or perhaps more aptly

---

[108]Lowie, 1920, pp. 210 ff.

[109]Wallace, 1947, p. 2; Heckewelder, 1881, p. 102, agreed with this concept of land possession.

[110]MacLeod, 1922, p. 463.

[111]Wallace, 1947, p. 3.

[112]*Ibid.*, p. 3; MacLeod, 1922, p. 463.

[113]Wallace, 1947, p. 4.

[114]*Ibid.*, p. 5.

[115]*Ibid.*, p. 6.

[116]MacLeod, 1922, p. 452.

"belonged to" the "individual" hunting territory.[117] The lineage, clan, and phratry are discussed in the next chapter. There is nothing incompatible in the existence of maternal lineages (or clans) and male-used hunting territories.

Material Culture

Villages.—There is little information concerning the villages and general settlement pattern of the early historic Delawares. Villages, or perhaps they might better be termed hamlets, were situated in bottom lands near the gardens or along the shores of bays.[118] These dispersed settlements were not palisaded.[119] Eighteenth-century and later information seems to reflect the original condition in that these settlements had no regular plan or arrangement, and that houses were not built close together.[120] There is no information concerning the length of time these villages were inhabited. If their garden plots were fertilized, residence in the villages may have been relatively permanent, but the fertilizer issue is in doubt. By the eighteenth century, after extensive migrations, villages were occupied until it became "troublesome to secure wood for fuel" and, implicitly, until they became overburdened with filth.[121] The Evelin paper of 1648 described twenty-three communities in New Jersey, ranging in population from fourteen to six hundred persons.[122] Lindestrom noted community size as "several hundred men strong, under each chief, counting women and children, some being stronger, some weaker."[123]

Dwellings.—There seems to have been some diversity in the type of dwellings of the early seventeenth-century Delawares. A circular wigwam and a long house identical with the Iroquoian type have been described, although the latter seems to represent a late prehistoric diffusion. De Laet and Van der Donck depicted Delawares using a circular bark dwelling with vaulted ceiling.[124] In another place De Laet stated that the dwelling was oven-shaped, but large enough for several related families.[125] Penn and Pastorius also alluded to this style of dwelling, whereas Holm and Lindestrom mentioned what seems to be the Iroquoian long house.[126] Zeisberger in the eighteenth century distinguished between house types of the Iroquois and the Delawares, describing a "rounded, arched roof" for the Iroqouis and a "high-pitched, peaked roof" for the Delawares.[127] Harrington in 1913 characterized the house type current a few years previously as being similar to the Iroquois type.[128] The evidence, then, is not conclusive, but it seems probable

[117] Wallace, 1947, p. 18.
[118] Zeisberger, 1910, p. 87; Wallace, 1947, p. 18.
[119] Lindestrom, 1925, p. 241.
[120] Zeisberger, 1910, p. 87; O. A., J. T.
[121] Zeisberger, 1910, p. 87.
[122] Smith, 1877, p. 11.
[123] Lindestrom, 1925, p. 170.
[124] De Laet, 1909, p. 57; Van der Donck, 1909, p. 302.
[125] De Laet, 1909, p. 57.
[126] Penn, 1912, p. 232; Pastorius, 1912, p. 425; Holm, 1834, p. 123; Lindestrom, 1925, p. 211.
[127] Zeisberger, 1910, pp. 17-18.
[128] Harrington, 1913, pp. 217-18.

that the Delaware groups nearest to the Iroquois had been influenced by them. The Munsi were nearest to the Iroquois, and Harrington's informants were predominantly of this group. The various house styles, on the other hand, are possibly related to the seasonal movements of the Delawares, who, like the central Algonkians, may have utilized the rectangular, bark-covered long house in summer and the dome-shaped lodge in winter.[129]

The dome-shaped lodges were simple structures built by placing pieces of bark, preferably of linden or elm, over a sapling framework. The bark was stripped from the trees in summer in as large sheets as possible and dried. It then provided a watertight house.[130] House furnishings were rather meager. "They. . .make very fine, strong and artistic mats of finely painted spruce roots and strong straw, with all kinds of figures, to decorate and cover the walls with, and to place below their bed clothes."[131] Rush mats were painted and fastened to the walls in winter to keep out the cold. Some houses had "portraits and pictures somewhat rudely carved."[132] By the eighteenth century platforms made of poles, which encircled the walls and served as tables, benches, and beds, were mentioned.[133] The platform was covered by an untanned skin of bear or deer, or else with a mat.

Near each village was one or more sweat houses:

> When they wish to cleanse themselves of their foulness, they go in the autumn, when it begins to grow cold, and make, away off, near a running brook, a small oven, large enough for three or four men to lie in it. In making it they first take twigs of trees, and then cover them tight with clay, so that smoke cannot escape. This being done, they take a parcel of stones, which they heat in a fire, and then put in the oven, and when they think that it is sufficiently hot, they take the stones out again, and go and lie in it, men and women, boys and girls.[134]

Informants (O.A., J.T.) recalled small sweat lodges of this type. Skinner found "small beds of cracked stones and pebbles, without relics, often at some distance from other remains. . ."[135] Thus, archaeological remains tend to confirm the existence of this trait for the prehistoric people of Staten Island.

Clothing.— The amount of clothing worn by the Delawares varied with the season. In summer men wore only a leather breech cloth and women only a short skirt, and they frequently did without moccasins.[136] In colder seasons the principal garment was a skin of beaver, fox, deer, bear, elk, or raccoon.[137] The hair side was worn next to the body in

[129] Wissler, 1917, p. 221; Denton, 1845, p. 7.

[130] Thomas, 1912, p. 341; Heckewelder, 1881, p. 401; Mahr, 1954, pp. 381-82; O. A.

[131] Lindestrom, 1925, p. 222.

[132] O'Callaghan, 1850, I: 282; Hayes, 1954, p. 77.

[133] Zeisberger, 1910, p. 17.

[134] De Vries, 1909, pp. 217-18; Lindestrom, 1925, p. 257, described the sweat lodge in similar terms.

[135] Skinner, 1909, p. 48.

[136] Pastorius, 1912, p. 384; Lindestrom, 1925, pp. 191-92.

[137] De Laet, 1909, p. 57; De Rasieres, 1909, p. 106; Thomas, 1912, p. 341; Juet, 1909, p. 18; Van der Donck, 1909, p. 301.

cold weather and outside in warmer weather.[138] Perhaps the most exotic garments in the eyes of Europeans were the feather mantles which were used both as robes and as bedding.[139] Lindestrom said: "They also make very fine and beautiful quilts of painted bird feathers. In the first place they tie them with meshes like nets, yet very fine, then fasten the feathers in the meshes, so neat and strong that not one feather can come loose from it; it would sooner go clear off."[140] Besides robes, leggings that extended almost to the hips and moccasins were worn.[141] For winter wear "they say that shoes made of dressed bears skins, with the hair on and turned inside, are very warm, and in dry weather, durable."[142] One source mentioned cornhusk moccasins.[143] Women's dress differed from male attire in that a short skin skirt of a square wrap-around style was worn.[144] Clothing was highly decorated with colored designs of dyed porcupine quills, or it was painted.[145] Hats were not used, although one source mentioned "helmets of hard sticks and strong wood" used for defensive purposes in war.[146] Denton said: "They wear no Hats, but commonly wear about their Heads a Snake's skin, or a belt of their money, or a kind of a Ruff made with Deer's hair & died of a scarlet colour, which they esteem very rich."[147] Children wore little or no clothing in warm weather, but by the eighteenth century girls donned, as soon as they could walk, "a little frock" resembling their mother's costume. Boys at about the age of six began wearing the breech cloth.[148]

Adornment and ornamentation.—Men wore a scalp lock, that is, one tuft of hair was allowed to grow long. Other body and facial hair, if any, was plucked out.[149] "They root out the hair from the forehead backward so that the head is bald up to the crown, and only a hand-breadth of it in circular form is suffered to remain. . . ."[150] Women wore their hair in a bun at the back of the head; it was not cut and sometimes hung to the knees.[151] Face and hair of both sexes were smeared with grease.[152] There was no mention of tattooing during the seventeenth century, but since in the next century it was well established, it probably was an ancient custom:

> The process of tattooing, which I once saw performed, is quickly done, and does not seem to give much pain. They have poplar bark in readiness burnt and reduced to a powder, the figures that are to be tattooed are marked or designed

[138] De Vries, 1909, p. 217; Holm, 1834, p. 119; Heckewelder, 1881, p. 202.

[139] De Vries, 1909, p. 217; Juet, 1909, p. 18; Van der Donck, 1909, p. 301; Heckewelder, 1881, p. 203.

[140] Lindestrom, 1925, pp. 221-22.

[141] Zeisberger, 1910, p. 15; Lindestrom, 1925, p. 199.

[142] Heckewelder, 1881, p. 202.

[143] Van der Donck, 1909, p. 301.

[144] Zeisberger, 1910, p. 15; Skinner, 1947, p. 5.

[145] Heckewelder, 1881, p. 202; Skinner, 1947, pp. 3-4.

[146] Lindestrom, 1925, p. 222.

[147] Denton, 1845, p. 10; Holm, 1834, p. 120, noted the same customs.

[148] Johnson, 1917, p. 280; Zeisberger, 1910, p. 17.

[149] Thomas, 1912, p. 340; Lindestrom, 1925, pp. 195-96; Van der Donck, 1909, p. 300.

[150] Zeisberger, 1910, p. 12.

[151] Smith, 1877, p. 137; Lindestrom, 1925, p. 195.

[152] Van der Donck, 1909, p. 301; De Rasieres, 1909, p. 106; Pastorius, 1912, p. 433.

on the skin; the operator with a small stick, rather larger than a common match, to the end of which some sharp needles are fastened, quickly pricks over the whole so that blood is drawn, then a coat of this powder is laid and left on to dry. Before the whites came into this country, they scarified themselves for this purpose with flint stones, or pricked themselves with the sharp teeth of a fish.[153]

The men tatooed their arms, legs, and faces with figures of snakes, birds, and other animals. These were marks of distinction and commemorated some worthy deed or heroic action. Occasionally the women tattooed themselves.[154]

Both sexes painted their thighs, legs, breast, and face with streaks, lines, or circles. The usual colors were red, black, blue, and yellow.[155] Painting was mostly for festive occasions or for warfare. Women were more circumspect than men in the amount of paint used, since excessive or immodest painting was regarded as indicative of a wanton woman.[156] Both men and women wore numerous ornaments. Wampum in particular was a favorite; it was used as necklaces and wristlets and was hung from the ears. Sometimes it was woven in bands and worn on the head or clothing.[157] The helixes of men's ears were often pierced for wampum, metal, and other ornaments:

> They frequently cut the helix of the ear,[158] leaving the upper and lower ends intact and then hang bits of lead to it so that it is stretched. Then this curved border of the auricle is bound with brass wire, distending it considerably, and decorated with silver ornaments.[159]

Besides wampum, necklaces of dyed deer hair, stone, native copper, and shell gorgets were worn.[160] One source depicted men wearing "the thumbs of enemies they have killed."[161] Men carried tobacco pouches, often made from the whole skin of a loon, large enough to hold a pipe, tobacco, knife, a pair of depilatory shells, and other objects.[162]

Manufactures.— The bow and arrow, the war club or tomahawk, and the spear were the principal implements of the men.[163] The type of bow used is unknown, except for one vague reference to wooden bows and arrows.[164] The triangular stone projectile points were fastened to the shaft by means of resin.[165] Projectile points were usually made of quartz, but chert, slate, shale, granite, sandstone, and argillite points have been found. Some may even have been made of fish bones.[166] Stone, pottery, and copper pipes were noted, both from early documents and

---

[153]Heckewelder, 1881, p. 206.

[154]Zeisberger, 1910, p. 12.

[155]De Vries, 1909, p. 217; Holm, 1834, p. 119; Van der Donck, 1909, p. 301; Denton, 1845, p. 10.

[156]Heckewelder, 1881, p. 203.

[157]Van der Donck, 1909, p. 301; Pastorius, 1912, p. 434; Lindestrom, 1925, pp. 196-97.

[158]Heckewelder, 1881, p. 207; Luckenbach, 1938, p. 107.

[159]Zeisberger, 1910, p. 12.

[160]Abbott, 1875, p. 327; Heye and Pepper, 1915, pp. 32-42; Holm, 1834, p. 119.

[161]Holm, 1834, p. 119; Van der Donck, 1909, p. 301.

[162]Zeisberger, 1910, p. 68; Heckewelder, 1881, p. 204.

[163]Brinton, 1885, p. 53.

[164]Zeisberger, 1910, p. 29.

[165]De Laet, 1909, p. 48; Holm, 1834, p. 129; Zeisberger, 1910, p. 29.

[166]Smith, 1950, p. 119; De Laet, 1909, p. 57.

from archaeological sites attributed to the Delawares. Copper tobacco pipes were recorded early in the seventeenth century by Juet who said: "They had red Copper Tabacco pipes, and other things of Copper they did weare about their neckes."[167] Lindestrom described the pipes as painted and said that there were some "an ell in length, which are screwed together with leather, to lean on. . .and in these pipe-heads will go a handful of tobacco."[168] In another place he indicated that pipe heads were decorated with birds and animals "very beautifully painted and glazed."[169] Holm said that the pipes were "a fathom long, which they lean upon as a stick."[170] The pottery pipes found in archaeological sites were plainer, being "straight conical tubes, plain or stamped, to elbow-shaped forms decorated with incised or stamped lines."[171] De Laet said they had ". . .tubes for smoking tobacco formed. . .of flint stone ingeniously perforated."[172] Stone pipes, however, are relatively rare in archaeological sites.[173]

Agricultural implements of the women were simple; short-handled hoes were fashioned with a blade of dogwood, stone, tortoise shell, or the scapula of a deer (later bison).[174] The scapula hoe is remembered by living Delawares. The Delawares had pottery vessels, and according to archaeological information the paste varied from fine to medium coarse, grit temper was more common than shell temper, and sherds are usually gray or brown. Vessels had "conical and rounded bottoms" and were "straight walled or rounded." Shoulders were often absent, although some had pronounced shoulders when associated with a collared rim. Decoration, if present, was by roughening with a cord-wrapped paddle. Incised decorative designs were frequent.[175] Containers and other utensils were fashioned of wood, shell, bark, gourds, and tortoise shell.[176] Stone tools are common in archaeological deposits and include "plain or pitted hammerstones, anvil stones, abrading stones, sinew stones, pestles, shallow mortars, choppers (or hoes), picks, netsinkers, paint stones and amorphous pieces of mica."[177] They possessed "stone hatchets" that were hafted to a handle, and another type which was neither grooved nor hafted.[178] The women and old men manufactured the mats, ropes, tump lines, and baskets, which were made from wild hemp, nettle, silkweed, spruce roots, cornhusks, ash splints, papaw bark, elm bast, and rushes. Wooden bowls, dishes, and mortars were made of maple, buckeye, and elm wood.[179] Speck has described fully the block

---

[167]Juet, 1909, pp. 18-19; De Laet, 1909, p. 49.

[168]Lindestrom, 1925, p. 197.

[169]*Ibid.*, p. 221.

[170]Holm, 1834, p. 120.

[171]Smith, 1950, p. 119.

[172]De Laet, 1909, p. 57.

[173]Butler, 1947, p. 252.

[174]Johnson, 1917, p. 279; Jemison, 1918, p. 47; Zeisberger, 1910, p. 28; Mahr, 1954, pp. 385-86.

[175]Smith, 1950, pp. 117-18.

[176]Pastorius, 1912, p. 384; Lindestrom, 1925, p. 255; Johnson, 1917, p. 281; Speck, 1941, pp. 47, 76-79; Smith, 1950, p. 119.

[177]Smith, 1950, p. 119.

[178]Kalm, 1937, I: 229.

[179]Thomas, 1912, p. 341; Lindestrom, 1925, p. 221; De Laet, 1909, p. 57; Harrington, 1913, p. 224.

stamp ornamentation of basketry in historic times, possibly a diffusion from the Europeans.[180]

Boats.—Canoes were of two types, a solid dugout canoe and one of birch or other bark. The dugouts were made of tulip poplar, cedar, sycamore, and probably other suitable woods, which were hollowed out by fire.[181] When they wished to venture out to sea or into rough water, two canoes were lashed together. Sails on these vessels were reported, but seem to be post-European.[182] Zeisberger described the manufacture of the eighteenth-century bark canoe, which probably represented the earlier technique:

> These canows are fashioned of one piece of bast, the outer side of which is turned inward, both ends sharply pointed and securely sewn with bast, the inside being stretched out by a ribbing of bent wooden rods, which keeps the canow in its proper form. These canows are so light upon the water that they easily glide away from under the feet of one unaccustomed to them when attempting to stand. ... To make one they choose a tree according to the size of canow desired and peel the bark off carefully so that there may be no rent. If a canow gets out of repair or is punctured...the latter know how to repair it by securing a patch of bast over any opening. Besides, there is a kind of elm-wood bast which they crush or pound fine and which is of a sticky consistency, serving them in place of tar, to keep their canows water-tight so that they do not leak.[183]

These canoes were made of elm, black oak, and hickory bark.[184] Harrington said that for temporary use "six or more logs lashed together in the form of a raft with bark withes carried people and baggage across waters or down streams as required."[185]

Wampum.—The subject of wampum comes up in several different contexts, since its uses ranged all the way from individual ornamentation to negotiatory belts in peace and war. I shall merely examine its form and manufacture since its sociopolitical implications have been discussed fully by Speck and Snyderman.[186] Virtually all the early documents mentioned the possession and use of wampum (often called zeewan or sewan) by the Delawares. Lindestrom, for example, said they had "oblong stones, with holes drilled through them, and threaded on strings. . .one kind [is] black-blue, the other kind white.... In size they are about the length of a wheat kernel and somewhat thicker."[187] He added that it was made by specialists, but says no more on the subject.[188] Fortunately, however, Burggraf has reconstructed the manufacture of wampum from knowledge gained through the material found in Indian workshops on Long Island. The white wampum was made solely from "the central stock of both *F. carica* and *F. canaliculatas*":[189]

[180]Speck, 1947, pp. 17-19.

[181]Holm, 1834, p. 130; De Laet, 1909, pp. 38, 57; Van der Donck, 1909, p. 301; Mahr, 1954, pp. 382-83.

[182]Lindestrom, 1925, p. 237.

[183]Zeisberger, 1910, p. 23.

[184]Zeisberger, 1776, p. 33; Brinton, 1890, p. 185; Harrington, 1913, p. 223; Mahr, 1954, p. 382.

[185]Harrington, 1913, p. 223.

[186]Speck, 1919; Snyderman, 1955.

[187]Lindestrom, 1925, p. 229.

[188]*Ibid.*, p. 230.

[189]Burggraf, 1938, p. 54.

> The first stage in the course of manufacture was to break away all the outer whorls, leaving only the spiral center-stock. Next, with a chip of stone or a knife, the spire was cut off by sawing or notching around its circumference at the point where the first bead would be started. After this grooving had been carried far enough, the waste portion was broken off and discarded. In some cases this cutting seems to have been accomplished wholly with some abrasive implement, usually a bit of sharp-grained red sandstone. The fresh shiny surface of the interior of a periwinkel, as the shells are called locally, is of surprising hardness, and for this first step the quickest method would be employed. In severing finished beads, great care was shown and the narrow groove was carried deep enough to prevent any breakage in detaching the completed specimen. . . .[190]

Black wampum was made from the Quahog (*Mercenaria mercenaria*), and its manufacture was more difficult:

> The first step was to break off the anterior end of suitable dark-colored valves. Many fragments were never worked beyond this stage, most generally due to an insufficient thickness of the purple shell. Then, with some light hammer and perhaps a sort of percussion flaker, the thin edges of this bit of shell were chipped away leaving a slightly curving "stick" of purple . . . . The next step was to grind away the chipped edges, which could be easily accomplished with the sandstone "abradors" recovered.[191]

This tubular type was of late origin, replacing a disc type after 1620.[192]

[190] Burggraf, 1938, p. 55.
[191] *Ibid.*, p. 57.
[192] Speck, 1919, p. 4; Burggraf, 1938, p. 53.

III. DELAWARE SOCIOLOGY

As is true of all people on a comparable technological level, Delaware social organization was based upon ties of kinship. Or to put it another way, the organization by which the technology was operated and the ways in which individuals behaved toward one another were regulated and determined by ties of relationship. But "the records of departed civilizations, archeological and documentary, are relatively rich in evidences as to technology, economics, religion, and government but poor in information as to rules of descent, kinship terminology, and other aspects of social organization."[1] This general condition is true of early Delaware culture, but if reliance is placed upon Murdock's suggestions, it is possible to move from the documentarily known to the deductive probable and to reconstruct with some success the early kinship structure.

Life Cycle

Pregnancy and Birth

Marital abstinence was practiced during pregnancy.[2] Heckewelder stated that husbands were solicitous of the whims of their wives during pregnancy, citing a case in which a man traveled at least forty miles to obtain cranberries with which "to satisfy his wife's longings."[3] During pregnancy meat was not touched with the hands, but was eaten with a stick.[4] One of my informants (J.T.) said that bird and animal livers could not be eaten during pregnancy. This may well be a vestige of the early taboo on meat. According to Harrington's Munsi informants:

> The husband of an expectant mother was often accompanied on his hunting trips by the spirit of the unborn child, whose romping and playing about the bushes, invisible to mortal eye, would nevertheless frighten away the deer and send the hunter home empty-handed. To prevent this a little bow and arrow were made and attached to the prospective father's garments, in the hope that the little spirit would play with them and stay quietly with his parent. Should this precaution fail, the child was thought to be a girl, and a little corn mortar and pestle were substituted. . . .[5]

Birth, which was reported to be easy,[6] seems to have taken place away from the village, either in a menstrual hut or simply out of doors. Mary Jemison (a white captive of the eighteenth century, married at one time

---

[1] Murdock, 1949, p. 323.
[2] Thomas, 1912, p. 335; Penn, 1912, p. 232; Holm, 1834, p. 126.
[3] Heckewelder, 1881, p. 159.
[4] Holm, 1834, p. 126.
[5] Harrington, 1913, p. 212.
[6] Holm, 1834, p. 126.

to a Delaware) gave birth in a small "shed" on a riverbank, attended by two women.[7] Informants said that old experienced women who had gone through childbirth themselves assisted in delivering a woman. Immediately after birth the infant was washed by its mother.[8] Lindestrom alone among the early sources said:

> When the savage females bear their children, they tie around their waists a snake skin of the most poisonous kind of snakes, which are found in New Sweden and are called rattlesnakes, which has such an effect that they do not know of the least pain in their child birth, and are as healthy in an hour, as if they had never been through it.[9]

Immediately after the child was washed it was placed upon a cradleboard. Lindestrom said:

> [The mother] binds it... with three long and broad braids, and does not place the smallest particle of clothing under or above the child. The first braid she wraps over the forehead and around the board; the second braid, right over the arms and the board; the third braid, right over the knees and the board, tying it right strongly to the board.[10]

The child was kept bound to the cradleboard most of the time, including nursing periods, until it could walk.[11] Moss was used as an agent to absorb the child's excreta.[12] If it was necessary to carry the child after the cradleboard had been discarded, he was borne on the mother's back wrapped in a blanket.[13]

Harrington was told that a newborn child was not felt to be securely in the world, and that to ensure life it was disguised from the supernatural beings by being attired in adult clothing. According to Harrington:

> ... deerskin strings or strips of corn-husk were tied on the wrists of children so that the ghosts would think they were tied fast to the earth; and holes were cut in their little moccasins so that they could not follow the spirit trail. If the child's mother died shortly after its birth, these precautions were redoubled.[14]

The umbilical cord was specially treated; it was buried in the woods if a boy's, and near the lodge if a girl's. It was considered to be closely connected with a child's disposition, and hence if buried in the woods would ensure a boy's liking for the woods and the hunt; if buried near a lodge it would ensure the girl's attachment to womanly occupations.[15]

Naming.— Personal names were bestowed upon children or announced to the public during religious ceremonials, particularly the Big House Ceremony.[16] The meager information derived from the seventeenth-century sources indicates that these names were not given the children

[7]Jemison, 1918, p. 45.

[8]Penn, 1912, p. 231; Penn, 1882, p. 242; Holm, 1834, p. 126; O.A., M.B.

[9]Lindestrom, 1925, p. 194.

[10]*Ibid.*, p. 201.

[11]Penn, 1912, p. 231; Pastorius, 1912, p. 434; Lindestrom, 1925, p. 201; Trowbridge MS.

[12]Loskiel, 1794, p. 61.

[13]Lindestrom, 1925, p. 201.

[14]Harrington, 1913, p. 212; J.T. mentioned defacing moccasins for this purpose.

[15]Harrington, 1913, pp. 212-13.

[16]Zeisberger, 1910, p. 80; Loskiel, 1794, p. 62; Harrington, 1913, p. 213; Kinietz, 1946, p. 44; O.A., M.B.

until they were "pretty well grown,"[17] or until they were old enough to hunt.[18] Trowbridge in the nineteenth century said:

> Children are named at one of the grand worshipping councils, and as opportunities do not occur regularly, there is no particular age at which they are formally named. The child when about to be named is taken to the assembly . . . and there presented to one of the old men of the same tribe [phratry?] together with a fathom of wampum for his services.[19]

Information from the eighteenth century suggests that temporary childhood names were also given. These names were often derived from dreams:

> If it is left to the mother to give the child a name, she used little ceremony and calls it after some peculiar mark or character in it, for instance the Beautiful, the Good Child, the Great-Eye, sometimes giving it a name of unsavory meaning. If the father gives the child a name he pretends that it has been suggested to him in a dream.[20]

Van der Donck in the seventeenth century specified the mother as name-giver, but Loskiel in 1794 indicated the father in that capacity.[21] Kinietz has suggested that "part of the diversity may be accounted for by the fact that often two or more old people including the child's grandparents, dreamed a name, and on being presented with these the parents made a selection."[22] The shift away from a matrilineal, matrilocal emphasis in society may also have led to the naming of children by the father. According to informants, a friend of the parents, usually an aged person, was asked to give the child a name. This person was given a present; in the last century the present was dress goods or the like (M.B., O.A., J.T.). The name-giver did not name the child immediately, but waited until an auspicious dream had occurred.[23] Names for girls were "feminine sounding" and those for boys were "masculine sounding." "Coming into Full Bloom" was given as an example of a girl's name, and "Stands Before the Wind" was given as a boy's name (N.D.). One of Kinietz's informants said that animal names were used, and another said that children were named for the month in which they were born.[24] Masculine names could be feminized by adding an appropriate suffix.[25]

The use of an adult's name was restricted to the Big House Ceremony and analogous rites: childhood names did not have this restriction.[26] It was not uncommon for a person to select a new name upon becoming an adult. This might be because the old name no longer fitted, or the individual might merit a new name because of some worthy deed which he had performed. Denton said that "every one invents a name to himself, which he likes best. Some calling themselves *Rattlesnake*, *Skunk*,

[17]Holm, 1834, p. 127.
[18]Lindestrom, 1925, p. 202.
[19]Trowbridge MS.
[20]Zeisberger, 1910, p. 80
[21]Loskiel, 1794, p. 62.
[22]Kinietz, 1946, p. 45.
[23]Harrington, 1913, p. 213; Kinietz, 1946, p. 101; M.B., O.A., J.T.
[24]Kinietz, 1946, p. 101.
[25]Harrington, 1913, p. 213.
[26]Trowbridge MS; J.T., O.A.

Bucks-horn, or the like."[27] In everyday life kinship terms were used rather than personal names.[28] Denton also said:

> Any Indian being dead, his name dies with him, no person daring ever after to mention his name, it being not only a breach of their Law, but an abuse to his friends & relations present, as if it were done on purpose to renew their grief: And any other person whatsoever that is named after that name doth incontinently change his name & takes a new one.[29]

Education and Training of Children

Children were nursed until they were three or four years old, but were increasingly fed meat and other specially prepared foods. Holm said they were taught to walk when they were nine months old.[30] When boys were four or five years old, they were given their first instruction in hunting, warfare, and woodcraft, as well as in other phases of a man's life.[31] Girls at the same age were initiated into the duties of housekeeping and the planting and cultivating of gardens. Old people, particularly grandparents, played an important role in instructing the children in tradition, religion, and correct behavior (O.A., N.D.). According to Trowbridge, men took upon themselves the duty of instructing the young of their phratry.[32] The earlier documents are silent on these points, but there seems to be no reason why these more modern data do not represent the customs of a former period.

In earlier times physical punishment was seldom if ever used on the children; explanation, ridicule, exhortation, and threats took its place.[33] Obedience was sometimes enforced by threats of punishment by the Mask Being. If a child was slow to rise in the morning, for instance, the recalcitrant one was told that this supernatural creature would visit him and poke him with a stick (N.D.). It was also believed that the supernatural powers punished disobedient children by causing them to become weak and sickly (N.D.). The myth of a great, naked bear was frequently used, since disobedient children were said to be its particular victims.[34] Children were described as being well behaved; a captive brought up by the Delawares said that "honesty, bravery and hospitality are cardinal virtues with them... .Their young, in a remarkable degree, reverence and honor the aged, especially their parents."[35] Not only were the old respected, but game and various other presents were often given to them.[36]

As children grew older, the boys in particular were more and more exposed to a toughening program. Training was one of increasing hardship, up to and including the puberty rituals. Children were forced to

[27]Denton, 1845, p. 8.

[28]Trowbridge MS.

[29]Denton, 1845, p. 8.

[30]Holm, 1834, p. 127.

[31]Lindestrom, 1925, p. 202; Harrington, 1913, p. 213; Trowbridge MS.

[32]Trowbridge MS.

[33]Brickell, 1842, p. 47; Zeisberger, 1910, p. 81.

[34]Heckewelder, 1799, pp. 260-62.

[35]Brickell, 1842, p. 48.

[36]Zeisberger, 1910, p. 76.

take baths in streams, even if the water was covered with ice.[37] Trowbridge said "they believe it of the utmost consequence to their children to subject them to hardship in their infancy and youth."[38] If children were orphaned "the maternal grandfather or mother is bound by custom to take the children under protection; but if they also be dead the children are adopted by such relatives or friends as may be inclined to take charge of them."[39] Children born out of wedlock were normally cared for by the mother, but the father might contribute to their support. No stigma attached to illegitimacy.[40]

Puberty: boys.— The vision quest of the young boy was the climax of the more formal aspects of the educational system and served to usher the boy over the threshold into adult life. When a boy was about ten years old,[41] or when his voice began to change (N.D.), he began what can best be called a series of ordeals:

> [A boy] is put under an alternate course of physic and fasting, either taking no food whatever, or swallowing the most powerful and nauseous medicines, and occasionally he is made to drink decoctions of an intoxicating nature, until his mind becomes sufficiently bewildered, so that he sees or fancies that he sees visions, and has extraordinary dreams, for which, of course, he has been prepared beforehand.[42]

Parents insulted their sons, N.D. added, telling them that they were no good and that they should go out and "die." Boys were shamed, ridiculed, insulted, and all but physically driven from the village. It was felt that a humbled, miserable boy had a better opportunity to induce the supernatural spirits to feel sorry for him, and so reveal themselves to him and provide him with a supernatural guardian. Boys inevitably went into a lonely exile filled with despair at their own inadequacy and in the desperate hope of obtaining a supernatural being's assistance in a hostile world. If the vision quest produced a guardian spirit, a boy was restored to the good graces of the community, acquired a good deal of self-confidence, and the course of his life was known. Future occupations, for instance, were decided by these visions, whether a boy was to be a warrior, shaman, or something else.[43] Not all boys, however, were successful in the vision quest. Women frequently had visions, although they were not consciously solicited.[44]

Puberty: girls.— When a girl menstruated for the first time she was secluded in a hut.[45] Zeisberger said of the Munsis:

> ...being the more strict and having more ceremonies in the observance of the custom than the Miamis. They build for such a girl, a separate hut, apart from the rest, where her mother or some old female acquaintance cares for her

[37]Penn, 1912, p. 231; Pastorius, 1912, p. 434; Trowbridge MS; J.T., N.D., O.A.
[38]Trowbridge MS.
[39]*Ibid.*
[40]*Ibid.*
[41]Harrington, 1913, p. 214.
[42]Heckewelder, 1881, p. 245.
[43]*Ibid.*, pp. 245-47. See Chap. IV for a discussion of the supernatural beings encountered in visions.
[44]Zeisberger, 1910, p. 132; N.D.
[45]Zeisberger, 1910, p. 77; Beatty, 1798, pp. 84-85; Loskiel, 1794, p. 56; N.D., O.A.

and guards her so that none may see her... she is also kept within the hut the whole of the menstrual period, with the blanket over her head....[46]

De Vries also noted that these girls hid behind a garment "which they throw over their body drawing it over the head so that one can barely see their eyes."[47] The emphasis during menstruation was on uncleanliness and the necessity of isolation from society.[48] A girl could not touch her hair during her first isolation, food was eaten with a stick, and no meat was eaten.[49] In the last century, and perhaps earlier, a girl could not look in a mirror or talk to people (N.D.). At the end of the seclusion the girl's mother washed her hair, bathed her, and gave her new clothes. The idea was impressed upon the girl that she was now a woman and was henceforth to give up the toys and activities of childhood.[50] The same general restrictions applied to menstruating women.[51]

Little is known about premarital chastity in early historic times. Denton said, however: "Any maid before she is married doth lie with whom she please for money without any scandal, or the least aspersion to be cast upon her it being so customary, & their laws tolerating it."[52]

Marriage

After the boys had proved themselves to be adequate hunters and the girls had passed through their first seclusion, they were considered ready for marriage. This took place at about the age of seventeen or eighteen for boys and thirteen or fourteen for girls.[53] A girl showed her marriageability by wearing some sort of headpiece and by modestly covering the face with a portion of clothing when in public.[54] De Vries said further that girls "deck themselves with a quantity of zeewan [wampum] upon the body, head and neck; they then go and sit in some place, in company with some squaws, showing that they are up for a bargain."[55]

Several different ways of arranging marriages and several types of marriage ceremony have been recorded for the Delawares. Some of this variety was probably due to diffusion from other Indian cultures or from Euro-American civilization, but it was also possible that there were variations among the diverse Delawaran peoples. Four seventeenth-century sources stated that girls were courted with wampum.[56] In later times, at least, relatives or go-betweens arranged the marriage. According to Heckewelder the prospective bridegroom's mother usually initiated the negotiations; according to Trowbridge the father of the

[46] Zeisberger, 1910, p. 77.

[47] De Vries, 1909, p. 218; also Loskiel, 1794, p. 56.

[48] Zeisberger, 1910, p. 77; N.D., O.A.

[49] Penn, 1912, p. 232.

[50] N.D. See section on Mythology in Chap. IV for an account of a girl who refused to part with her dolls.

[51] Zeisberger, 1910, p. 77.

[52] Denton, 1845, p. 9.

[53] Penn, 1912, p. 231; Holm, 1834, pp. 127-28; Zeisberger, 1910, p. 75; Loskiel, 1794, p. 63.

[54] De Vries, 1909, p. 218; Pastorius, 1912, p. 434; Penn, 1912, p. 231.

[55] De Vries, 1909, p. 218.

[56] *Ibid.*; De Rasieres, 1909, p. 106; Denton, 1845, p. 9; Van der Donck, 1909, p. 302.

bridegroom carried out negotiations with the father of the bride.[57] My informants said that either parent of the prospective bridegroom could make wedding arrangements (N.D., O.A., M.B.). The prospective bridegroom, or the go-between seems to have taken some produce of the hunt, usually a choice cut of deer or bear, to the dwelling of the prospective bride and presented it to the girl's mother. If the match was favored, the girl's mother reciprocated with a gift of beans or corn. Both go-betweens, whether relatives or friends, emphasized in their negotiations that their respective children, or clients, had themselves procured the gifts. If, after this exchange, the couple signified that the gifts were acceptable, the bargain was considered concluded, although subsequent exchanges of food and clothing were made. The period of time between the betrothal and the marriage was fairly lengthy in the seventeenth century: "If she be a young virgin, he must wait six weeks more before he can sleep with her...all this time she sits with a blanket over her head, without wishing to look at any one, or any one being permitted to look at her...."[58] Heckewelder added:

> The friendship between the two families daily increasing, they do their domestic and field work jointly, and when the young people have agreed to live together, the parents supply them with necessaries, such as a kettle, dishes or bowls, and also what is required for the kitchen, and with axes, hoes, etc. to work in the field.[59]

De Rasieres rather cryptically said that in the marriage ceremony they "...eat together with friends, and sing and dance together...."[60] An even more informal ceremony was mentioned in this and subsequent centuries, in which a man simply asked a woman if she wanted to live with him. If she assented, they lived together and were considered to be married.[61] Trowbridge described the marriage ceremony of the nineteenth century by saying:

> The female was conducted by her relatives to the lodge of her intended husband and there delivered to him. The day succeeding was taken up by the relatives of the bride in carrying to those of the groom large presents of corn, squashes, etc., together with pouches and other ornaments, the products of female labor, and they also gave her a kettle for cooking. This was the conclusion of the ceremony.[62]

Other data from this century add that the couple, dressed in their finest and most elaborate clothing, appeared before a shaman, who made an offering of tobacco to the supernatural powers and sacrificed a beaver skin. He then addressed the bridal couple telling them to be good and not to mistreat each other. This was followed by a feast and dance sponsored by the friends and relatives of the bridal pair.[63] He might

---

[57]Heckewelder, 1881, pp. 161-62; De Smet, 1859, p. 238; Trowbridge MS.

[58]De Rasieres, 1909, p. 107.

[59]Heckewelder, 1881, p. 161.

[60]De Rasieres, 1909, p. 107.

[61]Van der Donck, 1909, p. 302; J.T., O.A.

[62]Trowbridge MS.

[63]De Smet, 1859, p. 239; Adams, 1905, pp. 17-19; M.B.

also speak to the couple on subsequent occasions, perhaps on the birth of a child (M.B.).

The place of residence of a newly married couple is something of a puzzle. In the nineteenth century it was temporarily patrilocal or matrilocal (bilocal), with friends, or by themselves (neolocal).[64] This was probably not true in early historic times; the evidence favors matrilocality. All sources are agreed that the Delawares were polygynous.[65] Polygyny seems to have been more frequent in the early days. "An *Indian* may have two wives or more if he please, but it is not much in use as it was since the English came amongst them they being ready in some measure to imitate the *English* in things both good & bad."[66] Van der Donck said that "ordinarily they have but one wife, sometimes two or three, but this is generally among the chiefs."[67] The sororate was sometimes practiced, and informants added that the levirate was known.[68] Trowbridge said that "many instances have been known where a man having married a widow also married her daughter, and this has sometimes been at the suggestion of the mother herself."[69]

Divorce.— Divorce was easy among the Delawares; either member of a marriage partnership could break the union.[70] Reasons for divorce were sterility, adultery, and any other type of incompatibility.[71] Divorce was not frequent when there were children, and in this event small children remained with the mother.[72] Heckewelder quoted a Delaware on marriage and divorce, and the account is both enlightening and entertaining:

> The Indians had not only a much easier way of getting a wife than the whites, but were also more certain of getting a good one; "For" (said he in his broken English), "White man court, — court, — may be one whole year! O may be two year before he marry! — well! — may be then got very good wife — but may be not! — may be very cross! — Well now, suppose cross! scold so soon as get awake in morning! scold all day! scold until sleep! — all one; he must keep him! White people have law forbidding throwing away wife, be he ever so cross! no! no! Squaw know too well what Indian do if he cross! — throw him away and take another! Squaw love to eat meat! no husband! no meat! Squaw do every thing to please husband! he do the same to please Squaw! live happy!"[73]

Marital fidelity on the part of men does not seem to have been a major social goal, particularly during a woman's pregnancy, menstruation, and lactation, when marital relations were forbidden.[74] During this period many husbands apparently had concubines. There is one report of the social sanction of a woman's divorce from an adulterous husband. In this isolated case the husband was accused before the chief; he was

[64] Zeisberger, 1910, p. 78; O.A., N.D.

[65] Holm, 1834, p. 126; Loskiel, 1794, p. 58; Trowbridge MS., O.A., M.B., N.D.

[66] Denton, 1845, p. 9.

[67] Van der Donck, 1909, p. 302.

[68] Zeisberger, 1910, p. 88; O.A., M.B.

[69] Trowbridge MS.

[70] De Vries, 1909, p. 218; Holm, 1834, p. 126; Brainerd, 1884, pp. 171-72; Trowbridge MS.

[71] Denton, 1845, p. 9; Zeisberger, 1910, p. 85; Heckewelder, 1881, p. 154; Trowbridge MS.

[72] De Rasieres, 1909, p. 108; Trowbridge MS; O.A.

[73] Heckewelder, 1881, p. 161.

[74] Penn, 1912, p. 232; Zeisberger, 1910, p. 80.

found guilty and the wife was "permitted to draw off his right shoe and left stocking...she then tears off the lappet that covers his private parts, gives him a kick behind, and so drives him out of the house...."[75] Husbands could punish adulterous wives by thrashing them, or could obtain a divorce by bringing them before the chief or sachem. The woman's hair was cut off, she was deprived of her property, and perhaps even of her life, if found guilty by the sachem.[76] But Denton remarked: "It is no offense for their married women to lie with another man provided she acquaint her husband, or some of her nearest Relations with it, but if not it is accounted such a fault that they sometimes punish it with death."[77] One of the culturally sanctioned mechanisms for obtaining revenge upon an adulterous spouse was suicide.[78] A man's retaliation for adultery could also be seduction of the adulterer's wife. If and when the injured husband was successful in this venture, he made the fact public so that the original adulterer would be held up for public scorn.[79]

A widow, prior to remarriage, whether his wife had died of natural or other causes, had to recompense her relatives for her loss.[80] The duration of mourning was about a year.[81] A widow during this time had to support herself; she could not be given meat since a hunter's weapons were supposed to fail if he had given meat to a widow.[82] When the year had passed, the deceased one's soul left the earth and remarriage could follow.

Death

As soon as a person died the fact of death was spread throughout the community by a crier. The crier was a woman especially appointed and paid for her services.[83] This announcement evoked loud outcrys and lamentations from the general populace. These lamentations were continued intermittently in the house where the deceased lay until burial.[84] In recent times and perhaps earlier the moccasin game was played in the dwelling where the corpse lay.[85] The body was not buried at once because it was necessary to give the supernatural forces an opportunity to restore life to the corpse.[86] The length of time the body was kept varied with the season; it was three days in summer and seven in winter.[87] During this interval the corpse was dressed in new clothes and richly adorned and painted. Before noon on the day of burial a number

[75]De Rasieres, 1909, p. 108.

[76]*Ibid.;* see also Pastorius, 1912, p. 434.

[77]Denton, 1845, p. 9.

[78]Penn, 1912, p. 232; Heckewelder, 1881, pp. 258-59; Loskiel, 1794, p. 58.

[79]Zeisberger, 1910, p. 77.

[80]Penn, 1912, p. 232.

[81]Pastorius, 1912, p. 435; Holm, 1834, p. 143; Brickell, 1842, p. 49; Trowbridge MS.

[82]Zeisberger, 1910, p. 88; Loskiel, 1794, p. 64.

[83]Lindestrom, 1925, p. 249; Heckewelder, 1881, p. 269.

[84]Zeisberger, 1910, p. 89; Heckewelder, 1881, p. 269.

[85]Harrington, 1913, p. 215; Kinietz, 1946, p. 72.

[86]Trowbridge MS; Kinietz, 1946, p. 51; J.T.

[87]Lindestrom, 1925, p. 249; Heckewelder, 1881, p. 269; Trowbridge MS; Kinietz, 1946, p. 51; M.B.

of tools and ornaments were placed in the grave (or coffin in later times).[88] "They put into the Ground with them some House-Utensils, and some Money (as Tokens of their Love and Affection) with other Things, expecting they shall have Occasion for them again in the other World."[89] Denton and Lindestrom described burials in which deep circular pits were dug, the corpse being placed "...upright, sitting upon a seat, with his Gun, money, & such goods as he hath with him, that he may be furnished in the other world."[90] As far as can be determined there is no archaeological confirmation for this trait. Voegelin said, however, that this custom was "pan-eastern North American, with the center of distribution in the north."[91] In later centuries the corpse was buried in an extended, or partly flexed, prone position. One source said that the body's hands were tied "one on each side of his head."[92] Heckewelder, who observed the burial of the wife of an important man, gave the clearest discussion of the eighteenth-century mortuary practices. Just prior to burial "a small bag of vermilion paint, with some flannel to lay it on, was then thrust into the coffin through the hole cut out at the head of it. This hole, the Indians say, is for the spirit of the deceased to go in and out at pleasure, until it has found the place of its future residence."[93] J.T. said that the hole is painted with a red paint made from a root.

In the ceremony in which Heckewelder participated, a procession carried the coffin to the cemetery, which was a little way from the village, the female mourners making "the air resound with their shrill cries."[94] The procession consisted of a leader, followed by men carrying the coffin, then the husband of the deceased, war chiefs, counselors, women, and children. Finally came two men bearing loads of European goods, and women with eating utensils and dried elk meat. The chief mourners took their separate way to the grave, on the right side of the procession, about fifteen or twenty yards off. At the grave the corpse was exposed, the multitude arranging themselves in a half circle on the south side of the grave. The bereaved widower retired "to a spot at some distance, where he was seen weeping, with his head bowed to the ground."[95] The female mourners sat down twelve to fifteen yards east of the grave. Two hours were spent without further activity. At about one o'clock six men stepped forward to place the lid on the coffin and lower it into the grave; they were prevented from doing so by the female mourners. These mourners called upon the deceased to return, even trying to pull the corpse from the casket. When these women had returned to their places, continuing their lament, the six men again stepped forward and lowered the coffin into the grave. The head of the

[88] Heckewelder, 1881, p. 271; Trowbridge MS; O.A., M.B.

[89] Thomas, 1912, p. 340; Penn, 1882, p. 244, and Holm, 1834, p. 143, recorded the same custom.

[90] Denton, 1845, p. 8; also Lindestrom, 1925, p. 249.

[91] Voegelin, 1944, pp. 344-45.

[92] Holm, 1834, p. 143.

[93] Heckewelder, 1881, p. 271. J.T., N.D., and O.A. mentioned this trait.

[94] Heckewelder, 1881, pp. 271-72; Zeisberger, 1910, p. 88.

[95] Heckewelder, 1881, p. 272.

deceased was oriented towards the east.[96] At this time they laid "two thin poles of about four inches (in) diameter, from which the bark had been taken off, lengthways and close together over the grave, after which they retired."[97] The widower then came up to the grave slowly and "walked over it on these poles, and proceeded forward in the same manner into an extensive adjoining prairie."[98] When he was gone, a painted post which signified the position and station of the deceased and her husband was "brought by two men and delivered to a third, a man of note,"[99] who placed it at the head of the coffin in the grave with its symbolism facing east.[100] Holm said, "If he was a good hunter, they put the figure in wood, of some wild animal, and if he was a good fisherman, that of a fish."[101] After the grave was filled with earth, palisades were set up "about breast-high, so as to secure it from. . .wild beasts."[102] Denton noted that ". . . .they fence their graves with a hedge, & cover the tops with mats, to shelter them from the rain."[103]

A meal, which had been prepared some distance from the grave, and a distribution of presents concluded the funeral rites. Everybody received a gift, although those who had performed various duties received the most valuable presents. Food was placed on the grave at dusk, and this was repeated every evening for three weeks. After this span of time "it was supposed that the traveller had found her place of residence."[104] For three weeks the mourning of the women continued, although it gradually decreased in intensity.

People of less social importance were given less elaborate funerals.[105] No matter how simple the funerary rites, however, the customs of mourning had to be observed. Blackening of the face is one of the few such customs with which we are familiar.[106] Denton's description is the most complete one available for the seventeenth century. He said:

> At his Burial his nearest relations attend the Hearse with their faces painted black, and do visit the grave once or twice a day, where they send forth sad lamentations so long till time hath wore the blackness off their faces, & afterwards every year once they view the grave, make a new mourning for him, trimming up of the Grave, not suffering of a Grass to grow by it. . . .[107]

A number of other sources from all periods confirm the care which was given the grave.[108] Food was occasionally left there, and annual feasts at the grave were common.[109] Trowbridge said that "it is customary among them to offer the first fine products of the hunting season and the first fruits of the earth at the grave of the deceased."[110] My informants said that Munsi feasts were more elaborate and that one was held twelve

[96] Zeisberger, 1910, p. 88; O.A., N.D., J.T., M.B.

[97] Heckewelder, 1881, p. 273.

[98] *Ibid.*

[99] *Ibid.*

[100] McClure, 1899, p. 90; Trowbridge MS.

[101] Holm, 1834, p. 143.

[102] Heckewelder, 1881, p. 274.

[103] Denton, 1845, p. 8.

[104] Heckewelder, 1881, p. 275.

[105] *Ibid.;* Trowbridge MS.

[106] Pastorius, 1912, p. 435; Penn, 1912, p. 234; Holm, 1834, p. 143.

[107] Denton, 1845, p. 8.

[108] Thomas, 1912, p. 340; Penn, 1912, p. 234; Zeisberger, 1910, p. 90; J.T., O.A.

[109] Penn, 1912, p. 234; Zeisberger, 1910, p. 90; J.T., O.A.

[110] Trowbridge MS.

days after burial (J.T.). The modern funerary feast may not be entirely representative of the aboriginal custom but it probably is a fairly accurate reflection of it.[111] These annual feasts are held at the home of the mourning relative and not at the cemetery. Friends and relatives eat, pray, and talk about the departed. Some person, unrelated to the deceased, is especially invited. (Trowbridge also noted this custom.) This guest, who has to be younger than the deceased at the time of death, but of the same sex, must sample all the foods which were favorites of the deceased. The feast, it is said, benefits the dead since the food the stand-in eats satisfies the spiritual appetite of the dead. The stand-in is not paid for his services (J.T., O.A.).

Another adjunct to funeral customs of the modern period, and perhaps one which existed in an earlier period, consists of rites of purification. Following a funeral, the immediate family burns a handful of sweet grass on the grave (O.A.). The members of the family also purify themselves by washing the arms, hands, and face with water and then symbolically rubbing the smoke from burned cedar leaves over these same parts. With cedar smoke they also purify the rooms of the dwelling where the person died. This is said to repel the soul of the departed if it should attempt to return (O.A., J.T., N.D.).

It seems reasonable to assume that prior to European contact the Delawares varied somewhat in their funerary rites. De Vries, for example, alluded to a form of secondary burial, but this cannot be specifically associated with the Delawares.[112] This account mentioned a funeral feast and the erection of four poles and shelves upon the grave. Lindestrom also described a grave upon which four poles were raised:[113]

> The dead man's money is placed upon him and he is set down in the pit upon the stool with a tobacco pipe, a fathom long, in his mouth, screwed together with leather, the head of green or black stone, which is lighted through by the fire in the pipe, so that we can see how the tobacco is consumed, and this pipe-head is so large that a handful of tobacco will go into it, which is to be his food on the journey. This pipe they dig down into the ground from the mouth of the man.[114]

Thomas mentioned that the bones of celebrated persons were carried considerable distances to be reinterred near their homes. Perhaps this is a reference to the well-known secondary burial of the Nanticokes.[115]

Suicide.—It has already been noted that suicide was a means of punishing an adulterous spouse. Heckewelder knew of four persons who committed suicide between 1771 and 1780; all were men and all ate the root of the May apple. Three were successful, and the other was given an emetic and survived. Two of the men committed suicide because of thwarted love lives; the other two were married to adulterous women.[116] Trowbridge early in the nineteenth century mentioned that suicide was

[111]Speck, 1937, p. 59, has discussed "Sacrifice Feasts" of which funeral feasts are an example and noted that their "ancient character is exhibited by the fact of [their] wide distribution in similar form over the entire territory inhabited by Algonkin-speaking peoples."

[112]De Vries, 1909, pp. 223-24.

[113]Lindestrom, 1925, p. 250.

[114]*Ibid.*, p. 249.

[115]Thomas, 1912, p. 340.

[116]Heckewelder, 1881, pp. 258-60.

not uncommon: "Mr. Conner knows of many instances of it having been committed, sometimes by shooting, but generally by eating the root of the may apple. It proceeds most frequently from excess of gref (sic) or from disappointment in love."[117] There are indications, then, of a pattern of sex-oriented suicide in Delaware culture at least as early as the eighteenth century.

Kin Groups

There is no way of knowing exactly how much Delaware kinship structure and terminology changed in the two and a half centuries following European invasion. That it did change during this period is virtually certain, since factors which induce change were present, such as altered rules of residence, decreased polygyny, and increased economic and political importance of men. The literature of the seventeenth and eighteenth centuries gives no description of the kinship structure. L. H. Morgan was the first investigator to furnish information on the subject, obtaining his data in 1859 on the Kansas reservation of the Delawares. Even at this time Morgan termed the system "deteriorated."[118] I shall first describe the system found by Morgan, then compare it with the modern one, and finally turn to a reconstruction of the early historic system. Kinship terms given by Zeisberger and other earlier authors are too scant to yield any information; these nuclear terms agree with Morgan's lists.

Nineteenth-Century Kinship Terms and Principles

The kinship system of both the Munsi and Unami has been called the "Mackenzie Basin" type by Spier, and would be termed Hawaiian by Murdock.[119] According to Morgan, the essential features of the Delaware (Unami) system (Fig. 1, p. 45: Fig. 2, p. 46) were:

1. A brother's son and daughter, whether Ego was male or female, were termed son and daughter.
2. A sister's son and daughter, Ego a male, were nephew and niece. Ego a female, they were son and daughter.
3. Parallel and cross-cousins were termed stepbrother and stepsister, "the males and females using different terms."[120]
4. A father's brother was termed little father.
5. A mother's brother was termed uncle.
6. Mother's sister, father's sister, and father's brother's wife were termed little mother.
7. All grandparents and all kin of the second ascending generation were called grandmother or grandfather.

[117] Trowbridge MS.

[118] Morgan, 1871, p. 221.

[119] Spier, 1925, p. 76; Murdock, 1949, pp. 223, 228.

[120] Morgan, 1871, pp. 221-22.

8. All grandchildren and kin of the second descending generation, irrespective of sex, were called by one term, grandchild.
9. If Ego was male, the children of male cousins were son and daughter, whereas children of female cousins were nephew and niece. If Ego was female, the children of siblings and cousins, irrespective of sex, were son and daughter.

Modern Kinship Terms

My data agree in the main with Morgan's, although there are some curious differences. (For comparative purposes the modern kinship terms are discussed here rather than under Acculturation.) The changes may be due to Munsi influence, since the modern system is like that of the Munsi, although the Unami dialect is employed. The changes may also be regarded as a further deterioration, particularly as the kinship society is no longer functional.

In terminology the major alteration has been in the classification of cousins. All cousins are now put in the sibling category, being termed older brother, older sister, or younger sibling. (Fig. 3, p. 47.) The children of those individuals whom Ego terms sibling are son and daughter, with the exception that male Ego calls a sister's son nephew. Male Ego does not call sister's daughter niece, as was true in Morgan's time, but calls her daughter. When cousins became brothers and sisters, it was only logical to extend the son and daughter term to their offspring. It might be noted that women in Morgan's time used the son and daughter terminology for all offspring of cousins. All of my informants were vague about the proper term for father's sister's husband and mother's sister's husband. It was given as "my little stepfather," but also as "my little father."

A Reconstruction of the Early Historic Kinship Terminology

Despite the lack of any early historic description of the Delaware kinship terminology, an attempt to reconstruct it is profitable. There is fairly extensive information concerning the other facts of social existence in early historic times, and, given these facts, only certain conditions were possible for the kinship structure. The kinds of forces that affected Delaware society between the time of first contact and 1859 are also known, as are the results that these forces generally have upon kinship systems. Moreover, Morgan's description of the kinship system in 1859 provides a point of departure.

There are strong indications that most if not all of the seventeenth-century peoples who were to become the Delaware tribe reckoned descent in the maternal line and practiced matrilocal residence.[121] It has been seen that horticulture was in the hands of women, a fact which emphasizes

[121] Wallace, 1947, pp. 1-35.

Delaware Kinship Terminology
Consanguineal

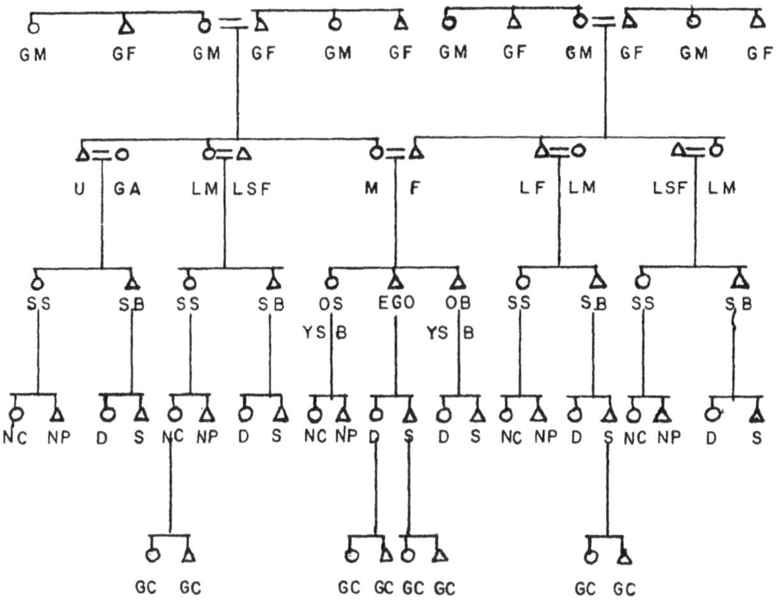

Fig. 1. Delaware terminological structure, consanguineal terms, male speaking (1859). The abbreviations are GF, grandfather; GM, grandmother; U, uncle; GA, great aunt, LM, little mother, LSF, little stepfather; M, mother; F, father; LF, little father; SS, stepsister; SB, stepbrother; OS, older sister; OB, older brother; YSB, younger sibling; NC, niece; NP, nephew; D, daughter; S, son, GC, grandchild. Δ = male; O = female. With Ego female, the only difference in terms is found for nephew and niece. They are called son and daughter, so that all kin of the first descending generation are son and daughter.

the maternal line.[122] There were other cultural traits which point to a maternal emphasis: avuncular succession of sachemship is one, as are the facts that orphaned children were cared for by maternal grandparents, that a widower had to reimburse the wife's family before remarriage, and possibly that childhood names were given by mothers rather than by fathers. The occasional polygyny of the early period did not favor either matrilocality or matrilineal descent, although if it was of a sororal type it was then compatible with matrilocality.

As has been noted, by the nineteenth century residence of a newly married couple was neolocal or bilocal, although probably it was matrilocal in early historic times. If a pre-European matrilocal society is assumed, what would cause an alteration to a neo- or bilocal rule? Murdock has said: "Rules of residence reflect general economic, social and cultural conditions. When underlying conditions change, rules of

[122]Murdock, 1949, pp. 204-5.

Delaware Kinship Terminology
Affinal

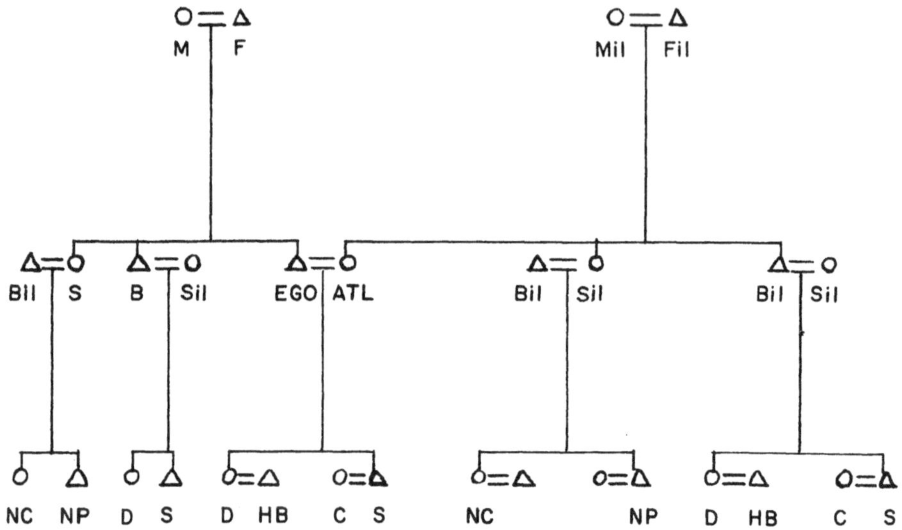

Fig. 2. Delaware terminological structure, affinal terms (1859). The abbreviations are Mil, mother-in-law; Fil, father-in-law; Bil, brother-in-law; Sil, sister-in-law; ATL, aid through life (spouse); HB, hunter for my benefit (son-in-law); C, cook (daughter-in-law). With Ego female, terms are the same. Other abbreviations as in Figure 1.

residence tend to be modified accordingly."[123] As he has pointed out further, the isolation and emphasis placed upon nuclear families, the decrease in polygyny, the scattering of kinsmen, and the individualistic emphasis placed upon economic activity, all favor the development of neolocal residence.[124] Bilocal residence is favored by "the adoption of a migratory life in unstable bands," and by the "approximate equality in status of the two sexes, especially with regard to the ownership and inheritance of property and privileges."[125] Almost all of the conditions which Murdock mentioned were prominent factors in Delaware life between 1600 and 1859. These forces are discussed at length under Acculturation; suffice it to say here that contact with Euro-American civilization caused extensive migrations, a new economic system emphasizing individual initiative, a decline in polygyny, breakup and decimation of geographically associated kinsmen, a decline in the importance of female-dominated horticulture, and increasing importance of men in subsistence. In short, residence rules of the Delawares in all probability altered from matrilocal to neolocal or bilocal.

The kinship terminology which Morgan described was in most of its

[123] Murdock, 1949, p. 17.
[124] *Ibid.*, p. 204.
[125] *Ibid.*

Modern Delaware Kinship
Terminology

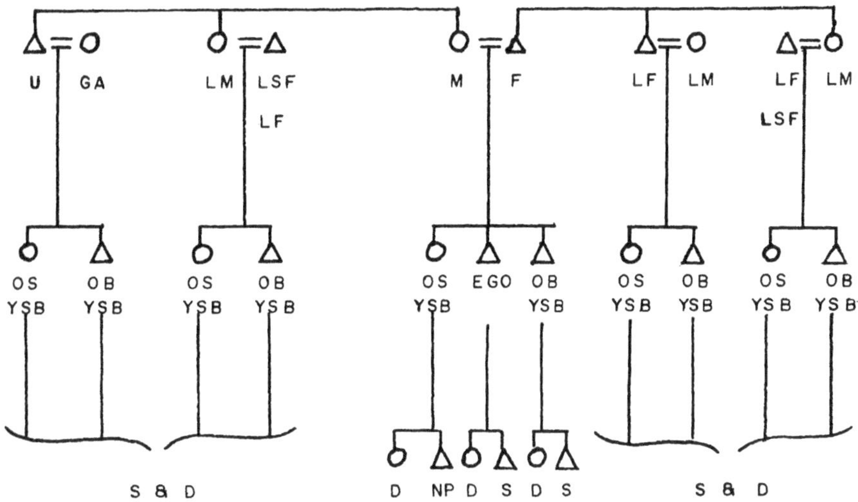

Fig. 3. Abbreviations are the same as for Figures 1 and 2. All cousins are called older brother or sister, or younger sibling. Sister's son is nephew, Ego male. Ego female, all kin of first descending generation are son or daughter. Mother's sister's husband and father's sister's husband may be called either little father, or little stepfather. A complete diagram is not given since there has been no change in other terms. Informants: O.A., M.B., J.T., F.W.

features in accord with the type which Murdock terms "Matri-Hawaiian."[126] It is apparent, however, that the early historic terminology was not Hawaiian, since descent must have been matrilineal instead of bilateral, as is required by a Hawaiian system. If an early historic system is now considered, with matrilineal descent and a matrilocal rule of residence, which by Morgan's time had evolved to a bilateral, Matri-Hawaiian type, is it possible to suggest the form of the early historic terminology? The most likely form would seem to be one of the "Iroquois" type, since the generation principle is not violated in either, and the other differences are relatively minor.[127] In an Iroquoian system cross-cousins are called by the same terms, which differ from those used for parallel cousins. Parallel cousins may or may not be called by the same terms which are used for siblings. The term applied to mother and mother's sister is different from the one applied to father's sister. If it is assumed that the Delawares had this system, with matrilocal residence and matrilineal descent, how would this alteration to the Hawaiian type take place? It may be postulated, for example, that Ego's

[126]Murdock, 1949, p. 229.
[127]White, 1939, pp. 568-70.

mother's brother upon marriage violates the traditional rule of matrilocal residence and brings his wife back to the group in which Ego is growing up. If this becomes a common occurrence, it is readily seen that a mother's brother's children might soon be confused, or aligned in Ego's mind with his parallel cousins, leading eventually to an alteration in cousin terminology. Or, if the rule of residence becomes neolocal, the same sort of alteration might take place. In this instance the reason for distinguishing between various kinds of cousins disappears, as with our own system. Neither paternal or maternal cross- or parallel cousins would in this case consistently be more familiar with Ego because of residence; they would be equals, receiving an equal emphasis in the kinship terminology. A logical accompaniment to this sort of alteration would be a change in Ego's terms for the first ascending generation. It is plain that a father's sister, who under an Iroquoian system had a special term, would now be the mother of children whom in a Hawaiian system Ego calls siblings, and hence she is called mother. It should be noted that the terminology employed in Morgan's time retained at least one feature of a previously unilateral system. This was the term for mother's brother, who was called uncle, instead of little father, as the logic of a bilateral system would lead one to expect. It may also be noted that the offspring of this uncle were placed in the sibling category by Ego. It may well be that the special, asymmetrical term for a mother's brother is a vestige of the once important avuncular relationship. It is difficult to arrive at a reasonable hypothesis for the similarly nonbilateral terminology applied to nepotic relatives in Morgan's time. First, there may have been no change in the terms employed for the children of siblings, for this is still a common Iroquoian type of terminology. I have not been able, however, to state the most probable terminology for the offspring of cousins; that the terms were different from the ones used in Morgan's time seems likely.

Clan and Phratry

The early historic Delawares seem to have had a rather weakly developed clan system. These named units probably consisted of a woman, her descendants, and collateral kin unilaterally reckoned in the maternal line. It cannot be determined whether these units should more properly be termed lineages, that is, unilateral descent groups tracing descent to a known ancestress, or clans, which may be defined as named, unilateral, exogamous descent groups, tracing ancestry to a mythically, or at least genetically, remote ancestor. Morgan termed these groups subgentes, since they were not totemic.[128] Wallace termed them lineages, and Harrington has called them clans.[129] Because of the diverse nature of the peoples who were to become the Delaware tribe any single characterization may be inaccurate.

[128]Morgan, 1877, p. 171.

[129]Wallace, 1947, p. 6; Harrington, 1913, p. 210.

The clans seem to have been territorial units of a loose sort. The family hunting territories were grouped together (See Chap. II) into larger "communal territories." These larger geographical units should probably be equated with the clans. The numerous small settlements were probably inhabited by subdivisions of the clans, either maternal lineages or extended families. It is possible that several different clan units, or subunits, inhabited these settlements, but it seems more likely, on the basis of their size, that this was not so. Men probably sought wives in nearby villages. If this was true, or if there was village endogamy because several clans occupied one village, then men could continue to hunt in their maternally inherited hunting territories. Even if this was not so, it seems entirely possible that in a relatively short space of time men could become well enough acquainted with a wife's hunting territory to be able to hunt there effectively.

Matrilineally related women communally tilled their outlying garden plots. In addition to co-operation in subsistence activities and mutual aid in general, clan members "were theoretically supposed to avenge the death of one of their number, or, in case of a kinsman's forfeiting his right to live through the murder of a member of another lineage, to buy back his life by the payment of blood money."[130] The leading matron of the clan was termed "chiefmaker,"[131] since it was she who could remove and appoint, within the rules of inheritance, the clan chief or sachem. Clans were not totemic, but were named for some "peculiarity of their ancestors or from some locality once frequented by them."[132] L.H. Morgan, the first investigator to list them, said that each clan was "composed of twelve subgentes, each having some of the attributes of a gens."[133] Morgan's "subgentes" are herein reproduced:[134]

1. Wolf. Took'-seat

1. Mä-an'-greet, Big Feet
2. Wee-sow-het'-ko, Yellow Tree
3. Pä-sa-kun-ä̆'-mon, Pulling Corn
4. We-yar-nih'-kä̆-to, Care Enterer
5. Toosh-war-ka'-ma, Across the River
6. O-lum'-a-ne, Vermilion
7. Pun-ar'-you, Dog standing by Fireside
8. Kwin-eek'cha, Long Body
9. Moon-har-tar'ne, Digging
10. Non-har'-min, Pulling up Stream
11. Long-ush-har-kar'-to, Brush Log
12. Maw-soo-toh', Bringing Along

2. Turtle. Poke-koo-un'go

1. O-ka-ho'-ki, Ruler
2. Ta-ko-ong'-o-to, High Bank Shore
3. See-har-ong'-o-to, Drawing down Hill
4. Ole-har-kar-me'kar-to, Elector
5. Mä̆-har-o-luk'-ti, Brave
6. Toosh-ki-pa-kwis-i, Green Leaves
7. Tung-ul-ung'-si, Smallest Turtle
8. We-lun-ŭng-sil, Little Turtle
9. Lee-kwin-ä̆-i', Snapping Turtle
10. Kwis-aese-kees'-to, Deer

The two remaining subgentes are extinct.

3. Turkey. Pul-la'-ook

1. Mo-har-ä̆'-lä, Big Bird
7. Tong-o-nä̆'-o-to, Drift Log

[130] Wallace, 1949, p. 8
[131] *Ibid.*
[132] Harrington, 1913, p. 210.
[133] Morgan, 1877, p. 171.
[134] *Ibid.*, p. 172.

2. Le-le-wa'-you, Bird's Cry
3. Moo-kwung-wa-ho'-ki, Eye Pain
4. Moo-har-mo-wi-kar'-nu, Scratch the Path
5. O-ping-ho'-ki, Opossum Ground
6. Muh-ho-we-kä'-ken, Old Shin
8. Nool-ă-mar-lar'-mo, Living in Water
9. Muh-krent-har'-ne, Root Digger
10. Mur-karm-huk-se, Red Face
11. Koo-wä-ho'ke, Pine Region
12. Oo-ckuk'-ham, Ground Scratcher

Harrington in 1913 found some of these clans still in existence in Canada. He added two that could not be associated with any of Morgan's. They were Mun'hat ko wi of the Turkey phratry and Ali 'ke, of the Wolf phratry.[135] There is no knowledge or memory of the clans today in Oklahoma.

Each clan was a member of one of the three phratries (Morgan's gentes), and phratry membership was a consequence of clan membership. Many of the clan names were obviously associated in meaning with their phratry: "Ground Scratcher" with Turkey phratry, "Snapping Turtle" with Turtle phratry, to give but two examples. No mention was made of the three phratries in the literature of the seventeenth century. Since the phratries had no political functions in the early period, Europeans probably did not come in contact with them. It seems unlikely that the association of every clan with a phratry in historic times represented the early pattern, when the social diversity and the spatial dispersion of the pretribal Delawares is considered. What it was like is unknown, although a looser, more informal association, probably with fewer clans in a phratry, might be postulated. As remnant peoples joined the tribe, they probably were considered kinship units, thus swelling the number of clans. In some fashion they became associated with one or another of the phratries.

In the eighteenth century phratry heads became political leaders of the Delaware tribe. This development is discussed further under Acculturation. The phratries were exogamous, at least in later historic times, since Morgan said that "in old times no man was allowed to marry a woman of his own tribe [phratry] and it was the law until within the last generation...."[136] The three phratries were totemic units named for qualities of animals rather than for the animals themselves. The Tuksit were named for a quality of the wolf, "round foot," the Pilea for a quality or attribute of the turkey, "don't chew," and the Pokuwango for the slow characteristics of the turtle, "crawling" or "dragging along."[137] For the sake of brevity, however, I shall continue the usage initiated by Morgan and refer to these groups as Wolf, Turkey, and Turtle.

The primary function of the phratries was ceremonial: "In ceremonial rites they each enjoy special privileges, have allotted duties to perform, segregated places of seating, the animal emblem as a name signature in common, and their own chiefs and council of three."[138] According to Harrington each phratry had a paramount leader, who had rather limited

[135] Harrington, 1913, p. 210.
[136] Morgan, 1859, MS.
[137] Harrington, 1913, p. 210; O.A., J.T.
[138] Speck, 1931, p. 75.

powers, serving primarily in the capacity of adviser.[139] This position was gained through inheritance.[140] Morgan agreed with him, saying:

> A Delaware woman, after stating to the author that she, with her children, belonged to the Wolf gens, and her husband to the Turtle, remarked that when Captain Ketchum... late head chief or sachem of the Turtle gens, died, he was succeeded by his nephew, John Conner... a son of one of the sisters of the deceased sachem, who was also of the Turtle gens. The decedent left a son, but he was of another gens and consequently incapable of succeeding. With the Delawares, as with the Iroquois, the office passed from brother to brother, or from uncle to nephew, because descent was in the female line.[141]

The three phratries have frequently been confused with the three geographical divisions of the Delawares. Heckewelder was the first to make this association, and his copyists have continued his correlation.[142] The association was Turtle with Unami, Turkey with Unalachtigo, and Wolf with Munsi.[143] Harrington dissented from this viewpoint on the basis that phratry members could be found among any of the geographical divisions.[144] As early as 1824 Trowbridge specifically denied this association and said that members of all three phratries were found in the Munsi group.[145] There can be little doubt that Heckewelder was mistaken in associating the geographical divisions with the phratries.

Social Control

Government

Relatively more information exists dealing with political organization and government of the early historic Delawares than concerning the kinship system. Europeans had an opportunity to observe the governmental machinery, participating in councils and the like, but their contact with the kinship system was so slight that they could not understand it.

Each social unit, or clan, had a leader, usually termed "sachem" in the literature, who had inherited his position through the maternal line. "When a king dies it is not his children who succeed him, but his brother by the same mother, or his sister's, or her daughter's male children."[146] Penn, who has given the clearest description of government, said:

> Their government is by kings, which they call sachama, and those by succession; but always of the mother's side. For instance, the children of him who is now king will not succeed, but his brother by the mother, or the children of his sister, whose sons (and after them the children of her daughters) will reign, for no woman inherits. The reason they render for this way of descent is, that their issue may not be spurious.[147]

---

[139] Harrington, 1913, p. 211.

[140] *Ibid.*

[141] Morgan, 1877, p. 173.

[142] Heckewelder, 1881, pp. 51-52; Brinton, 1885, p. 39.

[143] Heckewelder, 1881, pp. 51-52.

[144] Harrington, 1913, p. 209.

[145] Trowbridge MS.

[146] Holm, 1834, p. 133.

[147] Penn, 1882, p. 244; Thomas, 1912, p. 335, and Zeisberger, 1910, p. 98, agreed on the matriarchal succession of sachems.

In the seventeenth century sachems had limited power and authority and, incredibly in the eyes of Europeans, had no special servants, prerogatives, or the like.[148] Pastorius, for instance, in a letter written in 1694 said:

> These very kings go forth with the others to hunt, shoot the wild animals, and support themselves by the work of their own hands. They have neither servants nor lacqueys, neither housemaids nor court-ladies, and what use has one for a master of horse who keeps no horse, but always goes on foot? In like manner, no court-steward is needed, where there is no one to be cared for besides one's self and one's wife and children.[149]

In the seventeenth century these clan leaders owed allegiance to no higher authority; there were no tribal chiefs.[150] By the eighteenth century leaders had appeared who wielded much more power over larger groups.

Despite the little real authority which sachems had, their councils were solemn, ceremonial occasions. Penn and Denton provide early and clear descriptions of how these men governed; their accounts are confirmed by a number of other investigators:[151]

> Every king hath his council; and that consists of all the old and wise men of his nation, which perhaps is two hundred people. Nothing of moment is undertaken, be it war, peace, selling of land, or traffic, without advising with them, and, which is more, with the young men too. It is admirable to consider how powerful the kings are, and yet how they move by the breath of their people. I have had occasion to be in council with them upon treaties for land, and to adjust the terms of trade. Their order is thus: The king sits in the middle of an half-moon, and has his council, the old and wise, on each hand. Behind them, or at a little distance, sit the younger fry in the same figure.[152]

Denton said:

> When their King or Sachem sits in Council he hath a company of armed men to guard his person, great respect being shown him by the People, which is principally manifested by their silence: After he hath declared the cause of their convention he demands their opinion, ordering who shall begin: The person ordered to speak, after he hath declared his minde tells them he hath done: no man ever interrupting any person in his speech, nor offering to speak though he make never so many or long stops, till he says he hath no more to say: the Council having all declared their opinion, the King after some pause gives the definitive sentence, which is commonly seconded with a shout from the people, every one seeming to applaud & manifest their assent to what is determined: If any person be condemned to die, which is seldom, unless for Murder or Incest, the King himself goes in person (for you must understand they have no prisons, and the guilty person flies into the Woods) when they go in quest of him, & having found him, the King shoots first, though at never such a distance, & then happy is the man can shoot him down, & cut off his — which they commonly wear, who for his pains is made some Captain or other military officer.[153]

---

148 Lindestrom, 1925, p. 205; Thomas, 1912, p. 335; De Laet, 1909, pp. 57-58; Van der Donck, 1909, p. 302.

149 Pastorius, 1912, pp. 425-26.

150 Lindestrom, 1925, pp. 128-30.

151 Holm, 1834, p. 133; Thomas, 1912, p. 335; Heckewelder, 1881, pp. 107-11; Zeisberger, 1910, pp. 92-93; Harrington, 1913, p. 211.

152 Penn, 1882, pp. 244-45.

153 Denton, 1845, p. 10.

It should be noted, then, that a sachem's duties were administrative, legislative, and judicial. The duties of these chiefs were on the whole fairly simple; their power was in no sense autocratic. They carried out the wishes of the people directly through the council and indirectly through informal pressure. To retain their position they had to be "... gracious, hospitable, communicative, affable, and their house is open to every Indian."[154] It appears that incompetent chiefs could be deposed.[155]

Morgan stated that there were two war chiefs, subordinate to the principal chiefs in peacetime. War chiefs gained their rank through leading a number of successful war parties, and were often those individuals who had had visions indicating that war was their vocation.[156] By this time (1859) the phratry heads were the political leaders, and one of these men was the principal chief.[157] If the war chiefs unanimously favored war, the civil chief had to give his consent.[158] Political as well as military power was then in the hands of the war chiefs.

Informal Controls

Individual behavior was controlled primarily by family and kinship groups, rather than by special institutions. Europeans were surprised to learn that Indian behavior was so well regulated:

> Judged by the mere appearance of the Indians one is surprised how modest and careful they are in relation to each other and imagines that the whites, if they were as free a people and had neither government nor punishment to fear, would not be as united and peaceable as the Indians appear to be.[159]

Penn said:

> The justice they have is pecuniary. In case of any wrong or evil fact, be it murder itself, they atone by feasts and presents of their wampum, which is proportioned to the quality of the offence or person injured, or of the sex they are of. For, in case they kill a woman, they pay double; and the reason they render is, "that she breedeth children, which men cannot do." It is rare that they fall out if sober; and if drunk they forgive, saying, "It was the drink, and not the man, that abused them."[160]

A number of other sources have noted that the laws of the wergild were enforced.[161] Denton said:

> The friends of the murdered person do revenge upon the murderer unless he purchase his life with money, which they sometimes do: This money is made of a Periwinkle shell of which there is black & white, made much like unto beads & put upon strings.[162]

---

[154]Zeisberger, 1910, p. 93.

[155]Ruttenber, 1872, pp. 47-48; Zeisberger, 1910, pp. 93-95; Heckewelder, 1881, pp. 107-11; Harrington, 1913, p. 211.

[156]Zeisberger, 1910, p. 101; Loskiel, 1794, p. 142.

[157]Morgan, 1859, MS.

[158]Zeisberger, 1910, p. 98; Ruttenber, 1872, p. 48.

[159]Zeisberger, 1910, p. 122.

[160]Penn, 1882, p. 245.

[161]Pastorius, 1912, p. 434; De Rasieres, 1909, p. 109; Lindestrom, 1925, p. 205; Wallace, 1947, pp. 10-11.

[162]Denton, 1845, p. 7.

If peace could not be restored through the payment of "blood money," the interested kin, in case of murder, resolved the case by the murder of the guilty party or one of his kin.[163] From the scanty evidence available it would appear that only in the case of unresolved murders which were upsetting internal peace would society step in to halt the conflict.

Little is known about etiquette and the customary ways in which people behaved towards one another. Penn, however, said:

> In liberality they excel. Nothing is too good for their friend. Give them a fine gun, coat, or other thing, it may pass twenty hands before it sticks: light of heart, strong affections, but soon spent: the most merry creatures that live: they feast and dance perpetually; they never have much, nor want much. Wealth circulateth like the blood. All parts partake; and though none shall want what another hath, yet exact observers of property.[164]

Denton in the same vein said:

> They are extraordinary charitable one to another, one having nothing to spare, but he freely imparts it to his friends & whatsoever they get by gaming or any other way, they share one to another leaving themselves commonly the least share.[165]

This sort of behavior is, of course, to be expected in a society organized upon a kinship basis. Society was predicated, not on the competition between individuals, but upon mutual assistance and the unity of action of the kin group. Respect for, and solicitous care of, the aged has also been noted.[166]

War

Small-scale, probably infrequent raiding by a few warriors was the typical form of warfare in early historic times and undoubtedly in the pre-European period. This type of conflict was a personal, usually noneconomic feuding. An apt designation for it might be primitive war, since it seems to be characteristic of many cultures at this and lower technological levels of development. A special term for it is necessary since it generally differs in its causation, purpose, and form from total, modern warfare. There is little evidence that chronic, full-scale, economically caused warfare existed aboriginally in what is now northeastern United States. Hunt shared this point of view in writing of the Iroquois, generally considered to have been the most warlike of peoples in this area! He said:

> In the beginning intertribal rivalries were not keen, and intertribal war was purely private and social interprise. But before long the European trade was to create new rivalries, and whet old ones to the point where the issue became one of survival.[167]

[163] Van der Donck, 1909, p. 303.
[164] Penn, 1882, p. 243.
[165] Denton, 1845, p. 9. Also see Zeisberger, 1910, pp. 115-16.
[166] Zeisberger, 1910, p. 123; Heckewelder, 1881, p. 103.
[167] Hunt, 1939, p. 22.

Kroeber, on the other hand, has characterized warfare for the northeast as a whole as being of the modern, total kind:

> It was warfare that was insane, unending, continuously attritional, from our point of view; yet it was so integrated into the whole fabric of Eastern culture, so dominantly emphasized within it, that escape from it was well-nigh impossible.... This warfare, with its attendant unsettlement, confusion, destruction, and famines, was probably the most potent reason why population remained low in the East.[168]

There is no evidence which would support Kroeber's allegations, at least with respect to the prehistoric and early historic Delawares. Whether population density was low or not is conjectural, but even on the assumption that it was low, there is a much more realistic hypothesis available to explain it than the one offered by Kroeber. (See the Summary for this discussion.)

In the face of lack of evidence substantiating chronic and total warfare among the early Delawares, it is necessary to utilize indirect evidence to demonstrate that this type of conflict was minimal. The archaeology of the area offers little of a positive nature. Village sites of the East River Aspect, so far as can be determined, were not fortified or palisaded. They were "situated on or near tidal streams and bays."[169] A few sources mention palisades, but the evidence is not conclusive.[170] In Chapter I it was noted that Delaware villages were small, scattered, and on poorly defensible ground. During part of the year even village units did not exist, since family groups were away hunting. These facts do not suggest a martial atmosphere. If population densities were low, it seems unlikely that competition for agricultural land or for choice fishing locations existed. Disputes over hunting territories might have occurred, but these would have been primarily a family matter rather than of general concern. For chronic, vicious, and total war to exist there has to be a fairly strong motivation. As has been demonstrated elsewhere, cultures do not indulge in full-scale war, in the modern sense of the word, simply as an outlet for "psychological urges" or as a game.[171] As has been shown in the first chapter, Delaware culture in precontact times was in a political sense almost wholly unorganized. There was no tribe and there were apparently no institutions which in the event of invasion or attack could organize the people into an effective unit. It is difficult to believe that a people perilously and unendingly at war (for no apparent reason) would have as rudimentary a political and military organization as had the Delawares. Even in this cursory examination of the problem, it is clear that the precontact Delawares could have had only a small-scale, primitive war complex. This condition rapidly changed with the invasion of Europeans; chronic warfare of the most bitter kind soon came to be the daily pill of the Delawares. (This subject is taken up more fully in Chapter V.)

[168]Kroeber, 1947, p. 148.

[169]C. S. Smith, 1950, p. 116.

[170]Brinton, 1885, p. 51; Skinner, 1947, p. 7.

[171]Newcomb, 1950, pp. 317-30.

Daniel Denton's description of the Delawares' primitive war complex is the earliest one I have found. Most of the material is derived from later sources. It may be assumed that the customs of war in these later periods were largely derived from, or were elaborations upon, the earlier primitive war complex. Denton said of their warfare:

> In their wars they fight no pitcht fields; but when they have notice of an enemies approach, they endeavour to secure their wives and children upon some Island, or in some thick swamp, & then with their guns & hatchet they waylay their enemies, some lying behind one, some another & it is a great fight where seven or eight is slain.[172]

Warriors were recruited at a dance, those wishing to join the war party taking part in the dance:

> When those invited have assembled at the appointed place, one of the war chiefs holding the great belt in his hands, which is now covered with vermilion, rises and dances the war dance around the circle formed by the warriors. The council thus opened he explains to them the circumstances which occasion the meeting and with all his eloquence enforces the necessity of resorting to war for a redress of their injuries. He then repeats the dance and seats himself, when each one who chooses to declare his intention to join the party takes the belt and dances around the circle as his chief had done.[173]

This dance was repeated at the war party's first camp, the women having followed the expedition.[174] Trowbridge stated that cooks were taken along and added:

> Formerly no man joined a war party until he was twenty four winters old, as they were thought to be too imprudent at an earlier age; but of late years this custom has not obtained among them. The aged often continue to bear arms so long as their strength permits, and some have been known to join warparties when from their advanced age they were obligated to ride on horseback; but in these cases they did not approach the field of battle.[175]

The bow and arrow constituted the principal weapon; shields of elkhide or bark and helmets constructed of sticks were used.[176] War parties may have worn special regalia; Holm said that they wore red turkey feathers when going to war.[177]

War parties even when directed at Europeans were small in size. With perhaps a few exceptions, their size never exceeded two dozen men. This was in keeping with their military tactics in that a successful war party consisted of a rapid raid without loss and the capture of prisoners or plunder. A big battle was considered to have occurred if ten or eleven warriors were killed.[178] The taking of scalps was mentioned in the seventeenth century,[179] and prisoners were taken:

---

[172]Denton, 1845, p. 8; Van der Donck, 1909, pp. 300-301.

[173]Trowbridge MS.

[174]Heckewelder, 1881, p. 210.

[175]Trowbridge MS.

[176]Johnson, 1917, pp. 281-82; Holm, 1834, p. 138; Lindestrom, 1925, p. 197; Loskiel, 1794, p. 141.

[177]Holm, 1834, p. 137.

[178]*Ibid.*, pp. 137-38; Van der Donck, 1909, pp. 300-301.

[179]Holm, p. 138.

> They cut and slash them alive, cutting off their ears, their noses, their tongues, and their lips, and also their fingers and toes: they also cut off pieces of flesh from different parts of their bodies, and then they strew ashes over the wounds in order to prevent the blood from flowing.[180]

Charles Stuart, captured in the mid-eighteenth century, recounted the torture, motivated by revenge, through which he was to go. It bears a striking resemblance to Holm's account:

> The Deaths we were to Suffer were as Follows, First our Fingers were To be Cut off and we were To Be Forced to eat them, then our Eyes pull^d out wch we were also to Eat, after wch we were To Be Put on a Scaffold and Burnt, the Manner of Scaffolding is first To Tie Them To a Post or Tree with so much Length of Rope as will allow them ab^t 3 Foot to move about the Tree, then they raise them a little from the Ground on a Logg or what Else happens to be Most Convenient to Set them on then Puts Wood about them and burns them up-After the Council in Genl had agreed To Put us to this Death.[181]

Colonel William Crawford, who was tortured to death by the Delawares, underwent more or less the same rigors.[182] In general, torture was prolonged as long as was possible and was motivated entirely by revenge, particularly so in a case like Crawford's, since he had with him on his expedition men responsible for the Gnadenhutten massacre. Captives who escaped and were recaptured probably suffered the most ingenious tortures.[183]

Prisoners were adopted if they were not killed. One late source stated that a family might request a leader of a war party to bring back "a prisoner who shall fill the place of some deceased relative." Trowbridge went on to say that "in the adoption of prisoners no particular distinction is made on account of age, save that the person adopted must be youthful to supply the place of a son or daughter, and aged for a father or uncle."[184] According to Zeisberger, if white prisoners were intended for adoption, their hair was cut Indian fashion immediately after capture and their faces were painted red. These adopted individuals were well treated, but if they ran away they were liable to be tortured and killed.[185]

Prisoners were forced to run the gauntlet, whether they were to be killed or adopted. When the returning warriors approached a village, Indian prisoners were forced to dance while the warriors paraded booty and red painted scalps on poles. For white prisoners the dance was apparently not held.[186] The prisoners were made to pass through two lines of the general multitude to a hut or a painted post.[187] The men, women, and children were equipped with axes, sticks, clubs, and whatever else came to hand and would attempt to strike the prisoner as he passed by. Charles Stuart, who "ran the gauntlet," went through what is probably a typical experience:

---

180 Holm, p. 138.
181 Stuart, 1926, pp. 61-62.
182 Butterfield, 1882, p. 293.
183 Schweinitz, 1905, p. 410.
184 Trowbridge MS.
185 Zeisberger, 1910, p. 106.
186 *Ibid.*, p. 105; Trowbridge MS.
187 Zeisberger, 1910, p. 105.

> It was my Lott to Be Carried to Kittanning with other Prisoners, and on Entring into the Town we were obliged to Pass Between Two Rows of Indians Containing ab^{t} 100 on Each Side who were arm^{d} with various kind of Weapons such as Axes Tomhawks Cutlasses Hoop Poles, Pieces of Wood etc. But they did not strike wth Axes, and only Used the Heads and Handles of their Tomhawks, But used the Blades of the Cutlasses tho' not with so much Severity as To Kill, I had however the Misfortune to receive a Blow on the Side of my Forehead wth one of them wch Cut me To the Bone & a Billet of Wood Stikeing on the head ab^{t} the Same time Between Both I was Knock^{d} down to the Ground –It was only the more elderly People both Male and Female wch rece^{d} this Useage – the young prisoners of Both Sexes Escaped without it. . . .[188]

One girl captive (Marie Le Roy), intended for adoption, said:

> [We] received our welcome, according to Indian custom. It consisted of three blows each, on the back. They were, however, administered with great mercy. Indeed, we concluded that we were beaten merely in order to keep up an ancient usage, and not with the intention of injuring us.[189]

Whether running the gauntlet was a precontact trait is undetermined.

Peace was secured by a defeated group through the agency of an ambassador. This individual bore no arms, traveled openly, and had no distinguishing marks of office other than a white belt of wampum, "containing the speech with which he was entrusted."[190] When he reached the enemy's camp a council was called, and the wishes of the ambassador were made known. If agreement was reached the victors invited the vanquished to a council:

> At this council a grand feast was prepared and was accompanied with dancing. The weaker party made the necessary acknowledgements, the peace belt was delivered to the conquerors as a token of their superiority and the parties returned to their respective homes. They never have used the pipe as is customary among northern nations, nor had they anything like flags or ceremonial bearings before their knowledge of the whites.[191]

[188]Stuart, 1926, p. 66.
[189]Schweinitz, 1905, p. 409.
[190]Trowbridge MS.
[191]*Ibid.*

IV. DELAWARE IDEOLOGY

Religion and Magic

Of all the aspects of Delaware culture, religious ceremonies and beliefs have received the most extended treatment by anthropologists because this segment of culture has been better preserved than any other. F. G. Speck's *A Study of the Delaware Big House Ceremony* described the central religious ceremony of the Delawares, and his *Oklahoma Delaware Ceremonies, Dances, and Feasts* added to this account and described the minor ceremonies.[1] M. R. Harrington's *Religion and Ceremonies of the Lenape,* and his "Preliminary Sketch of Lenape Culture" dealt with the Big House Ceremony and a number of minor beliefs and practices.[2] It is hardly necessary, then, to present an extended treatment of Delaware religion; instead, particular attention will be paid to the early historic religious beliefs and practices.

Supernatural Beings

The Delawares believed in a single, all powerful, originally creative, supernatural power. He was called Gicelamu'kaong, which means "Great Spirit," "Great Power," or "Creator."[3] This supernatural figure was a remote one, somewhat removed from the affairs of men. He had appointed a number of agents who created the world and all upon it. He was capable of endowing any matter, either animate or inanimate, with supernatural attributes or power.[4] Lesser anthropomorphic deities, enjoying their authority through this primal power, were the Sun, the Moon, the Seven Thunders, the Four Directions, the Earth Mother, and the Mask Being, or Living Solid Face. The Sun and the Moon were addressed as Elder Brother, the former having the duty of providing light, and the latter that of protecting and guarding people at night.[5] Our Mother, the Earth, was Sun's sister, but not Moon's sister, and was charged with caring for and feeding the people.[6] The Seven Thunders, who combined features of men and birds, provided rain for crops, protected men from various water monsters, and were responsible for lightning.[7] The deities of the cardinal directions were associated with the wind and the

---

[1]Speck, 1931, 1937.

[2]Harrington, 1921; 1913, pp. 208-35.

[3]Penn, 1882, p. 244; Brainerd, 1884, pp. 244-45; Zeisberger, 1910, p. 128; Speck, 1931, p. 26; Harrington, 1921, pp. 18-24; Trowbridge MS. gives a literal translation, "Keshaallemoonkunk, he who created us by his thought" (Kinietz, 1946, p. 88). The Christian Delaware religious texts use Kitannowit, "great spirit," rather than this term.

[4]De Laet, 1909, pp. 49-50; Brainerd, 1884, pp. 244-45.

[5]Brainerd, 1884, p. 345; Trowbridge MS; Harrington, 1913, p. 226; Speck, 1931, pp. 29-33; M.B.

[6]Harrington, 1913, pp. 226-27; O.A., J.T., M.B.

[7]Harrington, 1913, pp. 226-27; 1921, pp. 29-30; M.B.

weather.[8] The Mask Being was the only deity who was made concrete by human impersonation. Brainerd saw this deity impersonated and gave a vivid description:

> He made his appearance in his pontifical garb, which was a coat of boar [bear] skins, dressed with the hair on, and hanging down to his toes; a pair of bearskin stockings; and a great wooden face painted, the one half black, and other half tawny, about the color of an Indian's skin, with an extravagant mouth, cut very much awry; the face fastened to a bearskin cap, which was drawn over his head. He advanced towards me with the instrument in his hand, which he used for music in his idolatrous worship; which was a dry tortoise-shell with some corn in it, and the neck of it drawn on to a piece of wood, which made a very convenient handle. As he came forward, he beat his tune with the rattle, and danced with all his might, but did not suffer any part of his body, not so much as his fingers, to be seen. No one would have imagined from his oppearance (sic) or actions, that he could have been a human creature, if they had not had some intimation of it otherwise. When he came near me, I could not but shrink away from him although it was then noonday, and I knew who it was: his appearance and gestures were so prodigiously frightful.[9]

The Mask Being was the guardian of animals and in recent times took part in the Big House Ceremony. It was this masked figure with which children were threatened.[10] The stone faces found in archaeological sites attributed to the Delawares bear a striking resemblance to it.[11] Speck said that they "may be thought of as prototypes of the small wooden and corn-husk masks still serving the Iroquois as 'guardians of health' and the Delawares as personal charms."[12] A multitude of lesser deities included Doll Beings, Tornado, Mother Corn, Snow Boy, Comet, animal spirits, plant spirits, and local genii.[13]

Approaches to the Supernatural

The principal means by which an individual got in contact with supernatural powers was in a dream or vision:

> Such dream no doubt has great effect during the life of its subject, and in his private worship all his songs are descriptive of some of the events which he saw in his dream. He often repeats them and does not fail to attribute his success to the deity whose wonderful appearance had foretold his good fortune, or any mishap to his own bad conduct which incensed his guardian.[14]

Not only was the guardian spirit the guiding force in an individual's life, the secret of whatever success he had, and aid in time of trouble, but the public recitation of visions was the basis for the major religious

---

[8]Harrington, 1921, p. 25.

[9]Brainerd, 1884, pp. 184-85. Luckenbach, 1938, p. 451, also described this masked figure.

[10]Harrington, 1921, pp. 31-34; Speck, 1931, pp. 61-62; 1950, pp. 32-34; L.F., O.A.

[11]Skinner, 1920, p. 5; Harrington, 1921, p. 36.

[12]Speck, 1950, p. 45.

[13]Harrington, 1921, pp. 43-51.

[14]Trowbridge MS.

ceremonials.[15] Subsequent to their initial vision men might have repeated contacts with their spiritual guardians. An informant's grandfather had multiple visions, and the account is reproduced here to demonstrate the type of vision and vision quest current in the nineteenth century; it probably is similar to earlier ones:

> My grandfather was hunting one time as a boy. He wounded a deer, but it got away. He was sad and felt very bad. He cried and cried. He happened to be standing near a grove of young pine trees. The pines sang a beautiful song to him. He stopped crying and listened to their singing and the things they were telling him. The song was so beautiful that he no longer cared that the deer had escaped. Later he had a second vision of a large bone in the sky. In a third vision he saw a serpent with twelve eyes. This serpent could see everything. His fourth vision was of tiny babies and of unborn babies. All the babies were glad to see him. When he was mature he became a shaman and excelled at curing the diseases of childhood. (M.B.)

Young men obtained guardian spirits by sacrifice, fasting, and isolation, as has been noted. The supplicant tried to cajole and flatter some supernatural being into pitying him and hence safeguarding him. Zeisberger, who understood the young man's attitude, said:

> Most extraordinary experiences have been met with by boys from twelve to fourteen years of age, when they have been alone in the forest in apprehension and in need. An old man in a gray beard may have appeared and said in soothing tone, "Do not fear, I am a rock and thou shalt call me by this name. I am the Lord of the whole earth and of every living creature therein, of the air and of the wind and weather. No one dare oppose me and I will give thee the same power. No one shall do thee harm and thou needest not to fear any man." Such and similar prophecies he makes. Such a boy ruminates upon what he has heard and is confirmed in the opinion as he grows up that a peculiar power has been imparted to him to perform extraordinary exploits, and he imagines that no one can do him injury.[16]

Guardian spirits were usually animals or birds, but could be plants, any of the deities, inanimate objects, or ghosts. Trowbridge mentioned as guardian spirits bear, wolf, dog, tree, cornstalk, "or anything else which the imagination can conceive"; Zeisberger, the moon, owls and other birds, fish, and "ridiculously insignificant creatures such as ants."[17] As Benedict has shown for the Central Algonkians, the Delawares felt that animal guardian spirits were ancestral prototypes rather than the animals themselves. Thus, guardian spirit animals were not necessarily taboo as food.[18]

The apparition that appeared in visions and in other hallucinations not only indicated what sort of supernatural being he was, but foretold the future of the one to whom he appeared — whether or not he was to

---

[15]Zeisberger, 1910, pp. 132-33; Trowbridge MS; Harrington, 1913, p. 227; Speck, 1931, pp. 51-54.

[16]Zeisberger, 1910, p. 127; Harrington, 1921, pp. 67-77, gave examples of a number of visions.

[17]Trowbridge MS; Zeisberger, 1910, p. 132.

[18]Benedict, 1923, p. 49.

become a shaman, chief, warrior, a person of riches, one with many relatives, or a failure.[19] The most unfortunate persons were those who had no guardian spirit. After one was granted a guardian spirit he commonly made an amulet or fetish. Frequently this was either a representation of the human figure or a stone or clay effigy of the human head. It also might be claws or teeth of an animal or bird.[20] Lindestrom said:

> They consider this their god, so sacred that no one is allowed to touch it.... In this their god they have such a strong faith, that the night he dreams about him, he will at once the following day be able to shoot as much game and catch as much fish as ever he wants to....[21]

Although most of our information about the vision quest is relatively recent, there seems to be no reason why it should not be valid for prehistoric and early historic times.

Apart from the influence that individuals wielded over supernatural powers as a consequence of obtaining a guardian spirit, favor could be curried and influence exerted through sacrifice, primarily by burning flesh and tobacco, but also by dances and songs. Sacrifices of first fruits were commonly mentioned in seventeenth-century sources. Penn said of these:

> Their sacrifice is their first fruits. The first and fattest buck they kill goeth to the fire, where he is all burnt, with a mournful ditty of him who performeth the ceremony, but with such marvellous fervency and labour of body, that he will even sweat to a foam. The other part [of their worship] is their cantico, performed by round dances, sometimes words, sometimes songs, then shouts; two being in the middle who begin, and by singing and drumming on a board, direct the chorus. Their postures in the dance are very antic and differing, but all keep measure. This is done with equal earnestness and labour, but great appearance of joy. In the fall, when the corn cometh in, they begin to feast one another.[23]

Trowbridge said:

> When the ice is about to leave the rivers they make an offering of Tobacco with a wooden bowl of parched corn, by placing it on the surface and telling their grandfather, as they call it, that they leave him a pipe to smoke and something to eat on his journey. They sometimes make this offering of tobacco to obtain a safe voyage across the ice and for the same reason they throw it into the water when danger is apprehended. When they go to hunt, at the first encampment an offering of tobacco is made by burning, to the seven masters of the game.[24]

There were also many magical methods by which supernatural powers were influenced, but they are not well recorded in the literature. There are some indications from modern ethnographic data which

---

[19] Luckenbach, 1938, p. 612.

[20] Zeisberger, 1910, pp. 132-33.

[21] Lindestrom, 1925, p. 207; Zeisberger, 1910, p. 141, stated the same thing.

[22] Lindestrom, 1925, p. 208; Pastorius, 1912, p. 434; Brickell, 1842, p. 49; M.B.

[23] Penn, 1882, p. 244.

[24] Trowbridge MS.

suggest, and may reproduce, early magical practices. The best-known remaining magical practice is a rain-making device. It is said that a scale from the mythical horned serpent when put in water would make it rain (F.W., J.T.). The scale has disappeared today, but there are a number of tales about its efficacy.[25] Speck noted a rain-making ritual in which a weasel skin was employed.[26]

It was possible to divine future events by magical methods. Whether a wounded warrior was going to die or get well, for example, was foretold by putting a piece of dried liver in a cup of water. If the resulting bloody solution circled the cup before sinking to the bottom, the wounded person would recover (J.T.). A magical procedure similar to this was used for extremely sick persons after all other curing methods had failed. Shavings from a tooth of an animal were dropped into a shell filled with water. If the shavings circled the shell before sinking, it was a good omen. This process was repeated four times; if the shavings circled the shell each time before sinking, the patient would get well. The water of the fourth trial was given to the patient to drink. Love medicines were regarded by one of our informants as being purely magical devices. In the one instance in which data were secured, some type of animal foot was used with herbs. An incantation was spoken and within three days an erring husband or wife returned to a prior love (N.D.). Zeisberger mentioned "love charms" similar to this one and also hunting charms.[27]

Soul Concept

The Delawares believed that every individual possessed two souls. The heart was the locus of one soul which after death remained near the body for eleven days. On the twelfth day it left the earth for a spirit world.[28] It is this soul which was offered food in a "Feast of the Dead" twelve days after death and again twelve months after death.[29] The symbolic number twelve is in all probability a historic diffusion; otherwise these concepts appear to be of Delaware origin.[30] The second soul, a resident of the blood, remained on the earth after death. It was this soul which was apt to become a malevolent ghost especially active at night. "They have an idea that the ghosts of their deceased friends appear to them in the night, particularly after a failure to offer the customary feast at the grave, and they immediately prepare to do what from neglect or disrespect had been left undone, when the ghost ceases the visits."[31] Harrington said that "the blood in the dead body draws up into globular form and floats about in the air as a luminous ball."[32] One informant said: "You see a dark something rolling around at night" (N.D.). This soul was also associated with paralysis, strokes, and

[25]Zeisberger, 1910, p. 83; J.T.
[26]Speck, 1950, pp. 70-72.
[27]Zeisberger, 1910, p. 83; J.T.
[28]Speck, 1931, p. 25; Harrington, 1921, p. 52; J.T., N.D.
[29]Speck, 1931, p. 25; O.A.
[30]Kinietz, 1940, p. 118.
[31]Trowbridge MS.
[32]Harrington, 1913, p. 228.

lameness.[33] For fear of this soul nobody ever eats in the dark or allows a sick person to be in a dark room (J.T., N.D.).

The Delawares believed in an after life, but what this existence was like is only vaguely described in the early literature and probably was only vaguely envisaged by them. De Vries said that "when they die they sing like the ravens; but this singing is entirely different from the singing of angels."[34] One source stated that "some" believed that after a soul had been in the other world for a time it might be reborn on earth in another individual.[35] Harrington said that on the twelfth day after death the spirit made its way to the twelfth or highest home, a beautiful place, without pain or sorrow, where there were magnificent dwellings, beautiful streams, and fertile lands. This paradise was only for the good; where bad or evil spirits went is unknown.[36] This concept was in all likelihood a diffusion from Christianity.

The Big House Ceremony

The Big House or Annual Ceremony has been the principal ceremony and the focal point of Delaware religious observances at least since the second half of the eighteenth century. Prior to the tribal consolidation of the Delawares (in the early decades of the eighteenth century), this Ceremony could not have existed as it is now known, since in its modern form it is a tribal or national religious event. I do not agree with Kinietz that the Big House Ceremony came into existence as an adjunct of the revivalistic nativism of the Delawares after 1762.[37] It seems much more likely that it was synthesized during the early decades of the century at the time when other parts of the culture were being unified and the tribal society was emerging. As far as I have been able to determine, the import and the meaning of this ceremony have not been nativistic as would be required by Kinietz's hypothesis. Its general purpose was to give thanks for past blessings and to ensure good fortune for the coming year.[38] Morgan said: "They believe unless they observe it once a year their crops will fail, and they will loose (sic) the favor of the Great Spirit."[39] I agree with Kinietz that "European civilization in contact with that of the Delawares was unconsciously responsible for the integration of the Big House Ceremony, the dropping and addition of many features . . . ,"[40] but I set the date for this integration half a century earlier than he does. The addition of the symbolic number twelve (from the twelve Apostles of Christianity?), the sacred number of the sweat lodge, and the appearance of the Mask Being during the ceremony are but two examples of historic additions to the ceremony.[41]

Unfortunately, the seventeenth-century documents contain little more than hints concerning the nature of the religious rites from which the the Big House Ceremony was synthesized. Denton, however, said:

[33]Speck, 1931, p. 25; Zeisberger, 1910, p. 131; J.T.

[34]De Vries, 1909, p. 224.

[35]Zeisberger, 1910, p. 131.

[36]Harrington, 1921, pp. 52-54.

[37]Kinietz, 1940, pp. 117-21.

[38]Speck, 1931, p. 21; R.W., O.A.

[39]Morgan, 1859, MS.

[40]Kinietz, 1940, p. 121.

[41]*Ibid.*, p. 118.

> For their worship which is diabolical, it is performed usually but once or twice a year, unless upon some extraordinary occasion, as upon making of war or the like; their usual time is about *Michaelmass*, when their corn is first ripe, the day being appointed by their chief Priest or pawaw, most of them go a hunting for venison: When they are all congregated, their priest tells them if he want money, their God will accept of no other offering, which the people believing, every one gives money according to their ability.[42]

This is the sort of description of a pretribal ceremony which one would expect from a seventeenth-century writer. The hunt for venison and the use of wampum were, for example, integral features of the later Big House Ceremony. Speck has suggested that the historic form of the ceremony developed from "rites managed by the ceremonial group (Turkey, Tortoise, Wolf)" which, in turn, developed from family or individual rites.[43] In historic times each phratry varied somewhat from the others in the performance of the ceremony; that of the Wolf phratry, for instance, lasted only eight days, whereas the ceremony of the Turkey phratry lasted twelve days.[44] In a sense, then, the ceremony never attained complete tribal integration. Since Speck's studies of the Big House Ceremony are relatively complete and are complemented by those of Zeisberger, Trowbridge, and Harrington, and by the eyewitness account by Luckenbach, it is not necessary here to give a detailed description of the historic ceremony; a brief synopsis taken from the accounts of these writers and from the descriptions given by my own informants should suffice.

After the Big House Ceremony became a tribal affair, it was held but once a year. It took place in a "big house," a building which also served as a council house and was similar in structure to the Iroquoian Long House. In the center of this structure was a pole, on the north and south sides of which were carved faces;[45] ten other identical faces were placed around the walls. Apparently this was the practice before 1763.[46] The participants camped near the Big House for the duration of the ceremony, the women to the north and the men to the south (M.B.). Throughout this period celibacy was practiced, participants were supposed to be in a pure and clean frame of mind, and menstruating women were not allowed inside the Big House. Offenders were removed from the building by the Mask Being or other officials.[47] One individual, known as the "bringer-in," sponsored and led the ceremony, and the phratry to which he belonged determined the exact form the ceremony was to take. One source stated that in each phratry there was a family which inherited the right to sponsor the annual ceremony;[48] possibly this was a vestige of the individual or family rites from which it evolved.

---

[42]Denton, 1845, p. 7.

[43]Speck, 1950, p. 27.

[44]*Ibid.*, p. 16; Harrington, 1913, p. 230.

[45]Zeisberger, 1910, p. 141.

[46]Kinietz, 1940, p. 118, dates this feature after 1824, but Bartram and Kenny apparently saw such a ceremonial structure in August, 1761 (Kenny, 1913, p. 22).

[47]Trowbridge MS; M.B.

[48]Trowbridge MS.

The ceremonies commenced, at least in historic times, when the caretakers lighted the fires in the Big House with a fire drill. Kinietz has suggested that this act became sacred in post-European times.[49] Sometime after dark the chief of the sponsoring phratry delivered a sermon in which the Great Spirit was thanked for success during the preceding year, and he also explained the rules of the meeting.[50] The meeting was then turned over to the "bringer-in":

> [Standing] by the great central post with its weird carved faces, [he] begins to shake a little rattle of box-turtle shell and chant, in a high monotone, the story of his vision. Meanwhile two drummers have taken their places before a peculiar drum made by rolling up a dry deer-hide and stuffing it with grass. As the chanter utters each word the drummers repeat it in the same tone, producing a very peculiar effect. Finally the recital is finished, and he starts his dance-song, which the drummers take up, beating time with flat drumsticks and dances about the fires, still shaking his rattle, followed by as many of the people as care to join.[51]

The dance was in a counterclockwise direction, and the dancer stopped at twelve spots in this circuit, each time reciting a verse of the song he had composed from his vision. The path that was followed by all those who recited their visions represented allegorically the White Path or the Great Spirit's road, the road of human existence, and the stages the soul took to the abode of the Great Spirit.[52] As was noted previously, the number twelve and perhaps the inferred idea of heaven may have represented diffusions from Christianity.

After the leader had finished his recitation, two caretakers symbolically swept the chamber with turkey feathers and built up the fire. There was then a brief recess in which people could go outside (R.W.). Following the recess, the rattle was passed from hand to hand in a counterclockwise direction until it reached another man who desired to recite his vision.[53] Toward morning, when the rattle had made a complete circuit of the Big House, twelve cries or calls were uttered. The twelfth cry was thought to be heard by the Great Spirit.[54] A feast was then held, and afterwards the throng dispersed until the following evening. (Trowbridge alone among the sources said that the worshippers remained throughout the day in the Big House, preserving silence.) On each of the succeeding nights the ritual was the same, although there may have been some variation in the persons who recited their visions, and on the fourth day deer were hunted to supply venison for a feast to be held on the seventh day.[55] At noon on the final day of the ceremony the participants filed out and formed a line facing the east. They raised their hands and twelve times called out the prayer word to the Great Spirit. The caretakers then swept the ashes from the fires out the west

[49]Kinietz, 1940, p. 121; Zeisberger, 1910, p. 30.

[50]Speck, 1931, p. 23.

[51]Harrington, 1913, pp. 228-29.

[52]Speck, 1931, p. 23.

[53]Harrington, 1921, p. 95; R. W.

[54]Harrington, 1913, p. 229.

[55]Harrington, 1921, pp. 97-100; O.A., R.W.

door of the Big House, the leader paid them in wampum for their services, and thus the ceremony was concluded.[56]

Minor Ceremonies

There must have been a host of minor family and other kin-group religious ceremonies in early times, but unfortunately the seventeenth-century sources are for the most part silent about them. Denton, however, said:

> At their *Canticas* or dancing matches, where all persons that come are freely entertained, it being a Festival time: Their custom is when they dance, every one but the Dancers to have a short stick in their hands & to knock the ground & sing altogether, whilst they that dance sometimes act war-like postures, & then they come in painted for War with their faces black & red, with some streaks of white under their eyes, & so jump & leap up & down without any order, uttering many expressions of their intended valour. For other dances they only shew what Antick tricks their ignorance will lead them to, swinging of their bodies & faces after a strange manner, sometimes jumping into the fire, sometimes catching up a Firebrand, & biting off a live coal, with many such tricks, that will affright. . . .[57]

Zeisberger described a number of minor religious ceremonies which probably are similar to those of the earlier period. Of the five ceremonials he mentioned, the first was a description of the Big House Ceremony; in the second, men danced in a breech clout and were "daubed all over with white clay."[58] In the third, tanned deerskins were given to ten or more old men and women, who wrapped themselves in these skins, stood in front of the Big House, faced east, and prayed. In this ceremony wampum was thrown on the ground, and the children scrambled for it.[59] The fourth was a feast of bear's flesh and melted fat, in which the large quantities consumed brought on vomiting and indigestion. Speck mentioned this ceremony "as a definite rite intended for the placation of the bear," and recounted the mythological tale responsible for its origin.[60] The fifth ceremony was a sweat bath held in the Big House. A sweat house, framed with twelve poles of diverse woods, was set up inside the Big House and was covered with blankets. "These twelve poles represent twelve Manittos, some of these being creatures, others plants."[61] After a meal a fire was built in the entrance of the sweat lodge, and twelve stones were heated and placed inside. Twelve pipes full of tobacco were thrown on the hot stones; twelve people then entered and remained as long as they were able. During this ceremony

[56] Harrington, 1913, pp. 228-30; 1921, p. 85; Trowbridge MS.

[57] Denton, 1845, p. 9.

[58] Zeisberger, 1910, pp. 137-38.

[59] *Ibid.*, p. 138; Harrington, 1921, p. 109, and the Trowbridge MS. stated that this ceremony concluded the Big House Ceremony; Post and Hayes noted these details in the observance of an annual ceremony on May 24-27, 1760 (Hayes, 1954, pp. 74-76).

[60] Speck, 1937, pp. 30-43.

[61] Zeisberger, 1910, p. 138.

"a whole buck-skin with the head and antlers is raised upon a pole, head and antlers resting on the pole, before which the Indians sing and pray."[62] Speck noted that the sweat lodge was erected in the Big House in the Wolf phratry ceremony and that "the sweating rite was held as a test of endurance for the men who had spiritual guidance."[63] Zeisberger also stated that there was a number of less important ceremonies arranged by individuals.[64]

A minor ceremony, continued until the twentieth century but unrecorded in the earlier literature except for a casual reference by Zeisberger, was the "Otter-Hog Dance."[65] This rite had to be given every few years by a certain family or else bad luck ensued (O.A.). The leader of this dance wore an otter hide which stretched from his head down his back to the ground. Special songs were sung, and the meat of the largest procurable hog was consumed during the dance. The hog's head was carried around in a pan by the leader during the dance and at the conclusion of the ceremony was consigned to the flames (O.A.). Harrington mentioned this ceremony and gave an origin myth for it, but his informants did not remember the dance itself.[66] Speck has also described this "Grease Drinking, or Otter Ceremony."[67]

Another series of minor ceremonies consisted of the Doll Dances. These dances probably originated in prehistoric times, but were not recorded in the early documents. The dolls seem to have had their origin in the visions of women and were passed down through the maternal line.[68] Doll owners had to give their dolls annual dances, usually in the spring. The doll was tied to a stick and the dancers carried it during the all-night ceremony. Both sexes participated; men danced in an inner circle, the women in an outer. They danced around a fire on either side of which two poles had been raised. The drum used in this ceremony was the "package" drum used in the Big House Ceremony (O.A., M.B., J.T., J.W.). Twelve songs were sung in the course of the ceremony, followed by a pause for a feast in which various corn dishes prepared by the owner of the doll were eaten. After this meal the songs were repeated, and just before dawn cornbread was scattered on the ground and was picked up and eaten by the dancers. Speck said that a Doll Dance "embodies the idea of appeasing the latent ill-will of the Spirit of Corn, aroused through innocent familiarity incurred in the past between the children of certain families and this sensitive Manitto."[69] Harrington described the Doll dances, but his description varies somewhat from mine.[70]

There were undoubtedly other dances and feasts, including first fruits rites,[71] given at different seasons by various family or other kin

[62] *Ibid.*, pp. 138-39; Kenny, 1913, pp. 196-97.
[63] Speck, 1937, p. 21.
[64] Zeisberger, 1910, p. 140.
[65] Zeisberger, 1871, p. 344.
[66] Harrington, 1921, pp. 176-82.
[67] Speck, 1937, pp. 44-48.
[68] The section on Mythology describes several origin tales for the Doll Dances.
[69] Speck, 1937, p. 61.
[70] Harrington, 1921, pp. 164-71.
[71] Hayes, 1954, p. 70 (first deer killed after an annual ceremony, on June 9, 1760); Loskiel, 1794, p. 40; Brickell, 1842, p. 49.

groups. The Mask Being was "feasted" annually (J.T.). Speck described a number of other feasts and dances including "The Mask Dance Ceremony," an "Opossum Dance Ceremony," the "Buffalo Dance Ceremony" (apparently a recent diffusion to the Delawares), a "Corn Harvest Ceremony," and "The Spring Prayer and Football Ceremony to Advance Vegetation."[72]

Shamans

There were two kinds of shamans, one devoted to curing and the other to divination.[73] Heckewelder distinguished the Medeu, or the individual associated with curing, from the Powwow or Juggler, who was higher in rank and was skilled in divination and magic.[74] The members of the latter group, according to Harrington, were organized into societies, but Trowbridge denied this, and there is no other confirmation to be found for the existence of societies. They probably represent a diffusion from the Iroquois to the Canadian Delawares.[75] Shamans might be of either sex and were generally old. Among their activities were weather forecasting, rain making, the preparation of "medicine" for hunters who were down on their luck, and curing. They also make "philters or love potions for such married persons as either do not, or think they cannot, love each other."[76] Before they performed their services, shamans had to be paid in wampum, tobacco, dressed deerskins, or the like. They wore costumes when treating the sick, and a tortoise shell rattle, dancing, singing, and "mumbling" were always a part of their performance.[77]

Lindestrom in the seventeenth century said that the "curing" shaman "runs back and forth, cries so that he is heard a long way off, rolls himself naked into the burning fire, takes fire brands with which he builds a wall all around the sick one, the sick one enduring such with patience."[78] Denton said of shamans:

> When any person is sick, after the means used by his friend, every one pretending skill in Physick, that proving ineffectual they send for a Pawaw or Priest, who sitting down by the sick person without the least enquiring after the distemper, waits for a gift which he proportions his work accordingly to: that being received, he first begins with a low voice to call upon his God, calling sometimes upon one sometimes on another, raising his voice higher & higher, beating of his naked breasts & sides, till the sweat runneth down, & his breath is almost gone, then that little which is remaining, he evaporates upon the face of the sick person three or four times together & so takes his leave.[79]

---

[72] Speck, 1937, pp. 49-87.

[73] Brainerd, 1884, p. 131; Heckewelder, 1881, p. 236; Brinton, 1885, pp. 70-71.

[74] Heckewelder, 1881, pp. 228 ff.

[75] Harrington, 1913, p. 217; Trowbridge MS.

[76] Harrington, 1913, p. 232; N.D.

[77] Harrington, 1913, pp. 232-34; M.B.

[78] Lindestrom, 1925, p. 248.

[79] Denton, 1845, pp. 8-9; Heckewelder, 1881, pp. 232-33, described the performance in similar terms.

Heckewelder described an occasion during a drought in 1799 in which the women of a village paid a shaman to produce a rain. The shaman constructed an enclosure about five feet square of sticks and bark and left an opening on the north side. He then murmured an incantation while facing the north, shutting the opening of the enclosure at the conclusion of the incantation. He "turned in the same manner, still muttering some words, towards the south, as if invoking some superior being, and having cut through the bark on the southwest corner, so as to make an opening of two feet, he said: 'Now we shall have rain enough!'"[80] Zeisberger described the malevolent conjurers and stated that they had learned their black arts from the Nanticokes, and Speck noted that this tradition is still current among the Delawares.[81] These shamans were able to injure and destroy either individuals or entire villages. Zeisberger said:

> [They use] a little piece of an old blanket or something else. This they rub in their hands until formed into a little ball. Naming the one who is marked for death, they throw this ball at him, saying that he shall die. They call this shooting the witchball. Any person wishing to get another whom he hates out of the way will hire a sorcerer or several of them to do it, paying them in wampum.[82]

In another place Zeisberger described an individual who had fallen into the hands of a "wizard" and become paralyzed. The shaman who was responsible had offered to cure the victim, but refrained from doing so since the patient could not afford the treatment.[83] Heckewelder said of these conjurers:

> All they can say is that the sorcerer makes use of a "deadening substance," which he discharges and conveys to the person that he means to "*strike*," through the air, by means of the wind or of his own breath, or throws at him in a manner which they can neither understand nor describe. The person thus "*stricken*," is immediately seized with an unaccountable terror, his spirits sink, his appetite fails, he is disturbed in his sleep, he pines and wastes away, or a fit of sickness seizes him, and he dies at last a miserable victim to the workings of his own imagination.[84]

This bit of belief has survived more or less in its original form, since at a "stomp dance" an informant (R.W.) blew or threw something at another man (J.W.) and stole his drum. J.W. suffered a stroke that evening from which he never fully recovered. His family attempted to recover the drum, thinking this would effect a cure, but they were never successful. An informant from the Anadarko band (M.B.) said that malevolent sorcerers had killed most of the children and that this was the reason for the decline of the Delawares. She also said that many of the Cherokee-Delawares were "witches" and for this reason the two groups did not maintain closer relations.

---

[80] Heckewelder, 1881, p. 237.
[81] Speck, 1937, pp. 135-42.
[82] Zeisberger, 1910, p. 126.
[83] Zeisberger, 1885, II: 94.
[84] Heckewelder, 1881, p. 240.

Curing

Although most serious ailments were treated magically by shamans, there was a considerable body of knowledge concerning various herbs, roots, and decoctions of one sort or another that did have a beneficial medicinal value. It should also be noted that wounds and external injuries were successfully treated.[85] This practical medicinal knowledge was the property of both ordinary individuals and shamans. Many of the curative practices, both magical and otherwise, were directed at the spirits, rather than derived from a real knowledge of physiology and pathology. This, of course, did not decrease the beneficial (or harmful) effects of the various remedies.[86]

Roots, herbs, and bark, particularly oak, walnut, cherry, dogwood, maple, and birch, were used as medicines.[87] These materials were prepared and compounded in a number of ways, and the knowledge of them was a closely guarded secret, passed on to one's children only when the owner was at death's door.[88] This secrecy remains, and my informants refused to do more than hint at the nature of their medicines. Emetics, blood letting, and perhaps cupping were common remedies in the eighteenth century.[89] The most common medicinal practice was sweat bathing. Men used the village sweat bath more frequently than did the women, who had their own.[90] A sweat bath was taken by an individual when he was tired or had contracted a cold or did not feel well. Men usually took one or two a week; women took them less frequently. Occasionally, a shaman would take a sweat bath while his patient lay outside, and frequently various medicines were taken during or immediately after a sweat bath.[91]

Folklore

Knowledge of Delaware folklore is imperfect and incomplete. The purely secular tales are little known; however, I obtained a few in the field. The mythology dealing with supernatural beings is only slightly better known. R. C. Adams published a number of tales current in the late nineteenth century; none of the stories he related was told to me.[92] The earliest origin story was obtained by Dankers in the seventeenth century, who had directed some questions at an old man of the Hackinsack division of the Unami:

[85]Van der Donck, 1909, p. 301; Thomas, 1912, p. 340; Zeisberger, 1910, p. 15. Tantaquidgeon, 1942, described medical practices and materia medica of the Delawares. Mahr, 1951, has summarized the early data on Delaware herbalism and healing; Mahr, 1955, has studied nonesoteric herb lore.

[86]Heckewelder, 1881, p. 224.

[87]Penn, 1882, p. 244; Zeisberger, 1910, p. 25; Heckewelder, 1881, p. 224; Luckenbach, 1938, p. 376; Tantaquidgeon, 1942, pp. 24-37.

[88]Zeisberger, 1910, p. 24; N.D.

[89]Zeisberger, 1910, p. 26; Heckewelder, 1881, p. 225.

[90]De Vries, 1909, pp. 217-18; Zeisberger, 1910, p. 26; Heckewelder, 1881, p. 226.

[91]Zeisberger, 1910, p. 26; Heckewelder, 1881, p. 225; O.A.

[92]Adams, 1905.

> He [the old man] took a piece of coal out of the fire where he sat, and began to write upon the floor. He first drew a circle, a little oval, to which he made four paws or feet, a head and a tail. "This," said he, "is a tortoise, lying in the water around it," and he moved his hand round the figure, continuing, "this was or is all water, and so at first was the world or the earth, when the tortoise gradually raised its round back up high, and the water ran off of it, and thus the earth became dry." He then took a little straw and placed it on end in the middle of the figure, and proceeded, "the earth was now dry, and there grew a tree in the middle of the earth, and the root of this tree sent forth a sprout beside it and there grew upon it a man, who was the first male. This man was then alone, and would have remained alone; but the tree bent over until its top touched the earth, and there shot therein another root, from which came forth another sprout, and there grew upon it the woman, and from these two are all men produced."[93]

A number of other writers have said that the turtle was responsible for the creation.[94] The Munsi, however, may have had a slightly different origin myth, as Heckewelder said:

> The *Minsi*... say that in the beginning, they dwelt in the earth under a lake, and were fortunately extricated from this unpleasant abode by the discovery which one of their men made of a hole, through which he ascended to the surface; on which, as he was walking, he found a deer, which he carried back with him into his subterraneous habitation; that there the deer was killed, and he and his companions found the meat so good, that they unanimously determined to leave their dark abode, and remove to a place where they could enjoy the light of heaven and have such excellent game in abundance.... The other two tribes... have much similar notions, but reject the story of the lake, which seems peculiar to the Minsi tribe.[95]

Harrington related a divergent tale which included a flood:

> Some time after Gicelamukaong [Great Spirit] had created the world it became flooded with water, and it seemed to be a difficult matter to find earth with which to commence a new one. The Great Spirit... began to send down the various water animals which still survived to try to bring earth up from the bottom, but one by one they failed, and floated up to the surface dead. At last the muskrat was sent, and he succeeded in bringing up a little dirt in his paws. This was placed on the back of a turtle, which, with the mud upon it, immediately began to increase in size, until the "great island upon which we live" was formed, round and flat, floating upon the waters.[96]

Several myths and tales were gathered from informants. These show many similarities to those of the Eastern and Central Algonkians,[97] but they may be late historic diffusions. Myths which were intended to be informative about supernatural subjects and also purely secular stories were told by the Delawares only during the winter and hence were called "winter tales" (J.T.). If myths were told out of season "the bugs

---

[93] Dankers, 1867, pp. 150-51.

[94] Zeisberger, 1910, pp. 131-32; Heckewelder, 1881, p. 250; Trowbridge MS; Brinton, 1885, p. 133.

[95] Heckewelder, 1881, p. 250.

[96] Harrington, 1913, pp. 232-37; M.B. related essentially the same myth.

[97] Fisher, 1946, pp. 226-62.

would chase you" (M.B.) or "all the worms would take after you" (J.T.). Tales were told by old men and women, and talented story tellers were much in demand. They were paid for their services by the audience who promised before the tales began to perform some service or donate a gift. One person would say, "I'll kill a rabbit for her tomorrow, another would say, "I'll fetch wood for her tomorrow" (O.A.). The stories began about nine in the evening and lasted five or six hours. Trowbridge said in this connection: "And it is said that they will entertain each other a whole night with the ingenious story of a wolf, a raccoon, or of some great hunter, whose deeds have been handed down by their traditions."[98] The audience lay around the fire in the house during the story telling, but the little children could not fall asleep unnoticed, for during the course of many of the stories the audience had to reply to the storyteller in chorus (O.A., M.B.).

Thunder Myths

Stories about thunder deities are common, and several were obtained. M.B. and F.W. both told the following tale, but F.W.'s is used since M.B.'s suffered in translation.[99]

An old woman and her six-year-old grandson lived together. The boy just played around camp with his bows and arrows. He wasn't anything but a little boy. At this time there was a drought, it was hot and dry, the creeks were dry and the crops had burned up. His grandmother was beginning to get after him for being such a worthless little boy.

One day as his grandma was berating him he looked up and said, "I can make it rain." His grandmother replied, "You can't do nothin'." And the other people just laughed at the little boy too. The boy said he was going off and "hope" four times for rain. The boy went off and soon a cloud came up. Soon it was thundering, the lightning flashed, and it started to rain.

The grandmother was in her wigwam bailing out the water when the little boy returned. He said, "I told you it was going to rain." Lightning was still striking every minute.

Then the boy told his grandmother, "I'm going with my friends, but someday I'll come back, although I won't be able to stay. When you hear the lightning cracking around you think of me 'cause it's me."

The old people say that the sharp cracking of thunder is the little boy playing, and that the heavy, rumbling thunder is the old thunder birds.

All the thunder birds live by making soup out of old bones, bones so old "they have holes in them" (J.T.). When the clouds were low or when it was misty, the birds could jump down out of them to earth. The informant J. T. told the following story:

There once was a man who said he could go and live with the thunders. The people asked him how he could go 'cause he didn't have no wings. He said he knew a way and named a day when the people could watch him.

---

[98]Trowbridge MS.

[99]All myths and tales are given as nearly as possible in the informants' words.

The day came, he had a big round rock, "as big as this table" (ordinary enameled kitchen table), and he built a fire on top of this rock on a bluff overlooking a creek. He heated the rock until it was almost red hot, then he pushed it over the bluff into the water. The water was heated and began to steam. The man stepped into the steam and disappeared. He later returned from the sky. (J.T.)

Great Horned Serpent Myths

Water monsters and snakes have their place in Delaware mythology. People are usually protected from these monsters, or are allowed to destroy them, through the agency of the Sun or the Thunder Gods:

While out hunting a man heard the call of a turkey near a large lake. People had been accustomed to get water from this lake, but nevertheless a monster snake lived there. The unwary hunter was attracted to the lake by what he thought was the call of the turkey, but it was the water monster. The monster killed him by drowning, and then ate him. Two or three other people were caught in the same way by this snake.

Several men got together who had power. One of the men had two "clean" (i.e., ritually clean) sons. (In another version by J.T. several little boys tell their elders that they will kill the snake.) The boys go to the Sun. When they approached the Sun, he told them not to come too close because of the heat. Sun told them to stand off to one side.

He then instructed them to take some sweepings (dirt swept to the west end of the Big House) and to sprinkle it around the lake inhabited by the great snake, and that this procedure would kill the snake.

When they returned, this was done. Immediately the water began to boil, the snake could be seen writhing in the water. Soon he floated on his back dead, and so they were rid of the monster. (J.T.)

The Horned Serpent was not always an enemy of the Delawares, although he seems to have been an adversary of the Thunders and some other deities, as the following story related by M.B. shows:

There was a little boy who was different from other little boys. He wouldn't go out to hunt like they did. People told his grandfather that the boy wasn't any good. The grandfather decided that he would take care of the boy. He built a boat of sticks, put the boy on the boat and took him to an island. The old man built a fire on the island and told the boy to go off and kill some birds. This was just a ruse to get rid of the boy. While the boy was gone the grandfather used Indian tobacco and prayed for the little boy in order to make the boy wise.

When the old man was finished he hollered for the little boy to tell him that he was going. The old man left the little boy all alone on the island. The boy was frantic, he cried and he cried. Day after day he cried, but on the fifth day he heard someone talking to him. It was a skunk who said he wanted to take the boy home. But another voice told skunk that he was too small to do this.

The boy began to cry again. The next day, however, another voice said he would take the boy home. This voice came from a large snake with horns. The snake told him to hold tight to his horns and to warn him immediately if he saw a cloud. The boy held on to the horns and they sped toward the shore. They got about halfway and a large black cloud appeared. The boy warned the snake as he had been told to do. The snake turned around so violently that the boy almost fell off. They returned to the island and the little boy was again very sad.

The boy decided that next day he would not tell the snake about any clouds. The next day the snake told him to hold tight to his horns and to warn him of any clouds. This time they reached the shore, although the boy neglected to tell the snake about a cloud he had seen. The snake had been going through the water so fast that he ran right up onto the beach. At that moment lightning struck the snake and killed him. The Thunder Gods had been wanting to eat the snake and the seven of them did so. One took the horns, the "least" thunder bird took the tail.

The boy got home, the people met him and doctored him as the lightning had hurt him a little bit. The grandfather told the boy to go to a burned tree and build a fire, then to shoot at a blackened log and he would kill a bear. Then he would have company and they would eat the bear.

The boy did all this, the company came and ate the bear and then the boy was like all other boys.

Another myth about the Horned Serpent, which was not related to me in its entirety, was a tale in which the malevolence of this being was circumvented by marrying an attractive girl to the monster. All the boys of the village were enamored of a beautiful girl, but none of the adults would let any of them marry her. In time the girl was married to the Horned Serpent and he no longer menaced the Delawares (M.B.).

Mythological Giants

Only one story concerned giants; in this the supernatural beings involved were not identified:

A party of women was out gathering firewood when an eagle flew down to them. They abused him by capturing him. He escaped, however, and told the powers of his treatment at the hands of the women.

Within ten days it snowed so much that the houses were covered up. The people soon had nothing to eat or to burn. They finally began to eat one another. The cannibals began to grow until they became vicious giants. It is these giants who are buried in the Indian mounds. Fortunately the giants finally died out.

Once a family was crossing a creek when one of them saw the reflection of one of the giants in the water. The giant was standing on a mountain looking down at them. He had a long walking cane and started coming for them. The family crossed back over the creek because they knew that these giants were afraid of water. The giant came down to the creek and instead of putting his cane vertically in the water to measure its depth he measured it horizontally. After doing this he mistakenly assumed that it was over his head. Actually a normal sized person could wade this creek. The family moved away from where this giant lived. (F.W.)

Certain constellations of stars had myths connected with them. Only one story, however, was given:

During the Big House Ceremony, as the participants were taking a recess, seven boys began to rise in the air. The people began to shout to them and managed to knock two of them back down, by throwing unclean clothing at them. The others rose into the heavens and became those stars (an unidentified group). (J.T.)

Origin of Dolls of the Doll Dances

The informant J.T. told the following stories:

In early times there was a girl who liked to play with dolls. She would pick up all sorts of things and pretend that they were dolls. Even after she was grown she continued to play with dolls. Then she became very ill. During her illness a voice spoke to her. The voice told her that in order to get well she would have to make a doll such as she would see in the dream. She opened her eyes and saw the doll she was to make, and the voice told her how to take care of the doll, to give it feasts. The voice went on to tell her that dolls were not things to play with when you are grown. You don't play with them because dolls take care of the crops. When the girl awoke she went to the woods and carved a doll like the one she saw in her vision. She got well.

Once when the old folks had gone to a doll dance and left their kids at home, the kids got together and decided to make their own doll and have a dance. A girl made a doll and they had their dance, even though they didn't know the proper songs. It was wrong to make a doll, this was dangerous. One spring these children didn't dance this doll and the next spring a child got "bad sick." The phratry chief, who was also a medicine man, came to treat her. He knew that it was the doll that was causing this child to be sick. So the child's parents had the children give the doll a dance. They did and the sick child recovered.[100]

The purely secular tales, which have nothing to do with supernatural forces, are not well remembered today, and perhaps always formed only a small part of the folklore. The following tale was considered extremely hilarious by informants.

There once was a woman who intensely disliked her son-in-law. This worried the son-in-law and finally he decided to do something about it. He went down to the pond from which his mother-in-law was accustomed to draw water. He tied all the lily pads together so that he could make them vibrate by pulling on a string. Then he hid himself in some bushes that were near by. Soon his mother-in-law came down to draw water. He vibrated the lily pads and disguised his voice saying: "Your son-in-law is going to die, your son-in-law is going to die." She, of course, thought the lily pads were speaking to her. She started back to the wigwam, but her son-in-law took a short cut and beat her back. He was sitting within when the tearful woman arrived. She started being very nice to him, she combed and brushed his clothes and softened his buckskin clothes, and was nice to him afterwards because she thought he was going to die. (J.T., M.B.)

[100] Harrington, 1921, pp. 162-63, described a myth which was very similar to this one.

A SUMMARY OF DELAWARE CULTURE

The means of subsistence of the Delawaran peoples at the opening of the historic period were fairly simple but richly diversified, so that it is difficult to conceive of any of them ever suffering a famine. If the crops of the women failed, they had but to rely more heavily upon the fish and game supplied by the men. There were, moreover, well-developed techniques for preserving and storing agricultural products and wild foods. In short, the techniques of subsistence in this rich habitat provided an abundant supply of foodstuffs for the relatively small population.

Small, semipermanent settlements dotted the coast and river valleys. These virtually autonomous settlements were probably composed of lineages and clans, which possessed fairly definite hunting territories adjacent to their settlements. Even smaller kin units, families, were ordinarily the largest social aggregate in the winter hunting season. The life of an individual centered around his mother's community; his hopes, fears, and aspirations were bound up and identified with this kinship group. The system by which food and goods were produced, distributed, and consumed was also identified with, and was an integral part of, the kinship system. Goods and food were produced by kin groups for their own use. The lineage and clan dealt effectively with most social problems, both economic and governmental, so that above the clan level there were few and but poorly developed institutions. Sachems were only the voice of the kinship units with no special prerogatives and no autocratic power. The clans were probably grouped into three phratries in early historic times, but their function seems to have been wholly ceremonial and not governmental. If a tribe is a grouping of peoples with a single language and dialect, a common culture, and a feeling of unity, then the early historic Delawaran peoples were not even a tribe.

There has been considerable dispute about why the population density for the Eastern Area as a whole was low when the subsistence potential was relatively high. Insofar as there has been an attempt to explain this anomaly, it has generally been in terms of chronic warfare. I have rejected this explanation and suggest that for the Delaware economy to support a larger population would have required male participation in agriculture, stronger governmental mechanisms to control larger cooperative groups of workers, various sorts of specialists, more effective political groupings for offense and defense, and perhaps other alterations in the social system. The small, individually oriented, kin group socioeconomic institutions were sufficient to operate the basically simple technology, but nothing more. There is no doubt that the same techniques of subsistence geared to a different sort of social system could have been more productive. In sum, the nature of the socioeconomic system was such that the productivity of the technological system had reached its peak. Why the population density was relatively low is no mystery; it would be a mystery instead, if a social structure such as this one could have supported a large population.

As White has suggested, "ideological, or philosophical systems are organizations of beliefs in which human experience finds its interpretation."[1] This was true of early Delaware ideology; most religious and magical rites, for instance, were performed by small groups, often families. The Big House Ceremony may possibly have been a partial exception, but even here I have suggested that the modern ceremony was a late synthesis of early clan, or even family, rites. The individualistic nature of the vision quest and shamanism, to mention two other examples, also reflects the loosely organized, individually oriented nature of Delaware society. Religious and magical rites held to promote gardening were no more stressed, or so it appears, than those dealing with hunting or fishing. It has been seen that gardening was for most Delawares the subsistence activity of greatest importance, but the people themselves, particularly the men, probably did not view it in this light. In general, Delaware supernaturalism was directed at influencing the forces that controlled subsistence activities, health, and welfare. Religious systems deal with uncontrollable and critical spheres of life; this the Delaware religion did, and in a fashion consonant with the life which has been described.

From this reconstruction there comes to view a people who had solved the most pressing problems of life, but not to the extent that they had created a paradise on Earth. Much of a person's life was employed in satisfying basic needs; the hunter's life was arduous, gardening and household duties were onerous, and sudden death was not uncommon. Real knowledge of the world was limited and was blinded to a degree by the common store of misinformation and mythology. In sum, when Europeans saw these people for the first time, they encountered the bearers of a culture well adjusted to a mechanically simple and a socially undifferentiated and individualized way of life, completely unprepared for dealing with the aggressive, technologically complex, well-organized, exploitative culture of Europe.

[1]White, 1949, p. 365.

PART II. DELAWARE CULTURE CHANGE

V. DELAWARE ACCULTURATION

The alteration of Delaware culture by contact with European and American civilization has been treated thus far simply as an obstacle to be overcome in the reconstruction of the early historic form of that culture. It is now my purpose to reverse the approach and examine cultural changes which occurred when this relatively small and technologically simple culture collided with the complex, behemoth, invading civilization from Europe. The impact of European civilization on Delaware culture had immediate and far-reaching effects upon the latter, and the subsequent prolonged and intimate contact with European civilization continued to affect every facet of it in numerous ways.

I shall attempt to deal with Delaware culture change only on a cultural level since the theoretic approach has consistently been culturological. My aim is to examine the collision, conflict, and competition of culture traits and complexes and the results of this culture contact within Delaware culture. The approach to acculturation, then, is from an extrasomatic, nonbiological, nonpsychological, culturological point of view.[1] This does not imply that other aspects of acculturation are unimportant; certainly there is much to learn, for example, about psychological maladjustments of individuals in all sorts of acculturative situations. My purpose also goes beyond the confines of a simple description of acculturation. I am interested not only in the cultural changes, but in the order in which they occurred and the reasons for their occurrence; therefore a brief analysis concludes this section.

The most useful definition and concept of acculturation is that held by A. L. Kroeber. He said: "Acculturation comprises those changes produced in a culture by the influence of another culture which result in an increased similarity of the two."[2] In the present context the term acculturation means the process of Delaware culture change which took place in response to continued contact with European-American culture. One should note at the outset several particular features of the situation in which culture change occurred. An advanced, superior European civilization invaded the home land of a relatively backward, inferior culture, as measured in terms of technological productivity and effectiveness. All Delaware culture was at first exposed to influences from only a small segment of European civilization, represented by the traders and colonists from several different countries. This meant that at least in the early decades of contact the native cultures were not exposed to the entire range of European culture. In the first century following European invasion, the Delawares came in contact with Dutch, Swedish, English, and French nationals, so that the acculturative process

[1] White, 1949, pp. 121-45.
[2] Kroeber, 1948, p. 425.

was not a simple one brought about by one relationship. By the end of the seventeenth century the Delaware tribe was coming under the domination of the United States alone, but this did not simplify the situation since the new nation was changing almost as rapidly as were its policies towards the Indians. Another important condition, perhaps the most important insofar as survival of Delaware culture was concerned, was the opportunity which the Delawares had to retreat beyond the frontier when they were too hard pressed by the whites. These successive migrations brought them into new environmental situations and into contact with a number of different tribes. These also had an effect upon Delaware culture change. In this study I can only hope to point out the major trends of the complex process of acculturation and some of the principal reasons for various kinds of alterations in Delaware culture.

The Contact Period (1524-1690)

Delaware acculturation naturally falls into four or five phases or periods. The existence of these periods is clear, although their duration in years may be but hazily defined. The first period, extending from 1524 to about 1690, I have termed the Contact Period. It was characterized by primary acculturation, that is, direct borrowing by the Delawares of a whole host of European traits, overwhelmingly of a technological nature. During this period forces which were partly or wholly extracultural were responsible for the appearance of a new sort of warfare, an altered economy, and extensive depopulation.

History

The first contact the Delawares had with Europeans seems to have been with Verrazzano in 1524. This explorer sailed into what may have been the Bay of New York and explored Bayonne Bay, but this brief encounter seems to have been culturally inconsequential.[3] The next contact was with Dutch traders in 1598, but Henry Hudson's visit in 1609 is often described as the beginning of regular intercourse between the Europeans and Delawares.[4] Hudson entered the Bay of New York, and one of his boats went as far up the Hudson River as Albany.[5] It has also been said that Hudson entered Delaware Bay in the same year. These early contacts cannot be described as particularly friendly; Hudson's mate was killed during an Indian attack on the East River in 1609, and strife between the Dutch and the Tappan and Raritan has been recorded in 1639-40.[6] Mey's fort near Philadelphia, built in 1631, was razed by the natives, and De Vries' colony on Cape Henlopen in the present state of Delaware was destroyed in 1632.[7] Despite the hostility which the natives occasionally showed towards the Europeans, relations were for

[3]Murphy, 1875, p. 176.

[4]Mooney, 1911, p. 331; Acrelius, 1876, xii.

[5]Acrelius, 1876, xii.

[6]Ruttenber, 1872, pp. 102-3.

[7]Acrelius, 1876, xiii.

the most part peaceful during the early decades of the seventeenth century because both peoples were fascinated with, and drawn irresistibly to, each other by their respective goods and possessions. The contact was not limited to a few Delawares casually trading with Europeans; rather, every Indian avidly desired to barter his plentiful furs, food, or whatever else he might have that the Europeans desired, for the strange, efficient, and rare European goods. As Hunt has demonstrated, every Indian could at this time easily acquire the wherewithal to procure these desired items.[8]

During the early decades of the seventeenth century the Delawares found themselves in an admirable trading position. The Swedes, Dutch, and English had purchased land, established colonies, and were competing vigorously with one another for the Indian trade. On the Hudson River in 1609 there was "a great traffick in the skins of beavers, otters, foxes, bears, minks, wild cats, and the like."[9] In 1638 the Swedes, in their first year in the New World, exported 30,000 skins, chiefly from the Delaware area.[10] The Delawares did not long remain favored trading partners of the Europeans, however, since they did not have easy access to the rich fur-bearing lands of the interior. By 1627 the Iroquois were supplying the Dutch with a large quantity of furs in the Albany area, and until 1655 the Swedes carried on an extensive fur trade with the Susquehannock (Conestoga) Indians.[11] These Iroquoian peoples acted as a barrier to the coastal peoples in quest of the furs of the interior. The Europeans were quick to recognize the value of close trade connections with these inland Iroquoian peoples, for the Swedes backed the Susquehannock with arms and the Dutch, the Iroquois.[12]

The Delawares could not placidly watch the coveted European merchandise, particularly arms and ammunition, go to their rivals in the interior. In the 1660's "a terrific contest was then raging between the Senecas and the Minsis, and the former came to Ft. Orange and demanded, by virtue of the treaty of Esopus (1660) a higher price for their furs."[13] By 1680 the Minisink and the Tappan were under "obligations of subjugation" to the Iroquois,[14] and other Delaware groups were probably experiencing similar pressures about this time. This marks the beginning of the ascendancy of the Iroquois over the Delawares. The political and military superiority of the Iroquois was then a function of "their fortunate but accidental position as a buffer group and a trading front for the Dutch and English, [it] enabled them to maintain their solidarity while other aboriginal tribes were being broken and having their society destroyed by settlers, soldiers, and epidemics."[15]

The competition among the European nations was also intense, and by 1655 the Dutch were able to attack and conquer the Swedes on the Delaware River. Nine years later, in 1664, the English were able to

[8]Hunt, 1939, p. 4.

[9]De Laet, 1909, p. 48.

[10]Sipe, 1931, p. 61; Acrelius, 1876, pp. 19-20.

[11]Hunt, 1939, p. 33; Sipe, 1931, p. 61.

[12]Sipe, 1931, p. 61.

[13]Ruttenber, 1872, p. 68.

[14]*Ibid.*, p. 69.

[15]Griffin, 1944, p. 361; see also Ruttenber, 1872, p. 66.

oust the Dutch from New Netherland.[16] When the English supplanted the Dutch on the Hudson, the condition of the Indians improved temporarily; treaties were concluded and peace restored.[17] The English, however, were acutely interested in expanding their colonial possessions, and from this time on the position of the Delawares became less and less enviable in their relationships both with the British and with other Indian tribes.[18] The last half of this century found the Delawares in a violent struggle with the British-supported Iroquois on the one hand and the land-hungry Europeans on the other.

Acculturation

From the time of their first contacts with the Europeans, the Indians had wanted to acquire guns, powder, cloth, lead, copper, kettles, axes, hoes, picks, spades, shovels, glass beads, awls, bodkins, scissors, knives, mirrors, and needles. William Penn, for example, purchased land in 1683 from Tamanend and other Delawares by the payment of:

> . . . 5 pairs of stockings, 20 bars of lead, 10 tobacco boxes, 6 coats, 2 guns, 8 shirts, 2 kettles, 12 awls, 5 hats, 25 pounds of powder, 1 peck of pipes, 38 yards of "duffields," 16 knives, 100 needles, 10 glasses, 5 caps, 15 combs, 5 hoes, 9 gimlets, 20 fish hooks, 10 tobacco tongs, 10 pairs of scissors, 7 half-gills, 6 axes, 2 blankets, 4 handfuls of bells, 4 yards of "stroudswaters" and 20 handfuls of wampum.[19]

Bolton, speaking of articles traded for land in the seventeenth century, said:

> The articles in greatest demand seem to have been more than three hundred knives of various kinds, followed by one hundred and eighty-five hatchets, axes, and adzes, and, to a much less extent, by one hundred and forty-one hoes. Doubtless the guns and fowling-pieces were the most coveted weapons, but of these they secured only sixty-seven in all, with two hundred and twenty-seven pounds of gunpowder and one hundred and thirty bars of lead, three melting ladles, and five bullet molds. . . . Of clothing, one hundred and eighty-two coats were in the majority, these being already made up, with more than three hundred yards of the trade cloths known as duffels, duzzons, and stroudwater, and one hundred and thirteen shirts, ninety-two pairs of stockings, and eighty-seven blankets, with ten corals or beads.
>
> There were one hundred and seventeen kettles of iron or brass, seventy-six earthenware and stoneware jugs, twelve "steels to strike fire," and twenty spoons. Among sundry small objects were one thousand fish-hooks, two hundred and twenty needles, one hundred and twenty awls or "muxes," used to drill holes in wampum (as one of the deeds states), one hundred and thirty clay pipes, ten bells, and ten jewsharps.
>
> A few rolls of tobacco were thrown in, with thirty-two tobacco boxes; and with this went another kind of solace in the form of twenty-five half-vats of strong beer, and sixteen ankers of the Indians' deadliest enemy, rum.[20]

[16] Myers, 1912, p. 54; Ruttenber, 1872, p. 158.

[17] Ruttenber, 1872, p. 158.

[18] *Ibid.*, p. 158.

[19] Sipe, 1931, p. 70.

[20] Bolton, 1920, pp. 299-300.

It is apparent from this list that the natives desired those material items which at first glance were superior to their own. The case for firearms was slightly different, since the Indian had no similar weapon and could have had but slight knowledge of the mechanical and physical principles involved. But the circumstances were such that this artifact came to be the most desired and treasured of European articles.[21] Both militarily and in the now vital quest for fur-bearing animals the tribes that obtained firearms were superior to those that were not so equipped. The have-nots, to preserve their existence and to maintain their new trading contacts, were forced to secure firearms.

There was a series of associated technological traits which did not diffuse to the seventeenth-century Delawares. These were the small grains (such as wheat, barley, oats, and buckwheat) and the plow-harrow, horse-oxen complex used in European agriculture. This complex was not adopted by the Delawares until late in the nineteenth century. Introduced domestic animals, as will be seen presently, were not harnessed for the utilization of their energy in horticulture. There is little evidence which would indicate that these animals were used for food during the Contact Period. Horses, cattle, and sheep were scarce; only swine may have been an exception.

The demands of European trade caused a rapid change in the native economic system. To obtain European artifacts the Indians had to supply the Europeans with furs, and to a much lesser extent with garden produce. Once the desire for European goods was established, and it should be noted that before the Contact Period was over these goods were considered necessities, the native men spent much more time in the hunt and sought animals which had previously been relatively unimportant. Of even more importance was the fact that new hunting territories had to be opened up in order to maintain the supply of furs. The production of food and the manufacture of all sorts of artifacts for kin group consumption rapidly became less important and were replaced by a more individualistic barter economy based upon the fur trade. The simple gardening-hunting, subsistence-for-use pattern was changed to a dependent, competitive, predominantly hunting-for-barter economy. Hunt has summed up the results of the early trade conditions, saying:

> The great desirability of the trade goods to the Indian who had once known them became shortly a necessity, a very urgent necessity that permitted no renunciation of the trade. As new desires wakened and old skills vanished, the Indian who had fur, or could get it, survived; he who could not get it died or moved away. But whatever he did, life for him could never again be what it had been: old institutions and economies had profoundly altered or disappeared completely at the electrifying touch of the white man's trade. . . .[22]

A new and much more serious form of warfare developed early in the Contact Period. This was war caused by economic competition between the Delawares and Iroquois and also by conflicts engendered over

[21] Van der Donck, 1909, p. 303.

[22] Hunt, 1939, pp. 4-5.

land matters. The latter conflicts were with both Europeans and other Indian groups. In short, the pre-European primitive war complex, which had been indulged in as a pastime more than anything else, soon gave way to a bitter, long-lasting, and desperate struggle for survival.[23] In the Contact Period the conflicts were primarily with the Iroquois and Susquehannock; in subsequent periods the Delawares fought the land-hungry Euro-American forces almost exclusively. War continued to be carried on in the same way (i.e., by small groups of skulking Indians) and in fact proved highly successful in temporarily terrorizing the frontiers, but it was ultimately disastrous to the numerically and technologically inferior Delawares. In sum, a new form of warfare made its appearance in the Contact Period as a result of the conditions of culture contact rather than as a diffusion of traits. For this early period there is little positive documentation concerning the diffusion of social institutions or religious beliefs and practices. It is clear, nevertheless, that little if any diffusion from European civilization occurred in these areas of culture.

The Period of Consolidation (1690-1750)

In the sixty years following the close of the Contact Period there was an amazing reorganization and consolidation of the Delawaran peoples. The political entity known as the Delaware tribe emerged early in the eighteenth century, and there are indications of consolidation and synthesis in other parts of culture. The Big House Ceremony, for example, was probably synthesized during this epoch. Consolidation and reorganization were the results of the catastrophic depopulation which had occurred in the seventeenth century, the migration of Delawares and their subsequent concentration, their subjugation by the Iroquois, and the necessity for mutual protection and unified action in dealing with other Indians and with the Europeans.[24]

Migration

It was not until late in the seventeenth century that Delaware migrations became of major importance, although there had been a movement and reshuffling of the natives ever since the Europeans had established colonies. In 1682, when William Penn made his first treaty with the Delawares, they were still in possession of much of the lower Delaware Valley. Small groups or bands were moving westward as early as 1690; in this year, for instance, "a band of the Minsi left for the far West, to unite with the Ottawas."[25] Even before the opening of the new century, there seems to have been an increasing concentration of population

[23]Snyderman, 1948.

[24]Hunter, 1954, pp. 341-44, has contributed much to an understanding of this period by his study of the growth of the Delaware nation from 1701 to 1757.

[25]Ruttenber, 1872, p. 177; Brinton, 1885, p. 122.

around the present Sunbury, in the Susquehanna Valley. By 1724 the Unami and Unalachtigo of this region had begun their migration to western Pennsylvania and the Allegheny River, below the mouth of the Mahoning, centering around the town of Kittaning.[26] In 1742 the Iroquois moved some of the remaining coastal Delawares to the Susquehanna Valley, and two years later by the treaty of Lancaster all of the Delawares remaining in the Delaware Valley were ordered by the Iroquois to "leave the waters of their river, and remove to Shamokin (now Sunbury) and Wyoming, and the Susquehanna, and most of them obeyed. The former was their chief town, and the residence of their 'king' Allemoebi."[27] After the Walking Purchase of 1737 the Munsi began their migration to the west.[28]

The geographical displacement, then, did not affect all the Delawares at once; small groups sold their land or were forced from it at various times. The scattered, decimated, demoralized, and unorganized bands, perhaps even families, of Delawares soon gathered, or were gathered, as they had never been in pre-European times. The "towns" that grew up in the river valleys of western Pennsylvania in the early decades of the eighteenth century were not formed from homogeneous cultural units. As early as 1694 part of the Shawnee became allied with the Munsi.[29] It is not known whether this association was only an alliance or whether it was something more. Mahican remnants became incorporated into the Delaware tribe; Hodge, for instance, said that "about 1730 a large body of them emigrated to Susquehanna r. and settled near Wyoming Pa., in the vicinity of the Delaware and Munsee, with whom they afterward removed to the Ohio region finally losing their identity."[30] The Conoy also about this time, and undoubtedly remnants from other tribes, were incorporated into the Delaware tribe.[31]

The westward migration of the Delawares set the stage for their more complete subjugation by the Iroquois. During the Period of Consolidation they were forced by the Iroquois to become "women." Weslager, who has made the most extensive study of this phenomenon, said that it occurred by conquest before 1712.[32] Whatever the date and method of subjugation, the Iroquois between this date and 1756 barred the Delawares from making treaties or going to war. It is impossible to determine the exact time when these subjugated people became the Delaware tribe. There are scattered references to "Delaware Indians" in the later decades of the seventeenth century, but it is not clear whether these indicate a political and cultural unit or their geographical location.[33] By 1736 the term Delaware was being used in treaties for at least some of these subjugated, but relatively unified peoples.[34] Before 1750 "chiefs" appeared who seem to have had considerable authority.

[26]Sipe, 1931, p. 42.

[27]Brinton, 1885, p. 123.

[28]Sipe, 1931, p. 43.

[29]Ruttenber, 1872, pp. 180-81.

[30]Hodge, 1907, Pt. 1, p. 786; see also Harrington, 1913, p. 209.

[31]Hodge, 1907, Pt. 2, p. 25.

[32]Weslager, 1944, pp. 381-88.

[33]See, for example, Browne, 1896, XV: 174-75, XVII: 14, 210-11, 221.

[34]Franklin, 1939, p. 7.

Teedyuscung by 1756 claimed authority over the entire tribe, including the Munsi.[35]

Apart from this secondary, political acculturation there are indications of other cultural changes. It is apparent, for example, that a number of technological items had completely replaced their native counterparts and had become necessities. This foreshadowed the dependence upon the dominant culture which has constantly increased since that time. Kalm in the first half of the eighteenth century said:

> Before the Europeans settled in North America the Indians had no other vessels to boil their meat in than these earthen pots of their own making; but since their arrival the savages have always bought pots, kettles and other necessary vessels of the Europeans, and no longer take the pains of making any, so that this art is entirely lost among them.[36]

Although the kinship structure of society survived this period, it was probably undergoing some alteration away from its early matrilineal, matrilocal emphasis. The number of clans probably increased as the Delaware tribe made its appearance. The tribal and village leaders developed considerable authority in external affairs, but they had no more power or control over internal affairs or over individual persons than they had traditionally possessed. In this period of turmoil it is apparent that stronger internal controls and a more highly developed apparatus of government were needed. Stronger external relations were formed by the emergence of chiefs and the tribe, but there is no indication of a similar strengthening of internal governmental institutions.

In the ideological sphere of culture there seems to have been no direct diffusion from European to Delaware culture. There was acculturation of a derived or secondary type, however, as is noted in Chapter IV. The Big House Ceremony as a tribal affair was probably synthesized during the early part of this period. It was also at this time that missionary activity was initiated among the Delawares. The first brief and futile attempt was made by David Brainerd, a missionary of the Society for Propagating Christian Knowledge, a Scotch organization. The attitude of the Delawares was expressed in a conversation Brainerd had with a Munsi chief in 1744. Brainerd said:

> ...he inquired why I desired the Indians to become Christians, seeing the Christians were so much worse than the Indians are in their present state. The Christians, he said, would lie, steal, and drink, worse than the Indians. It was they first taught the Indians to be drunk: and they stole from one another, to that degree, that their rulers were obliged to hang them for it... he said, they would live as their fathers had lived, and go where their fathers were when they died.[37]

Later on Brainerd said:

[35]Wallace, 1949, pp. 103-15; Sipe, 1931, p. 262.

[36]Kalm, 1937, I: 173.

[37]Brainerd, 1884, p. 127.

> ...the manner of their living is likewise a great disadvantage to the design of their being Christianized. They are almost continually roving from place to place; and it is but rare that an opportunity can be had with some of them for their instruction. There is scarcely any time of the year, wherein the men can be found generally at home, except about six weeks before, and in the season of planting corn, and about two months in the latter part of summer, from the time they begin to roast their corn, until it is fit to gather in.[38]

By the closing decades of this period the Moravians had entered the missionary field and were to become important, although on the whole unsuccessful, agents of religious diffusion.

Nativistic Period (1750-1814)

The Nativistic Period is one of the most interesting epochs in Delaware history because the Delawares by the opening of this period had risen, Phoenix-like, from the ashes of their subjugation and removal and had forged themselves into a tribe which was able to defy the Six Nations and the Europeans. This was the period of Delaware militarism, and although they were on the losing end of every war in which they took part, the prowess of the Delaware warrior became know from the Atlantic seaboard to the Mississippi. In a more general way this period was characterized by secondary acculturation, or culture change and modification caused by, and a result of, earlier acculturation. In this period the stresses and strains of acculturation culminated in a nativistic movement.

History

The English had disposed of their European rivals on the Atlantic seaboard in the seventeenth century, but by the middle of the next century they were confronted with the much more serious competition of the French in the interior. War began between these two powers in 1754 with the surrender of Washington at Fort Necessity. The Five Nations continued their alliance with the English and promised the aid of their subjugated tribes, including the Delawares. Since the Delawares were now mainly in the Ohio Valley, they were not as amenable to Iroquoian pressure and were more easily influenced by the French. Their most immediate reason for finally taking the French side was probably the Albany purchase of 1754. Settlers from Connecticut had explored the Susquehanna River and decided to locate at Wyoming, land which had been assigned to the Delawares by the Iroquois. The purchase was made from a few drunken chiefs and "included the whole valley of Wyoming and the country westward to the sources of the Allegheny."[39] After Braddock's defeat in July, 1755, the Delawares with many other Ohio Valley Indians joined the French cause.[40] By this

[38] Brainerd, 1884, p. 131.
[39] Ruttenber, 1872, p. 216.
[40] Sipe, 1931, pp. 203 ff.

action they literally and figuratively threw off the title of "women" and henceforth could not be regarded as docile subjects of the Iroquois. During this struggle the Delawares were split in two divisions, an eastern wing under Teedyuscung and a western one under Shingas. The western division was the more formidable in numbers and in proximity to the French and made the first raid against the frontier in the fall of 1755. The eastern division soon followed with raids into the Lehigh and Delaware valleys.[41] By 1756 the "Indians had cleared the Pennsylvania, Maryland, and Virginia frontiers of settlers."[42] The French estimated that from July, 1755, until March, 1756, more than seven hundred people in Pennsylvania, Virginia, and North Carolina were captured or killed by the Delawares and Shawnees.[43] By 1758 the French could no longer support the marauding Indians, and a few days after the fall of Fort Duquesne in the autumn of 1758 the eastern Delawares and Shawnees made peace with the English in a council at Easton.[44] These Delawares accepted peace on the basis of English withdrawal east of the Alleghenies following the expulsion of the French.[45]

This peace was uneasy and of short duration for the English had no real intention of abandoning the rich Ohio and Allegheny valleys, and the western Delawares remained hostile.[46] Additional reasons for the renewal of hostilities were that the English were less friendly and sociable towards the Indians than had been the French, they gave less for skins and furs, they wanted to settle on the land instead of merely establishing trading posts, and they did not wish to part with guns and ammunition.[47] In 1763 the Indian allies were militarily successful, but by 1764 the Delawares had been subdued by Boquet.[48] In the spring of 1765 the Delawares "submitted to a treaty that represented a complete surrender." The principal features of the treaty were "cession of land in reparation for the losses caused by Indian attacks in 1763" and the stipulation that the Delawares should abide by "any cession of their lands made by the Iroquois."[49] This treaty deprived the Delawares of the use and ownership of all lands south and east of the Ohio River. Some Delawares lived on the upper reaches of the Susquehanna at this time with Nanticoke, Conoy, and Mahican, but the great body of the tribe lived in scattered settlements on Beaver Creek and the Muskingum in what is now Ohio.[50]

From the end of Pontiac's War until 1774 the Delawares were relatively peaceful; they had been soundly beaten by Boquet at Bushy Run, French influence was decreasing, and both Indians and the English needed to resume trading. The English, nevertheless, were unwilling to keep the Indians peaceful with expensive gifts, and the relentless

[41] Sipe, 1931, pp. 204-14; Ruttenber, 1872, pp. 219-20; Downes, 1940, p. 75; Acrelius, 1876, pp. 137-38.

[42] Downes, 1940, p. 80.

[43] Sipe, 1931, p. 275.

[44] *Ibid.*, pp. 408-9; Parkman, 1893, I: 143.

[45] Sipe, 1931, pp. 407-12.

[46] Ruttenber, 1872, pp. 242-43.

[47] Sipe, 1931, p. 407; Parkman, 1893, I: 172-90.

[48] Ruttenber, 1872, pp. 246-47; Downes, 1940, pp. 120-21; Thompson, 1937, pp. 4-5.

[49] Downes, 1940, pp. 121-22.

[50] *Ibid.*, p. 134; Parkman, 1893, I: 150.

westward tide of immigration was increasing, particularly after 1770.[51]

During the Revolutionary War the Delawares were the only Indian tribe in the Ohio Valley which, for a time, supported the Americans.[52] The Delawares eventually joined the British for the following reasons. The Americans were unable to aid them either with goods or with protection from pro-British Indians, some Delawares had been killed by Americans, including White Eyes, a pro-American leader, and squatters had invaded Delaware hunting grounds west of the Ohio. The Munsi consistently seem to have been pro-British, raiding the Kentucky border as early as 1777.[53] In February of 1781 Captain Pipe, the leader of the war faction among the Munsi, persuaded the rest of the Delawares in a council held at Coshocton to formally go over to the British.[54] Heckewelder, the Moravian missionary, informed the Americans of this defection, and the Americans decided to forestall the Delawares by destroying their central town, Coshocton, on the Tuscarawas. This was done and some captives and much plunder were taken. In the meantime Delawares had successfully raided Wheeling and the frontier.[55] As a result of these hostilities, the main body of Delawares from the Coshocton community migrated to the Sandusky, Scioto, and the Mad rivers to the northwest, taking with them the Moravian missionaries and their disciples.[56] From this region the Delawares sent raiding parties to the Pennsylvania and Virginia frontiers. The infamous Gnadenhutten massacre seems to have been a retaliation for these raids. On the Tuscarawas River near Coshocton, ninety-six friendly and for the most part Christian Delawares of both sexes and all ages were clubbed to death by militia or "border outlaws."[57] The English capitulated in the fall of 1782, and the jurisdiction of the territory northwest of the Ohio fell to the newly created United States.[58] Delaware hostility was brought to a close in August, 1794, by the defeat of the allied Indians in the battle of Fallen Timbers. With this victory General Wayne was able to conclude the Treaty of Greenville (August, 1795), which marked the end of the conflict for the upper Ohio.[59] Although this area was ceded, the Indians were regarded as the "recognized owners of most of the present Ohio, Indiana, and Illinois."[60]

After the Treaty of Greenville white immigrants poured into the upper Ohio Valley, and the Delawares moved westward. As far back as 1770 the Delawares, in what is now Ohio, had received permission from the Piankashaw to migrate to lands between the Ohio and White rivers in the modern state of Indiana.[61] In 1781 Buckongahelas, a war chief,

---

[51]Zeisberger, 1871, p. 257.

[52]Thompson, 1937, p. 19; Heckewelder, 1881, p. 151.

[53]Downes, 1940, pp. 211-17, 241, 263; Butterfield, 1882, pp. 25-26.

[54]Sipe, 1931, p. 627; Butterfield, 1882, pp. 50-51.

[55]Downes, 1940, pp. 265, 271; Sipe, 1931, pp. 628-29; Butterfield, 1882, pp. 51-52.

[56]Butterfield, 1882, p. 52; Downes, 1940, p. 271; Sipe, 1931, p. 629.

[57]Mooney, 1911, p. 335.

[58]Zeisberger, 1871, pp. 566-72; Downes, 1940, pp. 273-75.

[59]Downes, 1940, p. 337; G. Foreman, 1946, p. 18.

[60]G. Foreman, 1946, pp. 18-19.

[61]*Ibid.*, p. 42.

had urged this westward movement, and soon after the Treaty of Greenville many of the Delawares moved to the West Fork of the White River. Other Delawares, with associated Shawnees, moved to Missouri in 1789 with the permission of the Spanish government.[62] In 1792 Zeisberger had moved his colony of Christian Indians to Canada and founded the town of Fairfield on the Thames River.[63] Zeisberger's group settled near some pagan Munsi who had migrated to this region somewhat earlier. Today there is a threefold division of Delawares in Canada; the Moravians of the Thames, the Munsi, and a few Delawares settled on the Six Nations Reserve.[64] The subsequent history and acculturation of these groups has not been pursued further in the present study.

General W. H. Harrison, as early as 1803, undertook negotiations with the Indian tribes in the Northwest Territory with a view to gaining their land. From that date until the War of 1812 Harrison entered into numerous treaties with the Indians of this area, and the Delawares were forced to cede land, but were able to retain enough so that another westward migration was not necessary.[65] Of all the tribes in the territory of Indiana, the Delawares were the only one which Harrison was able to keep neutral during the War of 1812.[66] The Shawnees and other hostile Indians attempted to induce the Delawares to enter this war, but they were unsuccessful.[67] Chief Anderson, a principal chief, seems to have been persuasive in the cause for peace, as were the Moravians, but past military defeats and cultural decay in general were probably the basic reasons for the peaceful inclination of the Delawares.

Acculturation

During this period there was a continuous flow of European technological articles, yet there was no diffusion of new kinds of technological traits. Zeisberger's list of items which the Indians acquired from traders was similar to that given for the Contact Period:

> For their skins the Indians get from the traders powder, lead, rifle-barrelled guns — for other weapons they do not value — blankets, strouds, linen, shirts, cotton, callemanco, knives, needles, thread, woolen and silken ribbon, wire and kettles of brass, silver buckles . . . bracelets, thimbles, rings, combs, mirrors, axes, hatchets and other tools.[68]

The plow complex had not diffused to the Delawares even by the end of the period.[69] They acquired the domestic animals of the Europeans, although not all the skills of caring for them.[70] During the wars of this period they plundered the frontier settlements and acquired horses, cattle, and other animals. Charles Stuart, captive of the Delawares between 1755 and 1757, said in this connection:

[62]Hodge, 1907, Pt. 1, p. 385.
[63]Zeisberger, 1871, p. 631.
[64]Harrington, 1908, p. 408.
[65]G. Foreman, 1946, p. 23 ff.
[66]Thompson, 1937, p. 64.
[67]Luckenbach, 1938, pp. 16-17.
[68]Zeisberger, 1910, p. 118.
[69]Luckenbach, 1938, pp. 598-99.
[70]*Ibid.*, pp. 60, 598.

...this Morning the Delawares, Shawnese & Mingos Divided their Prisoners & Plunder, At the Time of Divideing they had abt 110 Horses & Mares Includeing those they Brot with them from their Towns wch might in the whole amt to abt 10 or 12 - So that those Plundred from the Inhabitants was abt 100.[71]

Other livestock taken in this raid were eaten or otherwise destroyed.[72] Horses were considered more desirable than other animals and were ridden, but were not used in farming. Their chief use was in hunting, enabling the hunter to cover considerably greater distances.[73] They were poorly fed and when not in use were turned loose to forage as best they could.[74] Some Indians kept cattle for their milk and butter, "but most Indians are satisfied with dogs, pigs and horses."[75] Cattle were difficult to keep since "as they [the Delawares] move about almost the whole year hunting, it is hard for them, they cannot take care of them."[76] Although these animals must be counted as an increment to Delaware subsistence, other factors tended to offset the gains. First, the use of sea food had long since been abandoned because of migration away from the coastal habitat. Second, less produce was grown because war and migration upset gardening activities. Third, in order to obtain the necessary European manufactures, men had to hunt fur bearers, such as beaver, relatively more and food producers, such as deer, relatively less. The Moravians in their journals record the want and starvation that occurred sporadically during this period.

The Delawares also gained a more complete understanding of European artifacts. Zeisberger, for example, said:

The Delaware Indians use no other than rifle-barrelled guns, having satisfied themselves that these are the best for shooting at long range, in which they are very skillful and shooting accurately. They have acquired considerable skill in making minor repairs when their weapons get out of order. Some have even learned to furnish them with stocks, neatly and well made.[77]

Native weapons did not disappear, however, since the use of such weapons as the bow and arrow on smaller animals conserved powder.[78] The technological dependence of the Delawares upon the Europeans was shown, however, in a speech made to Charles Stuart and a number of other captives:

Shingas Proceeded to Say that they did not want to Carry on the War against the English and were now willing again To make Peace with them and restore all their Captives and Everything Else they had from them Provided the English wou'd Comply with the Following Proposals Vizt 1st the English shou'd send 5 Men among the Indians who shoud live well at the Indians expence with them, But [should] work for them without any other Pay from the Indians than Supporting Said Workmen and their Familys with Provisss and all other necessaries

[71] Stuart, 1926, p. 62; also see Schweinitz, 1905, p. 408.

[72] Stuart, 1926, pp. 59-60.

[73] Zeisberger, 1885, I: 310.

[74] Loskiel, 1794, p. 74.

[75] *Ibid.*; Brickell, 1842, p. 47.

[76] Zeisberger, 1885, II: 65.

[77] Zeisberger, 1910, p. 85.

[78] *Ibid.*, p. 29.

that they stood in need of — the Business said men were to Be Employ^{d} in were — Makeing of Powder, Smelting of Lead from the Ore, and Indians wou^{d} Engage not only to find them Lead Mines But Mines of Every other Metal that was necessary — Weaveing of Blanketts — Makeing and Mending Guns for them — and Mr. Stuart thinks the Other Man was to Be Employ^{d} in Makeing of Iron — the 2^{d} Condition was that the English shou^{d} Come and Settle among them with their Families and Promote Spinning for Shirts and In Genl shou^{d} Bring all Kinds of Trades among them that they might be Supplied with what they want near home, and that they and the English shou'd Live Together in Love and Friendship and Become one people But the Indians did not Insist nor Desire that the English sho^{d} Be obliged to Intermarry with them — That on these Terms they wou'd be glad to Be at Peace with the English, and desired the Prisoners to write to the Gov^{or} of Pennsylv^{a} about it. . . .[79]

The technology of the Delawares was, then, dependent upon that of the Europeans, so much so that an assured flow of European goods was a primary objective of war. When the desires of the Delawares were not granted, an interesting alteration in feeling took place. Heckewelder said:

They, however, acknowledge that the whites are ingenious, that they make axes, guns, knives, hoes, shovels, pots and kettles, blankets, shirts, and other very convenient articles, to which they have now become accustomed, and which they can no longer do without. "Yet," say they, "our forefathers did without all these things, and we have never heard, nor has any tradition informed us that they were at a loss for the want of them; therefore we must conclude that they also were ingenious; and, indeed, we know that they were; for they made axes of stone to cut with, and bows and arrows to kill the game; they made knives and arrows' points with sharp flint stones and bones, hoes and shovels from the shoulder blade of the elk and buffaloe; they made pots of clay, garments of skins, and ornaments with the feathers of the turkey, goose and other birds. They were not in want of anything, the game was plenty and tame, the dart shot from our arrows did not frighten them as the report of the gun now does; we had therefore everything that we could reasonably require; we lived happy!"[80]

There are some references in the literature of this period which indicate that there was acculturation in housing. Zeisberger noted that the Delawares "have learned to build block houses or have hired whites to build them."[81] It has been noted, however, that the aboriginal dwelling was used in the nineteenth century, and that it was even built during the twentieth century. The extensive migrations during and following the Nativistic Period probably prevented frequent use of European style dwellings. At least one attempt was made to lay out a village "in orderly fashion" as white settlers and Christian Indians did, but this attempt was unsuccessful.[82]

Piercing and cutting the ears went out of style, as did the scalp lock.

---

[79] Stuart, 1926, pp. 64-65.

[80] Heckewelder, 1881, pp. 191-92.

[81] Zeisberger, 1910, p. 18; Brickell, 1842, p. 47.

[82] Zeisberger, 1910, p. 87.

Tattooing was practiced until 1762.[83] "Dress up" clothing was resplendent with all kinds of ornamentation:

> The garments of some of their principal actors are singular, and decorated with such a number of gewgaws and trinkets, that it is impossible to give a precise description of them. Neither are they all alike in taste, every one dressing himself according to his fancy, or the custom of the tribe to which he belongs. While the women, as I have already said, have thimbles and little bells rattling at their ancles, the men have deers' claws fixed to their braced garters or knee bands, and also to their shoes, for the same purpose; for they consider jingling and rattling as indispensably necessary to their performances in the way of dancing.[84]

Silver broaches, spangles, bracelets, and clasps for the hair were obtained from traders. European hats could also be obtained from traders, although headgear was not generally worn.[85] European ornaments had undoubtedly been obtained much earlier than this period, but the first descriptions of how these were worn come from the Moravians. The cradleboard had been abandoned by Zeisberger's time.[86]

It is apparent that there was a continuing decline in the effectiveness of the control of society over its members during the Nativistic Period. At various times during this period the Delawares were without a strong leader or leaders.[87] This lack, combined with military disasters and unfavorable treaties, caused control over external political relationships to disintegrate. Tribal solidarity and unity of action, insofar as they had ever existed, disappeared during this period of war, dispersion, and upheaval. The chiefs who traditionally had little authority over individual behavior – or misbehavior – seem to have been incapable of restoring order. Drunkenness had become a serious problem, and the weak chiefs were unable to deal with it. Zeisberger said:

> Frequently, the chiefs have prohibited the sale of strong drink in their towns; but it is always brought in in some manner, against which the chiefs are powerless to protest. For instance, they may appoint a sacrifice of rum, in which nothing but rum is used. This the chiefs cannot hinder owing to established custom. When once the Indians, who gather in large number for such a sacrifice, have tasted the strong drink but have not satisfied themselves, they will go to the old women who deal in liquor. The latter will often obtain everything that an Indian owns except his Breechclout.[88]

Divorce was more frequent than in earlier times, thievery was common, and respect for the aged was no longer an honored custom.[89] In brief, all sorts of institutions had seriously deteriorated; the Delawares themselves were acutely aware of this disintegration, a fact which is important in the context of nativistic reaction. As Zeisberger said, "Impurity

[83] *Ibid.*, p. 12; Heckewelder, 1881, pp. 205-7.

[84] Heckewelder, 1881, p. 205.

[85] Zeisberger, 1910, p. 15.

[86] *Ibid.*, p. 85.

[87] Zeisberger, 1885, II: 29.

[88] Zeisberger, 1910, pp. 117-18.

[89] *Ibid.*; Zeisberger, 1885, I: 129.

and immorality, even gross sensuality and unnatural vice flourish among them, according to the testimony of the Indians themselves, more than was the case formerly."[90]

About 1750 prophets began to appear among the Delawares, and these individuals continued to appear sporadically until 1812.[91] The Shawnee prophet of the early nineteenth century, although of another tribe, may be regarded as representing the end of this phase of acculturation. No prophets appeared before 1750 and none after 1812, if exception is made of the initiators of peyotism in the late nineteenth century. This anti-acculturative movement and the wars of this period were closely associated: some of the messages of the prophets fostered war, and, conversely, military defeats probably furthered their appearance. During this phase of acculturation the Delawares were desperately trying to save what was left of their cultural and social integrity and to turn back the clock to a mythical age when war, personal demoralization, and cultural chaos were unknown. One way of attaining this end was to follow the dictates of the supernatural powers as revealed by prophets. This the Delawares did in nativistic movements of a type which has been described as "revivalistic nativism."[92] This form of nativism is defined as "an attempt to revive extinct or at least moribund elements of culture . . . ."[93] All of these prophets taught that by following supernatural injunctions as revealed to them, acculturation could be halted and even reversed. The most successful was known as the Delaware Prophet or the Imposter, whose career reached its zenith about 1762.[94] In a vision this man received instructions from the Great Spirit on how to restore his people to their former state. His message was made concrete by a number of symbolic devices painted on a tanned deer hide or on a wooden stick. Copies of the deer-hide map were made, some on paper, and were sold by the Delaware Prophet. Some of the purchasers, in turn, seem to have become minor prophets. Heckewelder's description of this symbolic device is the most detailed:

> The size of this map was about fifteen inches square, or, perhaps, something more. An inside square was formed by lines drawn within it, of about eight inches each way, two of those lines, however, were not closed by about half an inch at the corners. Across these inside lines, others of about an inch in length were drawn with sundry other lines and marks, all which was intended to represent a strong inaccessible barrier, to prevent those without from entering the space within, otherwise than at the place appointed for that purpose. When the map was held as he directed, the corners which were not closed lay at the left hand side, directly opposite to each other, the one being at the south-east by south, and the nearest at the north-east by north. In explaining or describing the particular points on this map, with his fingers always pointing to "the heavenly re-

[90] Zeisberger, 1910, p. 20.

[91] Zeisberger, 1871, p. 265, gives this date, but the Delaware prophet did not appear until a decade later, in 1760. (Hayes, 1954, pp. 76-77, said, however, that Papunhang, the christianized Delaware preacher, had established his religious group before 1752).

[92] Linton, 1943, pp. 230-40.

[93] *Ibid.*, p. 231.

[94] Peckham, 1947, p. 98; Heckewelder, 1881, p. 291.

> gions," or the place destined by the great Spirit for the habitation of the Indians in future life; the space left open at the south-east corner, he called the "avenue," which had been intended for the Indians to enter into this heaven, but which was now in the possession of the white people, wherefore the great Spirit had since caused another "avenue" to be made on the opposite side, at which, however, it was both difficult and dangerous for them to enter, there being many impediments in their way....The space on the outside of this interior square was intended to represent the country given to the Indians to hunt, fish and dwell in while in this world; the east side of it was called the ocean or "great salt water Lake."[95]

The prophet discussed before his public this representation of the supernatural world and pointed out that through neglect and disobedience the Great Spirit had turned his benevolent attention to the whites. He had allowed the whites to usurp Indian land and to bar passage of the Indian to the spirit world.[96] To correct this state of affairs the prophet advocated several courses of action:

> Hear what the great Spirit has ordered me to tell you! You are to make sacrifices, in the manner that I shall direct; to put off entirely from yourselves the customs which you have adopted since the white people came among us; you are to return to that former happy state, in which we lived in peace and plenty, before these strangers came to disturb us, and above all, you must abstain from drinking their deadly *beson* [poison, alcohol], which they have forced upon us, for the sake of increasing their gains and diminishing our numbers. Then will the great Spirit give success to our arms; then he will give us strength to conquer our enemies, to drive them from hence, and recover the passage to the heavenly regions which they have taken from us.[97]

James Kenny, a Pittsburgh trader, emphasized that the prophet advocated the cessation of trade with whites, and said:

> ...its agree'd to by their Whole Nation, to follow their new Plan of Religion, & all their Boys are to be Train'd to yeuse of the Bow & Arrow for Seven Years Then to Live entirely on dry'd Meat & a Sort of Bitter Drink made of Roots & Plants & Water ye Women & Antient Men may Raise & Eat Corn at ye Expiration of ye Seven Years, to quit all Commerce with ye White People & Clothe themselves with Skins.[98]

Another prophet, a Munsi called Wangomend, appeared in 1766 and met Zeisberger in 1767. Relatively little is known about this man, although Heckewelder mentioned him:

> This man also pretended that his call as a preacher was not of his own choice, but that he had been moved to it by the great and good Spirit, in order to teach

[95] Heckewelder, 1881, pp. 291-92; Loudon published a purported reproduction of the prophet's book along with McCullough's description of the prophet and his works (Loudon, 1808, pp. 324-25, and tipped-in engraving). Hayes, 1954, pp. 76-77, saw the "old priest's" book in 1760. Zeisberger, 1910, p. 133, and Kenny, 1913, p. 171, also described the prophet's symbolic world portrait.

[96] Heckewelder, 1881, pp. 292-93.

[97] *Ibid.*, p. 293.

[98] Kenny, 1913, p. 188; also see pp. 171-72.

his countrymen, who were on the way to perdition, how they could become reconciled to their God. He would make his followers believe that he had once been taken so near to heaven, that he could distinctly hear the crowing of the cocks, and that at another time he had been borne by unseen hands to where he had been permitted to take a peep into the heavens, of which there were three, one for the Indians, one for the negroes, and another for the white people.[99]

The last of the prophets associated with the Delawares was Tenskawatawa, a Shawnee and brother of Tecumseh. These two Shawnees had established their headquarters and lived for several years, beginning in 1798, at one of the Delaware villages on White River in present-day Indiana.[100] The prophet preached against drunkenness, racial intermarriage, "release of Indian lands to the whites by sale, and the sin of witchcraft."[101] Luckenbach in 1805 said of him:

> We heard that a Schawano Indian had arisen among the heathen as teacher, and that a large number of Delawares and Schawanos had come together in Woapicamikunk to hear what this heathen teacher had to say. As usual his teaching consists of all sorts of ancient heathenism. In addition he forbids all sins, and insists that parents should not strike their children. He also urges most strongly that the Indians should sacrifice; that they should do away with their cattle and keep horses only; that the heathen should shave their heads and live as did the Indians in olden days. He assured the Indians that God had shown him the deer were half a tree's length under the ground and that these would soon appear again on earth if the Indians did what he told them to do, and then there would be an abundance of deer once more. He also related in an address that God had shown him a crab whose claws were quite full of seaweeds; that the spirit had told him, "Look! this crab is from Boston and has brought with it something of the land there. If you Indians will do everything I tell you I will turn over the land so that the white people are covered and you alone shall possess the land."[102]

Some diffusion from Christianity had occurred, although the prophets vehemently rejected Christianity and most of Euro-American civilization. The idea of a heaven and a hell, common in the messages of the prophets, is a case in point, as is the symbolic number twelve, which has been mentioned. Other traits of this sort may have diffused about this time. It seems certain that the revivalistic nativism did much to strengthen the Big House Ceremony, and, as Kinietz has shown, many minor elements seem to have been added to it by the prophets. Shaking hands with the left hand and the addition of ten carved heads in the Big House, bringing the total to twelve, are examples which he mentioned.[103] These changes in religion do not mean that any of the native ceremonies lost their force or vitality. According to Zeisberger:

---

[99]Heckewelder, 1881, p. 294.
[100]Thompson, 1937, p. 45.
[101]*Ibid.*
[102]Luckenbach, 1938, p. 392; also see p. 262.
[103]Kinietz, 1940, pp. 118-19.

> Though in the detail of the ceremony there has been change, as the Indians are more divided now than at that time [i.e., prehistorically] worship and sacrifice have continued as practiced in the early days, for the Indians believe that they would draw all manner of disease and misfortune upon themselves if they omitted to observe the ancestral rites.[104]

By the time the Shawnee prophet appeared the Delawares seem to have passed somewhat beyond the nativistic phase of acculturation.

Decadent Period (1814-1867)

The military defeats of the Delawares during the Nativistic Period and the disillusionment following the unsuccessful religious revivals set the stage for a phase of acculturation which is best described as one of decadence. By the second decade of the nineteenth century the Delawares were no longer an independent tribe, but were politically and militarily dominated by, and at the mercy of, the United States. In a social sense the tendencies towards dispersal first noted in the preceding period persisted, as small groups continued to desert the main body of the tribe. In other respects cultural decay and disintegration continued, although further acculturation is best described as halting. From this time on the Delawares underwent continuous, overt pressure to become "civilized" Americans.

History

In 1814 the British and Americans concluded a treaty of peace, one article of which stipulated that the Indian allies of the British would have their rights, privileges, and property restored.[105] In compliance with this treaty, in 1816 "A Treaty of Peace and Friendship" was entered into with the Delawares, as well as with other tribes.[106] This treaty did not long prevent the alienation of Indian lands, however, for during the administration of Monroe (1817-25) "a policy was inaugurated looking to increased westward emigration of Indians from east of the Mississippi."[107] Before the War of 1812 the Delawares had bitterly opposed the cession of land, but after the war they did not have the strength to resist the demands of the United States.[108]

In the Treaty of St. Mary's of 1818 the Delawares, including remnants of the Mahicans and Nanticokes, sold their land in Indiana to the government "without reserve." The government agreed to remove them to the west side of the Mississippi and give them land there, although no location or emigration date was set.[109] In 1820 Delawares from the

[104]Zeisberger, 1910, p. 136. Mahr, 1952, has documented the community responsibility of ritual leaders, as demonstrated in the experience of a Moravian convert of 1772.

[105]Thompson, 1937, p. 81; G. Foreman, 1946, pp. 27-28.

[106]G. Foreman, 1946, p. 29.

[107]*Ibid.*, pp. 32-47.

[108]Thompson, 1937, p. 81.

[109]Brinton, 1885, pp. 124-25; Mooney, 1911, p. 337; G. Foreman, 1946, p. 37.

Whitewater River region in southeastern Indiana and some Shawnees arrived at Kaskaskia. In November the Indian agent at Kaskaskia "paid for ferrying 1,346 Delawares and their 1,499 horses across the Mississippi."[110] Sickness hampered this migration as did also thievery of horses by whites.[111] They spent the winter of 1820 on the Current River in Carter and Shannon counties, Missouri, and they remained in this vicinity a second winter, despite the failure of their corn crop. During the early summer of 1821 the remaining White River Delawares began their trek to Missouri, but because of sickness and other difficulties they did not reach the Mississippi until winter.

In 1821 the Delawares were assigned land in western Missouri, but unfortunately this land possessed a lead mine which was coveted by whites.[112] Their Osage neighbors to the west also resented their presence, and hostilities resulted. During the second decade of this century the remaining Delawares in Ohio experienced increased pressure for emigration. The Delawares in Missouri urged them to migrate in a "correspondence by means of wampum."[113] The Indians of Missouri apparently were planning an alliance with these eastern Indians in order to strengthen themselves and dispossess the Osage. While negotiations were going on for removal of the eastern Indians, Senator Benton of Missouri proposed that land be provided west of Missouri for all Indians. By 1829 the Missouri Delawares and Ohio emigrants had consented to move to Kansas. The land reserved for them was in "the fork of the Kansas and Missouri rivers, extending up the Kansas to the Kansas line and up the Missouri to "Camp Leavenworth"; and thence by a line drawn westwardly, leaving a space of ten miles wide north of the Kansas boundary for an outlet."[114] This treaty provided that the Indians would be assisted in their removal with "ox teams, farming utensils, and provisions . . . ."[115] but some were so anxious that they moved on their own initiative. In 1829 the remaining Delawares in Ohio, chiefly Munsi, in a council with Cass at Detroit agreed to emigrate to Kansas.[116] In 1831 small bands were still moving west, including the band of the venerable Captain Pipe.[117]

As was noted earlier, some Delawares as early as 1789 had moved to Missouri under a Spanish grant. It appears to have been this band which was located on the Red River in the present-day McCurtain County, Oklahoma, in the early part of the nineteenth century. White settlers in 1828 petitioned the authorities for the removal of the Shawnees and Delawares in this area, the Shawnees having joined the Delawares subsequent to the War of 1812.[118] Under threat of armed might the Indians were driven from this locality to Texas. Samuel Houston attempted to supply the immigrant Cherokees, Shawnees, Delawares, Kickapoos, and others with land embracing present-day Cherokee and

[110] G. Foreman, 1946, p. 41.
[111] *Ibid.*, p. 43.
[112] *Ibid.*
[113] *Ibid.*, p. 48.
[114] *Ibid.*, p. 54.
[115] *Ibid.*, p. 55.
[116] *Ibid.*, pp. 55-56.
[117] *Ibid.*, p. 69.
[118] *Ibid.*, pp. 159-60.

Smith counties along the Neches and Angelina rivers in eastern Texas. The Texas senate refused to ratify Houston's treaty, however, and Mirabeau B. Lamar, Houston's successor, attacked and defeated these Indians.[119] They fled across the Red River to the vicinity of the Washita and Blue rivers in the lands of the Choctaw and Chickasaw. In the 1840's most of them settled in Creek territory on the north side of the Canadian River.[120] Colonel Ethan Allen Hitchcock reported in 1841 and 1842 that there were 700 Delawares "living sixty miles above the mouth of Little River."[121] They were at this time carrying on extensive intercourse with the Comanches and other western Indians. Foreman, quoting from the *Arkansas Intelligencer*, said that these Delawares "are in a semi-barbarous state, and entirely uneducated, but show great shrewdness and intelligence in their intercourse with the whites. As hunters and warriors they have a higher reputation than any other Indians on the frontier."[122]

Another small group of Texas Delawares had allied with the Caddos and they had intermarried. These, along with Tawakonis, Wacos, Shawnees, and Comanches, had been granted a reservation in Texas by the government. Texans resented their presence, however, and in 1859 the government moved them to the Washita River near the present town of Anadarko.[123] During the Civil War the agency responsible for the move was broken up, and the Indians fled to Butler County, Kansas. After the war they returned to the Washita much reduced in numbers; only 471 of the 1,492 who had emigrated from Texas were left. In 1874 the Delawares, Caddos, and Iowas near Anadarko joined forces under the Caddos, with a Caddo chief.[124] By 1886 the agency report listed only forty-one Delawares.[125] There appear to be no more than this number of Delawares in the Anadarko area today; they are culturally and biologically mixed with allied Indians.

Another group which was partly Delaware deserves mention here. This group, known as the Stockbridge, was originally the Mahican Housatonic of Massachusetts. After the American Revolution they joined the Oneida in New York, and in 1832, with a band of Oneida, confederated with a Christianized Munsi band on a reservation near Lake Winnebago in Wisconsin.[126] In 1839 the combined tribe of about 400 moved to Kansas, settling on Delaware lands. They were later reported as part of the Delaware tribe.[127] In 1853 the agent stated that there were only eighteen or twenty left. In 1859 the Stockbridge, variously known as Munsi or Christian Indians, confederated with two bands of Chippewa Indians in Kansas. After the Civil War the Cherokees took them into the Cherokee Nation. I found only one person who claimed to be a Stockbridge Indian living among the "Cherokee-Delawares."

Some Delawares served with the United States in the Seminole wars,

[119] G. Foreman, 1946, p. 161.
[120] *Ibid.*, p. 162.
[121] *Ibid.*, p. 162.
[122] *Ibid.*, p. 164, as quoted in the *Arkansas Intelligencer*, Feb. 7, 1846, p. 1, col. 4.
[123] G. Foreman, 1946, p. 282.
[124] *Ibid.*, pp. 282-84
[125] *Ann. Rep.*, 1886, p. 128.
[126] Wright, 1951, p. 246.
[127] G. Foreman, 1946, pp. 337-38.

and according to Adams some were employed by the Hudson Bay Company and not only entered the far northwest, but settled there. He said that their descendants lived in Idaho, Montana, and Oregon in affiliation with the Crow and Nez Percé and "other northwestern tribes." He estimated their number at thirty-five.[128]

In 1838 there were 1,050 Delawares on their reservation at the mouth of the Kansas River.[129] There were also several hundred living along the Red River, as has been noted. These seem to have forsaken agriculture and were dependent upon the chase for most of their livelihood. The main body of Delawares, at the confluence of the Kansas and Missouri rivers, found no more tranquility or isolation from white contacts than they had found in Missouri, Indiana, or Ohio. Until 1833, when Indian agents concluded a treaty of peace, the Pawnees and Delawares were hostile to each other.[130] During the Gold Rush, and until the Delawares were forced from Kansas, white immigrants continually harassed them. Their horses were stolen, their timber cut, and their property violated. By 1854, in one of the Manypenny treaties, the Delawares were coerced into ceding much of their reservation. Adams said of this cession:

> They were encompassed on every side by settlers, and the history of their difficulties and discouragements was again repeated, their lands coveted and trespassed upon, their timber cut and destroyed. They were denied the protection of the law to either their property or persons, and in the hope of satisfying the demands of their neighbors and of the Government were persuaded, in 1854, to enter into a treaty with the United States by which they ceded 558,555.46 acres of the choicest of their lands in trust, which brought them $1,054,943.37, and at the same time to cede to the United States what was known as the "Outlet," a tract containing more than 1,000,000 acres, for the paltry sum of $10,000.[131]

In subsequent years the plight of the Delawares in Kansas became even more exasperating, for the railroads and the white settlers continued to covet their land.[132] In 1860 more Delaware lands were alienated by allotting to each Delaware eighty acres. The surplus land was to be purchased by the Pawnee and Western Railroad Company for $1.25 per acre.[133] In 1864 another treaty was made for the benefit of a railroad, resulting in the alienation of more land. By 1863 the harassed Delawares petitioned the Commissioner of Indian Affairs for money to send a delegation to the Rocky Mountains in search of a new home.[134] This request was refused, and a location in Indian Territory was suggested by the Commissioner, William P. Dole. Nothing could be done to further this movement until after the Civil War. Adams said that nearly all the able-bodied men enlisted in the Northern Army.[135]

On July 4, 1866, the Delaware tribe and the United States entered into another treaty providing for the removal of the Delawares to Indian

[128] Adams, 1906, p. 35.

[129] G. Foreman, 1946, p. 182; *Ann. Rep.*, 1838, p. 447.

[130] G. Foreman, 1946, p. 182.

[131] Adams, 1906, pp. 40-41.

[132] *Ibid.*, pp. 42 ff.

[133] G. Foreman, 1946, p. 185.

[134] Adams, 1906, p. 42; *Ann. Rep.*, 1863, p. 235.

[135] Adams, 1906, p. 42.

Territory. Every person carried upon a roll to be made up by February 18, 1867, was to be given one hundred and sixty acres of land purchased from the Cherokee Nation.[136] The Senate was slow in acting upon this treaty, and the Delawares in April, 1867, took the matter into their own hands and entered into the contract with the Cherokee Nation.[137] A Delaware delegation examined land in the Cherokee Nation and selected a strip of land lying along the Little Verdigris, or Caney, River. This tract comprises the northern four-fifths of present-day Washington County in northeastern Oklahoma.[138] The Delawares from tribal funds paid one dollar per acre for this land. When the roll was compiled there were nine hundred and eighty-five Delawares, who henceforth became part of the Cherokee tribe.[139]

During the fall and winter of 1867 the migration to Indian Territory was begun. The more prosperous individuals were the first to leave; some of the poorer Delawares did not arrive until the next summer.[140] This last migration is remembered by aged informants and is recalled as a journey of extreme hardship. It typifies the condition of the Delawares at this time, for it was the migration of a dispersed, erratically led, destitute remnant.

Acculturation

Acculturation during the Decadent Period is in one sense more complicated than at any other time. As has been seen, during this period the Delawares were more widely scattered and dispersed than they had been previously, and they were never able to regroup or reunite. The forces which affected these various remnants varied; the group which finally settled in the Anadarko vicinity, for example, had close contacts with the "wild" tribes (Comanche, Cheyenne, Arapaho), whereas the main body had more intimate relationships with the whites. For this and other reasons the subsequent culture change of these groups differed. Since my field work was principally with the descendants of the main body (the "Cherokee-Delaware"), my discussion principally concerns this group. It might be remarked in passing, however, that today all Delawares, whatever their antecedents, seem to have reached approximately the same stage of social and cultural assimilation.

It was during the Decadent Period that the aboriginal gardening techniques were finally abandoned. With the settlement of the main body of Delawares on reservations, and with closer association of Indians and whites, the opportunity to become acquainted with the horse-plow complex and the small grains increased immensely. The government agents and missionaries did everything within their power to transform the Delawares into sedentary, farming people. The men were reluctant, however, to alter their traditional role as hunters and warriors and

[136] *Ibid.*, p. 43; G. Foreman, 1946, pp. 186-87.

[137] G. Foreman, 1946, p. 188.

[138] Adams, 1906, p. 43.

[139] G. Foreman, 1946, p. 188.

[140] Adams, 1906, p. 43; G. Foreman, 1946, pp. 188-89; *Ann. Rep.*, 1868, p. 263.

become farmers. They preferred "with a few exceptions, a nomadic, wandering life to that of tranquility and peace."[141] There was a special attraction in hunting since magnificent herds of bison still roamed west of the Mississippi. As late as 1866 the Delawares were having successful hunts on the plains.[142] The vast majority of men, both of the main body and of the "absentee" bands, at least during the early years of this period, concentrated their activities upon hunting bison, scouting for the Army, and trading with the Indians of the plains. One agent said in this connection: "The Delawares are brave, chivalrous, enterprising Indians. They hunt and roam throughout the length and breadth of the great western plains, some as far as California."[143] They became famous as trappers and scouts, both for the fur companies and for the government. They learned the skills of the Plains Indians and became fearless fighters and exploiters of the West and its native peoples.[144] The Delaware men were ideally suited for a successful life on the plains; acculturation had not yet proceeded far enough to impair their skill in hunting, scouting, and tracking. By this time the Delawares also shared the motives of the white trader. Speck has said in this connection:

> Having suffered expulsions, burnings, broken agreements, deceptions and massacres provoked by the vicious but nobly interpreted land-lust settlers in the East, they had learned the lessons involved in such transactions ... they knew and practiced commerce, had acquired the economy of European colonists.... This means that the Delawares had acquired a peculiar status by the middle of the nineteenth century.... They appeared on the frontiers of the Indian nations ... equipped and motivated much as the whites had been on their own frontiers a century before in Pennsylvania, New Jersey, and New York.[145]

Not only did the men prefer the hunt and a roving-trading life to agricultural pursuits, but there seems to have been difficulty in getting the Delawares to raise anything but corn.[146] It was not until 1863 that a reportable amount of wheat was grown, and then only one hundred and forty acres were planted, compared to 2,522 acres of corn.[147] Increasing numbers of livestock were kept, cattle in particular becoming more common.[148] In 1865 the agent reported that they had 554 horses, 989 cattle, 1,807 swine, and 92 sheep.[149]

Although the Delawares were able to resist complete assimilation in subsistence habits, technological assimilation was otherwise almost complete. Frame and log houses had replaced the bark wigwam before 1859. Morgan in this year said:

---

[141] *Ann. Rep.*, 1864, p. 357.

[142] *Ann. Rep.*, 1866, p. 247.

[143] *Ann. Rep.*, 1852, p. 75.

[144] DeVoto, 1947, p. 56, has briefly characterized the Delawares at this time. C. T. Foreman, 1946, also contains an interesting biography of the most famous of the Delaware guides and scouts of this period, Black Beaver.

[145] Speck, 1943, p. 322.

[146] *Ann. Rep.*, 1857, p. 454.

[147] *Ann. Rep.*, 1863, p. 233.

[148] *Ann. Rep.*, 1852, p. 77.

[149] *Ann. Rep.*, 1865, p. 366.

When Mr. Pratt came among them 12 years ago, as he informs me, they were living in bark houses. Now many of them are living in frame houses two stories and $2\frac{1}{2}$ stories high, some with a veranda in front the whole length, and they have good barns and outbuildings.[150]

Morgan described the attire of the Delawares on a gala "Payment Day" as resembling dress of the whites in cut, but varying in other respects. He said:

The Delaware women have usually dropped the Indian skirt, and put on the long dress of the white female.... Their dresses are of all colors, and some of them are of rich materials. A few were dressed in colored muslin with silk shawls, and looked quite becomingly, but the most of them were, strange to say, dressed in silk gowns, some of which were brocade patterns of rich brocade silk, some were black, these looked the best. Some were crimson and black, some fiery plaid; the most of them were in bright colors. Over these they wore silk shawls of every color and shade, most of them fringed.... They appeared to have put on all they had, to show it, the quantity of dress being of more importance in their sight than its style, or quality.[151]

Morgan also described male attire:

The men were more fantastically dressed than the women, and did not appear half as well. Their fancy dresses were cheap and absurd, rendering their general appearance ridiculous.... Some of the old men and some of the young men had on colored calico frock coats of the most gaudy colors. Many had vermilion on their faces, thus giving them a low appearance, and I saw a few girls with spots of it in their cheeks. One man I saw with a silver ornament in his nose, which covered part of his mouth. Many of the men wore leggins with a wide side projection, ornamented, and the breech cloth, over which they wore a vest or shirt, and perhaps one of the frock coats of calico above named, with head bands of bead work over the shoulder and meeting in a large bead work pocket on the right hand side.[152]

Social and political institutions continued their decline during the Decadent Period. In Chapter III the deteriorated kinship system of the mid-nineteenth century and the changes it subsequently underwent were examined in detail. The most noteworthy change politically was the surrender of political independence for the security, or anticipated security, of the reservation. There was no mention during the nineteenth century or subsequently of strong native leaders; they had ceased to exist. Many other features of Delaware social organization must have been seriously altered, or were completely replaced during this period. Unfortunately, information is limited. As early as 1824 Trowbridge observed:

In days of yore children were considered as bound to obey their parents, and were not suffered to marry until the age of thirty if males or twenty four if females; but to use their own language, a boy begins to grow hoarse he assumes the practices of a man, declares himself independent and marries.[153]

---

[150] Morgan, 1859, MS.
[151] *Ibid.*
[152] *Ibid.*
[153] Trowbridge MS.

Trowbridge also added that "there is no ceremony of courtship and marriage in these degenerate days."[154] Morgan noted that there were only two cases of polygamy and that other Delawares were "inclined to make a fuss about it." He also said that Indian women were "quick to marry white husbands."[155] He noted in another place, however, that "the Delawares are quite vigorous against intermarriage with the whites, and also against unlawful intercourse."[156] It is apparent that in 1859 society was still based on kinship ties, but dispersal, the efforts of whites, and other causes were bringing about its collapse. This state of affairs is apparent in such statements as: ". . . the Delawares thought a good deal more of their relationships than we did, and if there was the least particle of relationship they were glad to find it. He says that in old times near relatives could not marry, but now they married as near as our cousins."[157] It is also apparent from the following statement of the Commissioner of Indian Affairs, who realized that to some the bonds of communal possession of lands were still strong: "There are, however, amongst the tribe many who are unwilling to give up their old habits, and who insist upon continuing their tribal relations, refusing to select for themselves the lands to which they are entitled, and claiming that they will be happier with their lands in common."[158]

In July, 1866, just prior to the final removal to Indian Territory the chiefs and council adopted a code of laws. It consisted of ten articles, each with a number of subheadings. This code provided for the punishment of criminals and established a law code which included the regulation of marriage, divorce, domestic relations, and the like.[159] There is no indication that this code was forced upon the Delawares from above, rather it seems to have been a desperate attempt on the part of the members of a moribund society to re-establish order and regularity. It reflects better than anything else the chaotic, decadent state of Delaware culture at the close of this period.

This period also seems to mark the beginning of a social phenomenon which was not particularly apparent in earlier times. It was the unequal, disharmonious character of acculturation; some Delawares had adopted many more white customs than had others. This led to a lack of harmony between individuals and differences in interests which have persisted, resulting in the social atomization of the Delawares today. As early as 1856 the Delawares were living as widely scattered as the reserve permitted, probably a result of this disunity.[160] Time and again the agents reported that "some" individuals had become "civilized," whereas others were but "savages."[161]

All of the specific changes in social organization cannot be described. It is known, however, that the school established in 1835 overtly tried to discourage the continuance of old customs. This school was initiated

[154]Trowbridge MS.

[155]Morgan, 1859, MS.

[156] *Ibid.*

[157] *Ibid.*

[158]*Ann. Rep.*, 1861, p. 11.

[159]*Ann. Rep.*, 1866, pp. 248-49.

[160]*Ann. Rep.*, 1856, p. 670.

[161]*Ann. Rep.*, 1862, p. 100; 1861, p. 11.

and supported until 1856 by the American Baptist Missionary Union.[162] The school was not particularly successful while in missionary hands, the enrollment being limited to about twenty-five students who were "mostly orphans."[163] After the government took over the school, the Delawares showed more interest in educating their children.[164] In 1858 there were fifty-two boys and thirty girls in the school, but their parents withdrew them as soon as they were old enough to be useful at home.[165] The school taught the three R's and little else. There was no formal instruction in mechanical or agricultural subjects, although a two-hundred-acre farm was operated in conjunction with the school.[166] Before 1856 the emphasis seems to have been on conversion to Christianity. Agent Robinson in 1858 noted:

> I am of the opinion schools disconnected from the missionary management would likely prove of greater utility than the present system. The eradication of their own national religion before the mind is sufficiently enlightened to receive and comprehend the sublime principles of the Christian religion, has a demoralizing effect. It leaves the poor, ignorant Indian frequently without any religion whatever, and consequently without any moral restraint.[167]

There are no figures available which indicate how many Delawares were converted to Christianity during the Decadent Period. The number must have been considerable, although enough Delawares clung to the traditional religion for it to survive well into the twentieth century.

The individual demoralization resulting from cultural decay is probably reflected in the extensiveness of drunkenness. This problem is mentioned in virtually every *Annual Report*. An agent in 1854 summed up as well as anybody the condition of the Delawares during this phase of acculturation:

> The progress in agriculture and mechanic industry is but slow. Indolence and drunkenness cling to them with a tenacity which baffles the perseverance and benevolent zeal of the missionary. Civilization, it is true, has decorated their persons with more comely garments than the breech-clout and blanket, and banished many of the customs of savage life, but nevertheless much remains to be done. They are still the children of nature, easily led astray and seduced into vicious habits, difficult to be taught and slow to embrace the Christian code of morals.[168]

[162] *Ann. Rep.*, 1862, p. 101.
[163] *Ann. Rep.*, 1852, p. 77.
[164] *Ann. Rep.*, 1858, p. 110.
[165] *Ann. Rep.*, 1862, p. 101.
[166] Morgan, 1859, MS.
[167] *Ann. Rep.*, 1858, pp. 110-11.
[168] *Ann. Rep.*, 1854, p. 106.

VI. DELAWARE ASSIMILATION

The final flight to the Caney River Valley in Indian Territory in 1867 was the last movement of the Delawares as a tribe, and it also marked a stage of culture change which is more aptly termed assimilation than acculturation. Contact with the white man became even more intensive and extensive because the Delawares could no longer flee from his presence. Delaware technology had long since disappeared, and the old social organization was in an advanced state of decay. The religion had been attacked, and an increasing number of Delawares were becoming Christians. War, plunder by whites, disease, and poverty had reduced their numbers to less than a thousand persons. The last chapter of this saga does not, however, lack interest. Although the tribal society has disintegrated, the culture has not become extinct; the Delawares retain or remember a number of ancient cultural traits. They are also active participants in what has been termed a Pan-Indian society.

Settlement Pattern

According to the treaty which the Delawares made with the Cherokee Nation, each enrolled Delaware was to receive one hundred and sixty acres of land in the specified area of Indian Territory. The crucial fact is that the Delawares did not settle upon this land as a unit; some even settled on Osage land and some on land already claimed by Cherokee settlers.[1] There were several reasons for this scattered settlement pattern; the Delawares did not come to Oklahoma as a unit, they lacked leadership and straggled to it as individuals over more than a year's time. The shape of the purchased land, which was long and narrow, may have been a deterrent to settlement as a community. This settlement pattern was an important factor in the subsequent degeneration of Delaware society and culture.

Technological Assimilation

By the time the tribal remnant had settled in Indian Territory the old technology was hardly a memory. The Delawares had become by 1867, and were to remain for several decades of the twentieth century, essentially subsistence farmers. Old informants recalled that as soon as they were settled in Oklahoma, "squaw patches" were cultivated. These vegetable gardens, as was true in earlier times, ranged up to five acres in extent. Indian corn was the staple crop and is, in fact, still grown, although it is now of slight economic importance. Besides corn, informants related, sweet potatoes, beans, onions, peas, and Irish potatoes were raised. In time, however, subsistence farming was abandoned by most of the Delawares. Kinietz said of their subsistence:

[1]G. Foreman, 1946, pp. 188-89.

> Very few of them were fortunate enough to have oil on their lands. They either farm their fields or cash rent them. Judging from the state of repair of the houses, those that farm their own fields are more prosperous than those who rent them out. . . . The majority probably rent their fields and subsist on the small cash return, aided by the produce from their gardens, old age pensions, and other occasional sources of income.[2]

I have never seen a farming enterprise among the Cherokee-Delawares which could be considered a successful commercial venture. Some subsistence farming continues, but a large proportion of the adult males work in the various industries of the county, such as the Dewey Portland Cement Company, or the Phillips Petroleum Company. The older Delawares, who have remained in the area, appear to have done so mainly because they possessed no special training which would allow them to rise on the economic ladder or to leave for higher paid employment elsewhere. The older generation also seems to have had no culturally inspired incentives to acquire special skills.

There was considerable hunting in the early days in Oklahoma. Game was still fairly plentiful, and until about 1870 the Delawares had to hunt because their gardens yielded only a precarious livelihood. The chief object of the hunt was traditionally deer, and informants (J.T., O.A.) said that this was true in Oklahoma. They also ventured out onto the plains in quest of the bison. The Anadarko band, because of their location and probably because of their proximity to Plains tribes, made considerably more use of the bison. Besides these animals, prairie chickens, of which there were immense quantities in the early days, wild turkeys, quail, fish, beaver, and raccoon were utilized. In the Caney Valley the hunting was done on horseback, by individuals or at most by small groups. Communal bison hunts occasionally took place on the plains. These included women to do the butchering. Autumn was preferred for communal hunts since the cooler weather allowed the hunters to bring back fresh instead of jerked meat. Preparation, preservation, and storage of food followed the traditional patterns well into this century. Little or no food is dried or jerked by the Cherokee-Delawares at present; most food comes out of the can and is prepared in the Anglo-American tradition.

By the time the Delawares had migrated to Oklahoma the log house (about thirteen by twenty feet) had become the ordinary dwelling. A smaller log house was erected nearby and served as a cookhouse. The bark and sapling wigwam persisted as an auxiliary dwelling until this century, as old informants remember the details of these structures (O.A., M.B.). Small cookstoves were in general use by the time the Delawares appeared in Oklahoma, and the other furnishings were primarily of American origin and design. Gradually the early log buildings were replaced by small clapboard dwellings. Houses today are usually in poor repair and are overcrowded and small; they are comparable to those of the poorer whites of the area. No pottery was manufactured in

[2] Kinietz, 1946, p. 13.

Oklahoma by the Delawares, although some of the aged Delawares remember that their grandmothers made undecorated utility pottery. Dress and adornment had approximated that of the neighboring whites by the turn of the century. Men of the Cherokee-Delaware band, however, continued to wear their hair long until about 1920. Today, the only distinctive dress of the Delawares is worn at social and religious gatherings, and on these occasions it is of a miscellaneous Indian type rather than being specifically Delaware.

In sum, Delaware technology and material culture since 1867 have increasingly approximated the American pattern, particularly that of the poorer, rural, white groups. There are virtually no outward signs in subsistence, housing, or dress, which distinguish the Delawares from other Oklahomans.

Sociological Assimilation

It has already been noted that the social organization of the Delawares had undergone considerable alteration before the final flight to Indian Territory. Perhaps the most important change to take place after 1867 was the complete surrender of political authority. It should be recalled that the contract between the Cherokees and the Delawares provided for the admittance of the Delawares into the Cherokee tribe. Delaware chieftainship continued for a time, the last principal chief being Charles Journeycake, who served in this capacity from 1861 until he died in 1895.[3] After 1900 tribal chiefs were elected. Each of the three phratries nominated one candidate; the one who received the most votes became the chief. The principal duty of the chief was to act as a representative of the tribe in business dealings with the government. The last chief, Charles Elkhair, died in 1935 and has not been officially replaced. A business committee is the only formal governmental organization that continues in existence. It serves in an advisory capacity when there are claims against the government.[4]

The Delawares no longer have a society which is based upon ties of kinship. Outside of the immediate family there are no economic activities which depend upon the mutual aid of the clan, phratry, or other kinship groups. They have been completely assimilated into the American economic system. There is no feeling that care or assistance should be extended to other Delawares; in fact, in both Delaware communities there is a good deal of friction, jealousy, and antagonism between different individuals and family groups. This friction extends to all levels of organization, even to the business committee, with which there is always dissatisfaction. "They can't agree on a chief, they pull in different ways: if one person suggests something, somebody knocks him down" (O.A.). Probably this constant friction is a result of the heterogeneous degree of acculturation; some individuals are old, nearly illiterate, very

[3] Mitchell, 1895, pp. 7, 45. (This is a biography of the chief.)

[4] Wright, 1951, p. 153; J.T., O.A.

conservative, distrustful of whites, and, in general, less acculturated than others who are young, literate, moderately educated, progressive, and well assimilated. There is an antipeyote faction, and even within the peyote faction there is a schism between the Big Moon and Little Moon adherents. These various factions promote discord, so much so that any unified tribal activity is virtually impossible. The Delawares are, then, no longer a distinct social group. Delaware society has disappeared, although allegiance to a number of the ancient culture traits lingers.

The most notable remnant of socioreligious organization still perpetuated by both Oklahoma Delaware communities is the phratry. Adults still acknowledge membership in one or more of the phratries. Membership was originally determined by descent in the female line, but this is no longer true; a person inherits membership in both his mother's and father's phratry, so that many individuals consider themselves to be "half and half." An individual can belong to no more than two of the three phratries. Consequently, it is apparent that if this method of reckoning membership is carried on for many generations most people will belong to two of the three phratries. There is no memory of any other system of reckoning membership. Obviously, the shift in the method of determining phratry membership has been caused by the emphasis on the paternal line in American society. At least among the Cherokee-Delawares the pressure has not been strong enough to shift the system from simple matrilineal reckoning all the way to patrilineal, as in our patronymics; it has gone but an illogical part way. Phratry membership originally depended upon clan ties, but there is no knowledge of them today in either Delaware community. The conclusion is inescapable that the clan organization disappeared before the Delawares left Kansas.

An interesting factor contributing to the eventual extinction of Delaware culture and also to social heterogeneity is found in present marriage restrictions. It is considered incestuous for a person to marry anyone to whom he is related, however remotely. This means that in both Oklahoma communities the young Delaware boys and girls cannot marry other Delawares, since everybody is considered to be related to everyone else. Some of the feelings about this point were: "The young people are disgusted, can't find anybody they're not kin to" (O.A.). "We're disappearing as fast as we can 'cause we got nobody to marry" (O.A.). "It's awful when you marry kinfolks" (M.B.). Briefly, one generation hence there will be no person who is more than half Delaware biologically, and probably none more than half sociologically. (This subject is taken up more fully under Pan-Indianism.) Within the last several decades the Delawares have taken to marrying legally and are completely assimilated in this respect.

Religious Assimilation

Big House Ceremony. — Without a doubt the most tenacious and unchanging elements in Delaware culture, aside from language, have been in religion. According to Speck's exhaustive monograph composed from one informant's data on the Big House Ceremony in the early 1930's, the last full or "real" ceremony was held during the fall of 1924.[5] Since the Delawares knew that this ceremony was in danger of dying out, they attempted to put young people in "important positions" and in positions of leadership (R.W.). An abbreviated Big House Ceremony was, in fact, performed during the second World War.[6]

The wartime Big House Ceremonies were held three times: in the spring of 1944, the following fall, and just before the conclusion of the European War in the spring of 1945. The traditional season for the ceremony was the fall, but two of these meetings were held in the spring. R.W. said that the first one was held in the spring because of the seriousness of the war. No explanation was given for the final spring meeting. The meetings were held in order to induce the supernatural powers to provide a quick victory for the United States and to ensure the return of the Delaware soldiers unharmed. The purpose of the meetings, then, was within the traditional pattern. Many people remain convinced of the efficacy of these meetings; after all, the War was over shortly after the last meeting, and no Delaware servicemen were killed on the fields of battle.

The wartime ceremonies were held on a farm a few miles north of Dewey. The Big House itself was built of bark and canvas and was an arbor rather than a house (O.A.). The old log "church" or "meeting house" fell into disrepair sometime after the ceremony of 1924, and no trace of it exists today. The carved heads (Mesingkwa) and other paraphernalia had been removed and sold to museums by J.F.[7] Joe Washington was the leader, at least during the last two meetings; other men who played important parts were Ben Hill, Jim Thompson, and Reuben Wilson. Joe Washington tried to arouse interest and continuance of the ceremony by explaining in the Delaware language what they were doing and why they were doing it. This attempt was rewarded with little success.

The Delawares did not camp at the Big House, as was customary, but came to the ceremonies every evening. It was said that "lots of the younger people didn't go." They failed to attend either because they thought it "silly" or because they did not understand the Delaware language very well (O.A.). Vision recital, as was customary, played the principal role in the wartime ceremonies. Reuben Wilson, Joe Washington, Ben Hill, and perhaps others recited either their own or traditional visions. The vision recital of these men was ridiculed; it was said that although they might have had visions, they did not have the "power" that the traditional visions gave. In short, "they just went through the motions." "Although they knowed the songs they didn't have the right (spiritual) power" (J.T.). Women traditionally were seldom blessed with visions, but the few who had had them were allowed to recite them on the

[5]Speck, 1931, p. 18; F. W., O.A., R.W.

[6]The Anadarko Delawares never performed the Big House Ceremony. The following account refers only to the Cherokee-Delawares.

[7]I have seen ceremonial equipment in the Philbrook Art Center in Tulsa which supposedly came from the Big House. Other material has found its way into the collections of the Museum of the University of Pennsylvania.

final day of the ceremony. At the time of the wartime meetings there were no women left who had had visions. Perhaps this is why they were called upon to offer prayers instead.

There was friction in at least one of the meetings since the leader, J.W., sold the scarce, virtually sacred wampum donated by other Delawares. The people who purchased the wampum were frequently strangers or curiosity seekers; they were seldom donors. Friction also occurred when some peyotists prayed in their fashion. One individual said of this friction:

> Ben Hill asked people to get up and pray — to pray to the fire. Nobody did for awhile so I got up. I prayed like a white preacher does, but in Indian. I prayed to the fire, and asked that all the boys be returned safely. I prayed that my boy would come back safe. I went on praying and I got to crying. Then I sat down. Then E. J. got up and prayed the same way, then a man. After that T.M. got up and said he didn't believe you could pray that way in this meeting. I felt so funny, I was crushed. I didn't go back after that. (O.A.)

The form of prayer that O.A. described is common in the local version of the Big Moon peyote cult, with the exception that in the peyote ceremony the prayer is accompanied by the smoking of a Bull Durham cornhusk cigarette.

Even with what little is known about the wartime Big House ceremonies it is plain that they were more a reflection of the old rites than a faithful duplication of them. They lasted twelve days, visions were recited, some venison was eaten, but in almost every other respect they were changed. The few young people who attended did not know where to sit; even if they knew their phratry membership they probably did not know where that phratry belonged in the meeting house. The arbor was a poor substitute for the log Big House; there was room for only one fire, and the carved heads were missing. There could be no hunt for deer, because there were no deer. In one meeting O.A. persuaded a rancher to contribute a deer, but it was impossible to feed the participants for twelve days with one deer.

After 1924 the Big House Ceremony withered away. It was briefly revived because of the stimulus of the second world war, but this revival was only a dim reflection of the original ceremony. Joe Washington and Ben Hill, the spark plugs of the wartime meetings, are dead. The few remaining participants who are familiar with the ritual are old and are not imparting their knowledge to others; and many Delawares who formerly participated have focused their attentions on the peyote cult. Informants gave two reasons why they preferred peyotism to the traditional religious forms: first, peyotism is cheap, but in the Big House Ceremony the "Bringer-in" is primarily responsible for the cost which in 1930 was one hundred and fifty dollars.[8] In a peyote meeting the cost is negligible in comparison and is often shared by the participants. Second, only Delawares can participate in the Big House Ceremony, and individual Delawares often have only a few Delaware friends,

[8]Speck, 1931, p. 24.

although they have many Indian friends of other tribes. Any Indian can participate in peyote meetings, and a few people can hold one, whereas the Big House Ceremony requires a large co-operative group of people. Associated with the advantages of peyotism is the fact that the Delawares are even more scattered than they were during the war and would have a difficult time getting together for a twelve-day Big House Ceremony. The disintegration of the Big House Ceremony is regretted by many Delawares, but nothing is being done, or can be done, to revive it.

It is not entirely clear when most other elements of Delaware religion disappeared or were replaced. The reason for this is that no other ceremonies were as universal or as well known as the Big House Ceremony. Nevertheless, it is possible to make estimates which probably are reliable.

Vision quest.—The Delawares no longer seek visions, and apparently few people have unsolicited visions. Informants frequently claim that "no one can have visions because the earth is no longer clean" (M.B.), or that one has to be "morally clean" to obtain a vision (N.D.). Few people living in a white man's world can claim these virtues, informants add. No young people were encountered who had had visions, solicited or otherwise. Several middle-aged and old people claimed to have had visions, but their visions had not been solicited. The guardian spirit of one informant (R.W.), for instance, was the Mask Being. This deity had appeared when the man was in delirium following an automobile accident. The vision quest was probably declining in popularity before the Cherokee-Delawares reached Oklahoma and shortly thereafter disappeared entirely. Supernatural beings encountered in a peyote trance are not regarded as guardian spirits.

Sweat bathing, Shamanism.—Sweat bathing disappeared among the Cherokee-Delawares during the early decades of this century. O.A. was given a sweat bath as a child, as a cure for some childhood illness. Shamans often presided over sweat bathing, and the last Cherokee-Delaware shaman (Chief Elkhair) died almost two decades ago. M.B. of the Anadarko Delawares claimed that sweat baths were in vogue there until "a few years ago."

Curing.—Although shamans and sweat bathing have passed into oblivion there is still secular knowledge and perhaps use of native medicines and cures. These are useful in love, for fevers, hiccoughs, colic in children, and the like. One informant (N.D.), for example, had inherited from her mother some sort of animal foot plus rules and ritual which were used as "love medicine." N.D. used this magical device once successfully, but is reluctant to use it again. It is doubtful if she will pass these secrets along to her daughter. Peyote, government doctors, and hospitals seem to have supplemented native therapy — medicinal and supernatural — for more important illnesses.

Doll Dance.—According to Kinietz, "The Doll Dance which was a family responsibility has not been held since 1929."[9] This agrees with my information, although the last remaining doll owner had vowed to

[9]Kinietz, 1946, p. 14.

give a dance in the summer of 1951. The vow was probably brought on by the woman's illness but she died before the dance could take place At the present time the Cherokee-Delawares are in possession of only this one doll. All other dolls have been lost, given to missionaries, buried with their owners, or sold to museums.

Otter-Tail Dance.—This dance was unknown to the Anadarko Delawares, and it has been long defunct among the Cherokee-Delawares. O.A. saw it for the last time in 1902. According to her, the house in which the otter tail was kept burned down and the otter hide was destroyed, thus ending the dance.

Delaware Peyotism.—Petrullo has provided a description and analysis of the history and content of peyotism among the Delawares.[10] My concern, therefore is to indicate the importance and role of peyote in the religious assimilation of the Delawares, and also to describe what changes, if any, have taken place in Delaware peyotism since the time of Petrullo's investigation in 1929-30.

Peyote *(Lophophora williamsii)* is a spineless, carrot-shaped, grayish-green cactus, which in this country grows primarily in the lower Rio Grande Valley. When eaten, either green or dried, or drunk as tea, peyote has the property of heightening or sharpening the perception of color, form, and sound, or inducing visual and/or auditory hallucinations. A knowledge of the properties of peyote and its utilization in religious ceremonies antedates recorded history in Mexico. It was not until late in the nineteenth century, however, that knowledge of peyote and a new ceremonial use of it developed and spread widely among the demoralized reservation Indians of the United States. The modern peyote ceremony is essentially "a collective all-night vigil in which, through prayer, contemplation, and eating peyote, the peyotist receives a divine revelation."[11]

Peyotism was brought to the Cherokee-Delawares about 1885 by John Wilson, a part-Delaware from Anadarko. This man became a peyotist about 1880, and in subsequent years he converted many Delawares in the Anadarko and Dewey areas.[12] His influence spread far beyond tribal borders, however, and he has been called "the most significant figure in the diffusion of the religion in Oklahoma since 1885."[13] The John Wilson version of peyotism, variously termed Big Moon or Moonhead, is today the most important form of peyotism in number of adherents among the Cherokee-Delawares. The Anadarko Delawares also seem to favor a Big Moon variant. The more conservative, Little Moon version was introduced to the Cherokee-Delawares somewhat later than the Big Moon, and it still finds some adherents.[14] As far as being a causative agent in the decline and disappearance of traditional religion is concerned, peyote has played a negligible role. Many individuals practiced and believed in both religious creeds; Chief Elkhair,

[10] Petrullo, 1934.

[11] LaBarre, *et al.*, 1951, pp. 582-83.

[12] Petrullo, 1934, p. 83.

[13] *Ibid.*, pp. 78-79.

[14] *Ibid.*, p. 32; F.W.

for instance, the man who brought the Little Moon version to the Cherokee-Delawares, was a prominent participant in the Big House Ceremony. Peyote did not diffuse to the Delawares at the expense of traditional religious forms; instead, the gap left in Delaware existence following the decline of the traditional ceremonies was filled by peyotism. Peyotism was a creed born and tailored to fit into the ideological life of much acculturated societies. It was, as Petrullo said, "the natural but final recourse of a subjugated people who fully realize the inadequacy of their material means to restore their former world-state."[15] Peyotism was, after all, spawned in its modern form by the Kiowas and Comanches, who were facing the same sort of adjustment as were the Delawares. Small wonder, then, that it replaced the dissipated ceremonies and rites of the Delawares. Petrullo listed twenty-three elements which were common to both peyotism and the old Delaware religion. He found fifteen important elements of the traditional religion lacking in peyotism and eight important elements in peyotism lacking in the traditional forms.[16] In short, the majority of important traits of peyotism were already elements of Delaware cosmology. None of the important elements of peyotism, lacking in Delaware belief, can be said to be antagonistic to traditional Delaware customs. There has never been a rejection of the old forms of religion. "Their faith in the old doctrines and religious rites has remained unshaken, and they would revive the entire structure if they could."[17] One of Petrullo's informants, James C. Webber, put it rather succinctly when he said: "The old Delaware religion is too heavy for us who are becoming few and weak. It is too difficult; Peyote is easy in comparison. Therefore we who are weak take up this new Indian religion."[18]

It is not suggested, however, that peyotism has ever entirely replaced the defunct religion of the Delawares. The performance of the Big House Ceremony during World War II and the observance of this ceremonial and others earlier in this century suggest this point of view. When the national and world situation was felt to be desperate, the Delawares turned to the old rites; peyotism was not sufficient. Peyotism was originally and is now considered to be more efficacious at an individual level in curing both mental and physical ailments than in curing or ameliorating broad social and economic ills. In sum, because of the dissipation of the Delawares, both numerically and as a social unit, the old religious ceremonials could no longer be held; the belief in them has not died. Peyotism gradually took the place of the old ceremonials because it was understood and fitted in with the old religious concepts.

It was expected that during the twenty-two years since Petrullo's study there would be some sort of alteration in Delaware peyotism. By and large this did not occur. It is thought that fewer Delawares are participants in peyotism today, but no comparative data are available. I have a first-hand acquaintance only with the Big Moon version of

[15] Petrullo, 1934, p. 1.

[16] *Ibid.*, pp. 168-70.

[17] *Ibid.*, p. 26.

[18] *Ibid.*, p. 76.

peyotism, and in this there are no essential differences from those that Petrullo described. The Big Moon version is the more liberal and contains more Christian elements than does the Little Moon. Thus, if diffusion of Christian traits has continued, it more likely has occurred in the Big Moon version. In the Big Moon meeting which I attended, some features were present which were lacking in Petrullo's accounts, and some features were lacking which were present in Big Moon meetings attended by him. There were, however, no essential differences in these meetings separated by more than two decades. The meeting I attended might very well have taken place in 1930 instead of 1952. Since peyotism is essentially individualistic, and since there is no institutionalized priesthood or specific creed, minor differences in form and procedure are to be expected.[19] Petrullo found substantial, but inconsequential differences in the Big Moon meetings which he attended. He gave, for instance, eight variations of the Big Moon altar;[20] the altar I saw was not identical with any of these, yet the basic features of all the altars were similar.

Linguistic Assimilation

It has been said that of all culture traits language is the most persistent; this has been true for Delaware acculturation. During the earlier periods of acculturation there was virtually no replacement of language, although a few individuals learned English as a second language. In the Decadent Period there probably was an increase in the number of Delawares familiar with English. With permanent settlement in Oklahoma and the increased enrollment of Delaware children in government schools, this situation gradually altered. At the present time no Cherokee-Delaware, whatever his age or acculturative status, habitually speaks Delaware; all speak English. It is within the last generation that this change has taken place. I queried thirty-two persons and found that the native language of only three was English, and these three were thirty-five years old or younger. The youngest native speaker of Delaware was twenty-six. The native language of every person over thirty-five in the Cherokee-Delaware group was Delaware (or Munsi). Most of these people learned English when they were sent away to school. Present proficiency in Delaware varies tremendously, but there seems to be a correlation between age and proficiency (see Fig. 4). The people who speak Delaware well are usually older, but some of the younger people, because of individual inclination or association, speak it fluently. With the exception of three young persons, all people queried at least understood Delaware. Nine said they spoke Delaware well, five said their ability to speak Delaware was average, seven said it was poor, and eight understood but did not speak Delaware. These categories are admittedly imprecise, and the Delawares placed themselves on this linguistic scale, so that one person who said he spoke Delaware well may have been actually less fluent than another who said his ability was

[19]Petrullo, 1934, p. 149.
[20]*Ibid.*, Pls. 3-6.

The Relationship Between Language and Age Among
the Cherokee-Delawares

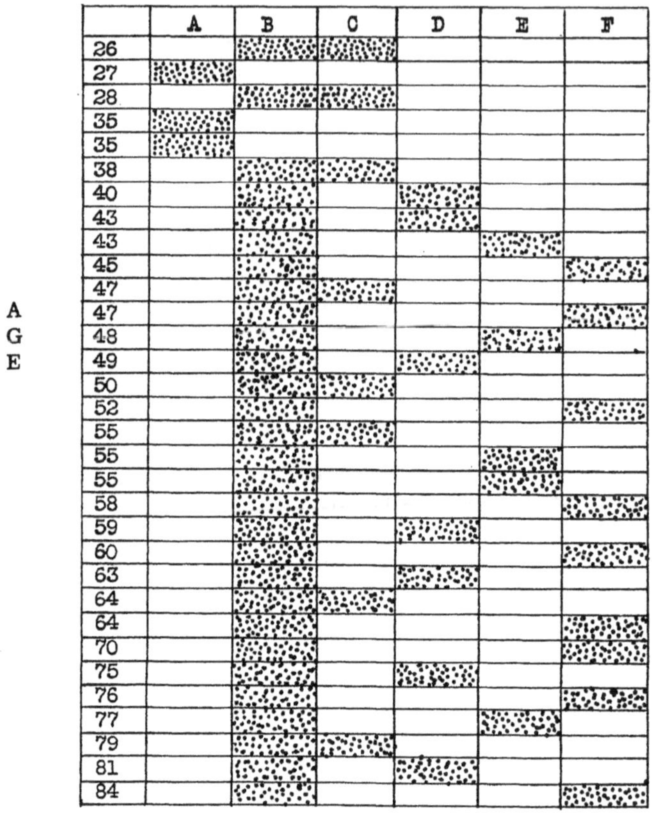

LINGUISTIC ABILITIES

Fig. 4. A. Native speaker of English. B. Native speaker of Delaware (or Munsi). C. Native speaker of Delaware, but only understands, does not speak Delaware. D. Native speaker of Delaware, speaks it poorly. E. Native speaker of Delaware, average ability. F. Native speaker of Delaware, speaks it fluently, or well.

average. No children were found who spoke Delaware, although a few possibly understood it simply because their parents used the native language when they were discussing topics not meant for juvenile ears. One parent said that this ruse no longer worked with her offspring (L.F.). At the same time the children of this woman absolutely refused to speak Delaware and as far as is known they have never done so. It is not known whether the Delawares of Anadarko are losing their language as rapidly as the Cherokee-Delawares. One informant (M.B.) habitually spoke Delaware, and several other elderly Delawares spoke only very halting English. Considering the small numbers of Delawares in this area and their close association with the Caddo, it seems probable that there, too, the Delaware language will rapidly disappear.

Pan-Indianism

As the preceding sections of this chapter indicate, the Delawares have arrived at what would seem to be a final stage of assimilation to American civilization; for all intents and purposes the Delaware culture and tribal society are things of the past. During the field work of 1951 with the Cherokee-Delawares it became increasingly clear, however, that they were not completely assimilated, nor did it seem likely that they would be in the near future. It was apparent that in the following summer's field work a survey of the phenomenon which was responsible for nonassimilation should be made. Since this survey was undertaken as peripheral to the major study, the reconstruction of Delaware culture, my conclusions should be regarded as tentative.

The Cherokee-Delawares have been participating in a number of customs and institutions which are describable only as Indian. Much time and a great deal of energy is consumed in activities which can be described as neither Delaware nor Anglo-American. There is, in short, wholehearted participation in and allegiance to what may be called a Pan-Indian society. This is a loosely knit, informally organized grouping of Indians, who, having partly lost their old cultural orientation, but not being fully assimilated into white society, have joined forces and are participating in and sharing a number of intertribal customs and institutions. These institutions were and are being synthesized from elements derived from Indian cultures, but also drawn from white civilization.

When I first wrote this section no published study had been specifically devoted to Pan-Indianism, although it had been mentioned explicitly or implied in a number of works.[21] Since that time a brief paper on the "Pan-Indian Culture of Oklahoma"[22] has appeared, and I have published an abbreviated account of Cherokee-Delaware Pan-Indianism.[23] Karl Schmitt read a paper entitled "A Possible Development of a Pan-Indian Culture in Oklahoma" at the Central States branch of the American Anthropological Association several years ago. He intended to publish the paper, but his untimely death temporarily halted this project. George Devereux in his book *Reality and Dream* approached the subject from a slightly different point of view, a psychoanalytical one. He suggested that "areal basic personalities" were being substituted for tribal ones, at least among Plains Indians.[24] Petrullo touched upon Pan-Indianism among the Delawares, saying:

[21]Brant, 1950, pp. 212-22; Devereux, 1951, p. 40; Mead, 1932, pp. 66-68.

[22]Howard, 1955.

[23]Newcomb, 1955*b*.

[24]Devereux, 1951, p. 40.

> ...there has arisen a sympathetic attitude of the various tribal units towards each other, with the result that intercourse between them has become common, and each other's rites are observed and studied with the avowed purpose of comparison. This constant interchanging of ideas is giving rise to a novel feeling for Indian nationality. . . . The Delawares are actively participating in this, and as a result not only have they assimilated many of the ideas emanating from other tribes, but have disseminated their own widely.[25]

Cherokee-Delaware Pan-Indianism

The peyote cult has always been essentially an intertribal phenomenon and this is true of Cherokee-Delaware peyotism today. It is probably the most important influence leading to Cherokee-Delaware participation in Pan-Indian society. Meetings are always held with Indians of other tribes, and in one which I attended, for example, besides the Delaware who sponsored it, a Winnebago (Roadman), Shawnees, and a Siouan couple from the Pine Ridge Reservation were present. Cherokee-Delaware peyotists frequently attend meetings with the Osages and Shawnees and also participate in meetings with Indians of many other tribes. Cherokee-Delaware peyotists feel closer and are more friendly to non-Delaware peyotists than they are to Delawares who are not members of the cult. Most Delaware peyotists belong to the more liberal and Christianized sect which has been termed Big Moon; a few are adherents of the Little Moon sect. Members of one sect ordinarily do not attend meetings of the other. The peyotists are ardent participants in, and often highly vocal advocates of, their cult, whereas the Protestants (who seem to be slightly more numerous) can be described as minimal or nominal members of their churches. The attractiveness of peyotism was especially apparent among the young men; none were encountered who were not peyotists. This may be partly explained by a feeling that peyotism is somewhat daring, and that it serves to announce to others that here is a person proud to be an Indian. The singing of peyote songs and the manufacture of peyote regalia are also pastimes of the young men. Membership in Protestant churches is not considered daring, it does not single out a member from his fellows, and it does not provide him with a pastime.

Brant has said that the peyote cult in southwestern Oklahoma "constitutes the religious symbol of what might be called a Pan-Indian movement."[26] LaBarre has summed up the Pan-Indian aspect of peyotism, and his remarks are also applicable to the Cherokee-Delawares: "The Indians feel, perhaps rightly, that peyotism is their last strong link with the aboriginal past, which others are trying to destroy. Hence it has contributed greatly to the sense of community and morale of the Indian groups in Oklahoma."[27]

Many social activities of the Cherokee-Delawares are expressions of

---

[25]Petrullo, 1934, p. 26.

[26]Brant, 1950, p. 222.

[27]LaBarre, 1938, p. 166.

Pan-Indianism and promote continued participation in the Pan-Indian society. Included here are the various powwows,[28] stomp dances,[29] and Indian associations of different sorts, from national organizations to the more or less informal Indian clubs, including women's clubs, sewing circles, and the like.

Powwows illustrate vividly the extent of Cherokee-Delaware Pan-Indianism. They are Indian fairs and in many respects are similar to the traditional county fair. Ordinarily, they are sponsored by inter-tribal Indian clubs. A powwow generally lasts from several days to a week, the participants camping on the premises. Social dancing is the principal activity, and many of the dances are modern syntheses of tribal and American elements. Dance costumes can seldom be identified with a specific tribe, as they have rapidly evolved during this century, with free borrowing going on between tribes.[30] Even the music of the powwow and of other similar gatherings has taken on a Pan-Indian flavor. Rhodes, commenting on Plains music, has said that "through the Dakotas and westward to Oregon, where social and ceremonial life function rather weakly in an acculturated pattern, there is to be observed a trend toward uniformization of musical style."[31] A list of the various tribes that attend these Indian fairs is impressive evidence of the extent of Indianism. The "Devils Promenade," a fair held annually over the fourth of July near Quapaw, attracts Indians from virtually every tribe in Oklahoma and sizable contingents of Indians from other states as well. A number of Sac and Fox from Tama, Iowa, for example, were present during the 1952 dance. The Oklahoma powwows are climaxed by the annual American Indian Exposition held at Anadarko in August; it attracts Indians from every quarter of the United States.

A number of powwows were attended in the second summer's field work and the presence of two families at these affairs was recorded. Both families in one month attended five powwows, for periods of time ranging from one to three days. Included were powwows in Tulsa, Pawhuska, Sperry, Quapaw, and Pawnee, some as far as eighty miles, from the Dewey area. In no instance was a Cherokee-Delaware found who was not an avid fan of powwows, despite the fact that neither the dances, the music, nor the costumes were Delaware, or were derived from Delaware culture. The Delawares do not hold any powwow of their own, or any in conjunction with other Indians. Moreover, their last stomp dance, which was held early in the summer of 1951, was unsuccessful. They are not even very active as dancers in the powwows which they attend, being interested spectators rather than active participants. The magnetism which these powwows have for the Cherokee-Delawares lies in the opportunity afforded them to be with others whom they consider to be like themselves, and the chance it gives them to act as "Indians," or at least to act as they think Indians should act. These Indian fairs, then,

[28]This term is used in Oklahoma for social gatherings; I use it in this sense.

[29]I am using this term for the smaller, more informal, less commercialized dances.

[30]See Gunther, 1950, pp. 174-79, for a detailed description of this diffusion.

[31]Rhodes, 1952, p. 132.

are of considerable importance to Cherokee-Delaware Pan-Indianism. They not only serve as a common meeting ground for Indians, but their effect reinforces membership and consciousness of membership in Indian society.

Contrary to what I had supposed, social clubs of various types were not an important factor in the development of Pan-Indianism among the Cherokee-Delawares. Not one person was ever found who belonged to any national Indian organization, such as the National Congress of American Indians. In fact, many people professed complete ignorance of such organizations. For this reason these formal Indian groups, which in a sense may be said to be lobbying for Indianism, have been disregarded here. In passing, it might be noted that these organizations are possibly some sort of concrete expression of this acculturative trend among other Indian groups. Informal social clubs have some bearing upon Cherokee-Delaware Pan-Indianism. A number of women at one time belonged to the Indian Women's Club, an intertribal extension club of Washington County, which holds monthly meetings, has rummage sales, luncheons, and the like. Significantly, proceeds of one rummage sale were sent to the Navaho. Membership in this organization has declined since the war and none of the women interviewed belonged to it. It should be emphasized that this organization was Indian in character and not tribal. There has never been a men's club.

Extratribal marriage is an important factor in Cherokee-Delaware Pan-Indianism and assimilation. The Cherokee-Delawares are at the present time tribally exogamous. The youngest all-Delaware marriage I could find was between a man of thirty-eight and a woman of thirty-five, and this seems to have been somewhat exceptional. Only three living couples were found in which both partners claimed to be entirely Delaware, although a number of old widows and widowers had had Delaware spouses. Marriage to Indians of other tribes is the usual custom, but marriage to whites is not uncommon. Cherokee-Delawares have married Comanches, Senecas, Shawnees, Cherokees, Creeks, Yuchis, Peorias, and undoubtedly Indians of other tribes. How the Indian parents in these mixed marriages classify their children is indicative of the feelings about Pan-Indianism. If parents are questioned about tribal affiliation of their children, they may simply reply without much thought, "Indian," or with a little thought they may say, "Yuchi-Creek-Delaware," or something similarly artificial. Occasionally, they will skirt the question by giving the tribe in which the children are enrolled by the government. The wholesale marriage of the younger generation of Delawares to Indians of other tribes must be considered an important influence in the growth of Pan-Indianism. On the other hand, the marriage of Delawares to whites naturally, perhaps inevitably, results in further culture loss and completed assimilation. This would be particularly true of the individual who marries a white person and moves to an all-white community. Those individuals who marry whites but remain in an Indian community have, of course, a much better opportunity to retain Indian ways, and white marriage partners may become participants in Indian society. In one instance a Delaware woman's white husband has become a peyotist; he sings peyote songs and has served as fire chief in meetings.

The minority role and the consciousness of this standing on the part of the Cherokee-Delawares has also promoted Pan-Indianism. Discrimination against the Indians would presumably lead to feelings of isolation, persecution, and difference, perhaps greater than actually existed, and hence strengthen Pan-Indian society.[32] It is difficult, however, to assess the extent of discrimination against the Cherokee-Delawares. It is becoming increasingly difficult to recognize an Indian, whether on a racial or social basis. With the high incidence of past miscegenation, the high frequency of present-day mixed marriages, and the assimilation in dress, speech, and manners, a race bigot must have a high degree of perception to recognize and act against this minority. A number of tales of alleged discrimination were current in the community, but only one of these incidents (in rental housing) could be substantiated. Actual discrimination of any sort is probably rare, but there is a fairly widespread knowledge or belief that it exists. A universal awareness of past discrimination and exploitation and a knowledge of discrimination against Indians elsewhere are factors which encourage Pan-Indianism.

There are several other conditions which set the Cherokee-Delawares and other Indians apart as a minority group, and so contribute to Pan-Indianism. The Cherokee-Delawares have access to free services of government hospitals and schools, which in itself sets them apart from the whites. It also provides an opportunity for the Cherokee-Delawares to become well acquainted with Indians of other tribes. This is particularly true in schools where the association may be continued over a number of years. Government schools, however, are attended by the Cherokee-Delawares less frequently than formerly. Some of the attitudes of whites toward the Indian minority also serve to foster Pan-Indianism. To many an Oklahoman an Indian is an Indian, not a Cherokee, Kickapoo, or Delaware. The movies, the magazines, and other outlets of public information are constantly impressing upon him that he is an American Indian; no public agency impresses upon him the fact that he is a Delaware.[33] Many whites in Washington County were totally unaware that such a tribe as the Delaware existed. They were well aware, however, that there were many Indians in the county.

There are forces which hinder and oppose the development of Pan-Indianism, but it is difficult to assess many of them because they are of a negative and subjective nature. It is difficult to estimate, for instance, the pressure exerted by the dominant society for complete conformity. Whatever the extent of pressure for "100 per cent Americanism," it is not at present particularly noticeable; it seems instead that the Delawares are sufficiently assimilated linguistically, economically, and in

[32] Wirth, 1945, pp. 348-49, contains a pertinent discussion of this subject.

[33] Mead, 1932, pp. 67-68, noted these factors more than two decades ago.

general behavior that no strong, overt pressure is brought to bear upon them to conform to all white customs. Perhaps the greatest deterrent to a more flourishing Pan-Indianism is found in the correlated facts of dispersion and assimilation. The majority of Cherokee-Delawares upon reaching maturity leave the area. They do so because there are no strong, culturally forceful ties which would hold them back, and there are many economic advantages to be gained elsewhere. They are far enough along the road of assimilation that they can go elsewhere and become nondistinctive participants in the majority society.

Even in a brief examination such as this, it is clear that a number of different circumstances and conditions have made participation in a Pan-Indian society a highly important part of Cherokee-Delaware life. As the old culture declined, as Delaware society disintegrated and its members became scattered, the void was partly bridged by participation in a Pan-Indian society. This amorphous and as yet unorganized grouping of Indians shares a mélange of traits which are Indian, as opposed to being tribal in their nature. The peyote cult was perhaps the first influence and is still one of the strongest elements furthering and cementing the bonds of Cherokee-Delaware Pan-Indianism. Intertribal gatherings such as powwows and Indian clubs and associations, tribal exogamy, the status of the Cherokee-Delawares as Indians rather than Delawares are all important, particularly in combination with one another, in contributing to Pan-Indianism. In sum, two sociocultural groups are rapidly obliterating the old culture and society of the Cherokee-Delawares; one is Pan-Indianism, the other is the Anglo-American culture. In general terms, more and more Cherokee-Delawares are becoming less and less Delaware and more and more white or Indian.

A SUMMARY AND ANALYSIS OF DELAWARE ACCULTURATION

A comparison of Delaware acculturation with that which other peoples have undergone at various times and places is beyond the scope of this study, but it is perhaps justifiable to attempt to analyze Delaware acculturation and to indulge in a few speculations concerning this general cultural process. The principal problem to be dealt with here is the reason for the occurrence of acculturation in some parts of Delaware culture before it appeared in others.

It has been seen that the technological part of Delaware culture changed radically and early. A new type of economic organization and economically motivated war also appeared in the early period, but they were not culture complexes that had been borrowed as such from the Europeans. The second stage of acculturation witnessed a reorganization and integration in Delaware society, particularly in political organization. The third stage was characterized by a revolt against the European interlopers and against prior acculturation. The defeats and disappointments of this period set the stage for the more rapid cultural disintegration which occurred in subsequent periods. The present phase of acculturation has been termed assimilation, since the Delawares have become, at least in external appearance, similar to their white neighbors. An important feature of this phase of acculturation is participation in a Pan-Indian society. In general, the technological and economic systems were destroyed and replaced at an early date. Deterioration of the kinship structure came later, but preceded the collapse of the ideological system.

The reasons for the rapid adoption by the early historic Delawares of numerous European technological traits are quite clear. The Delawares immediately appreciated the utility and general superiority of most of the tangible equipment of the Europeans. It was at once apparent to the Indians, for instance, that a steel axe or a cloth coat was immensely superior to its native counterpart. Direct comparison and rapid selection of artifacts of this sort could be made. The diffusion was, then, primarily of artifacts which had obviously inferior parallels in native culture and that could be readily understood in terms of native culture. Linton has noted this general condition. He said: "It seems that, other things being equal, certain sorts of culture elements are more readily transferable than others. Tangible objects such as tools, utensils or ornaments are taken over with great ease, in fact they are usually the first things transferred in contact situations."[1] Other technological items, particularly guns and gunpowder had no similar counterpart in Delaware culture, although, of course, they had functions analogous to native weapons. It has already been shown why this complex was rapidly adopted; suffice it to say here that if the Delawares

[1]Linton, 1940, p. 485.

were to survive in the new conditions imposed by contact they had to acquire European weapons.

Some technological items did not diffuse to the Delawares in the early period. The most important of these was the plow complex. First, this complex was an intricate, mechanical one, completely foreign to anything with which these simple gardeners were familiar. Second, the idea of using the energy of an ox or horse for utilitarian purposes was completely novel to them. Feeding, harnessing, and compelling obedience from these animals was in itself a complicated and difficult trait to acquire. Third, the Delaware women were not likely to associate the raising of wheat and other small grains with their own simple corn horticulture, even if they had observed the entire round of European farming. Other traits, such as houses and house furnishings, did not diffuse in the early period. It is apparent that permanent dwellings of European style were of little use to a people who were becoming more nomadic than they had been in precontact times.

The reasons why there was little diffusion sociologically or ideologically in the Contact Period are abundantly clear; either the traits were not present to be diffused, or if they were present they were not understood. If they had been present and understood, there would have been no stimulus to borrow them. The Delawares had little opportunity to observe such groups as the European family since their contacts were mostly with traders. It is hardly likely that the form and function of the family would be readily comprehended; even if it were, it is not probable that it would be considered worth imitating. The only hint of change in the native family was a possible lessening of polygyny. This alteration, if it took place, may not have been a direct diffusion, but a response to changed conditions. The natives in the early period had little opportunity to understand the structure and function of European political organization, since only the feeble arm of that organization was operating in America.

In some respects the diffusion of socioideological traits is different from the diffusion of technological items. An axe, whether steel or stone, is quickly recognizable as such by a person acquainted with axes, and he can readily choose the superior one. This type of reasoning cannot be carried over to the nonmaterial parts of culture. The family grouping or an economic organization can scarcely be seen, certainly not in the same way that one sees a concrete object. An axe can be readily understood and used apart from its original cultural context, but it is much more difficult for a kinship system to be understood and appreciated, much less voluntarily adopted, apart from its sociocultural context. It should also be noted that for a massive transfer of sociological or religious traits a shared language is a necessity; few Delawares spoke English or other European languages until well into the nineteenth century, and even fewer Europeans or Americans bothered to learn Delaware.

The same general comments can be made concerning ideological nonacculturation during the Contact Period. The native had little opportunity to observe or to embrace Christianity, the traders and settlers were of a social group which was neither interested in, nor particularly concerned with, the spread of Christianity to the Indian. These Europeans, although professing one or another brand of Christianity, were in the main poor examples to set before the heathen. One Dutchman in a letter written in 1657 said:

> We can say but little of the conversion of the heathens or Indians here, and see no way to accomplish it, until they are subdued by the numbers and power of our people, and reduced to some sort of civilization; and also unless our people set them a better example, than they have done heretofore.[2]

As the writer of this letter realized, until Indian culture had been extensively altered, voluntary conversion of the Indian was impossible. To be more precise, since a religion may be viewed as a reflection and interpretation of a way of life, ordinarily this way of life has to be altered before there will be a willing and wholesale change to some religious system which is an expression of a completely different sort of existence. Even if Christianity (church services, and so forth) were observed by the Indian, it is difficult to see how the Indian would judge it to be superior to native religious forms. Some few elements may have been borrowed from Christianity in the Contact Period, but there is no proof that any were.

The most important changes in the Contact Period, in terms of their far-reaching effects, were changes which occurred because of the conditions of the contact situation. Depopulation and migration were important in this connection, as were the economic relationships which developed between the Europeans and Indians and the rise of chronic warfare.

By the second half of the eighteenth century acculturation had forged the Delawares into a militant tribe, but one which was split by contradictions within and endangered by enemies without. Insofar as a culture must be integrated, it is plain that when revolutionary changes occur technologically and economically, other segments of the culture must in time change and become adapted to the new conditions. The Period of Consolidation was a time when Delaware culture was becoming adjusted, if only partly, to these drastic alterations. The most noticeable expression of consolidation was the appearance of the Delaware tribe as a political entity. At first glance it seems surprising that a people of such heterogeneous origins, whose ranks had been decimated and who had been forced from their homes, should in slightly more than a century become a relatively unified tribe. But when it is realized that the Delawaran peoples were concentrated in "towns" as they had never been in pre-European times, that the Iroquois and Europeans were treating them as a single entity, and that there was an acute necessity for some agency to deal with and combat the menacing forces arrayed against them, the political consolidation becomes understandable. That other parts of culture should become more standardized, and that such things as the Big

[2]Jameson, 1909, p. 399.

House Ceremony should be synthesized at this time is also more readily comprehensible from this viewpoint. This is not intended to imply that by the end of the period Delaware culture was well integrated or was well adjusted to the external world. On the contrary, external events were to prove too much for the crude political mechanisms the Delawares had evolved, and since the culture continued to change rapidly internal integration was never attained.

It was in the following Nativistic Period that the unresolved conflicts had their most convulsive expression; the revolutionary changes were causing repercussions in the kinship structure, chronic warfare was having effects upon every aspect of society, and the traditionally weak political institutions were unable to cope with the host of new internal problems. The Delawares, ever hard pressed by missionaries, militant whites, and the advancing frontier, were becoming increasingly aware of their inability to control or even to stabilize, by their own unaided efforts, the rapid changes and conflicts in their life. As the realization grew that there was nothing more they could do, that there was no practical way out of their difficulties, they turned as a final resort to the supernatural world and a revivalistic nativism. These nativistic movements were essentially attempts to obtain cultural reintegration and stability by rejecting much that had been accepted from the whites and most of the changes that had come about because of the conditions of contact. This sort of reaction was an almost inevitable consequence of the rapid and extensive acculturation of the earlier periods.

The failure of the revivalistic nativism set the stage for a more rapid disintegration and collapse of the Delaware culture. Acculturation in the subsequent Decadent Period was mostly within the realm of social organization; there seems to have been little breakdown or replacement religiously or in other areas of ideology. There have been several not entirely successful attempts to explain why Delaware ideology was so resistant to change.[3] It may be suggested that the Delaware social system altered more rapidly than the ideological system since the social system was more directly dependent upon the technological system than was the ideological system. When the technology altered, the social organization, or some parts of it, was sooner affected than were the religious ceremonies or myths. This is easily seen if it is noted, for instance, that with European weapons a native could kill many more game and fur-bearing animals than had previously been possible. This diffusion must rapidly have influenced such social institutions as hunting territories, clan organization, and the economic importance of women. With the gun a Delaware could quickly reduce the number of animals in his hunting territory. The necessity of trade and the disappearance of game would force him farther away from home, upsetting whatever common geographical base his clan had, perhaps irreparably damaging this institution. Since men were of the sex that obtained the fur-bearing animals, their importance grew at the expense of women.

---

[3]Kinietz, 1946, pp. 77-78; Speck,

Although a man could supply relatively more game for the same expenditure of energy, his wife was raising no more, and probably less, garden produce if they had moved from their original location. Hence, the economic position of the male was enhanced, that of the female was decreased. The result was probably a change from a matrilocal-matrilineal system to a bilateral or neolocal-bilateral system of kinship reckoning. In short, the effects upon social organization of this altered technology were relatively soon felt. The immediate effect upon the ideological system is much less clear. It is difficult to see, for example, how the diffusion of guns or other technological equipment would soon affect such traits as the vision quest, the soul concept, or other supernatural or ideological beliefs or practices. Perhaps eventually there would be major repercussions, but it is clear that they would be long delayed.

Another obvious reason why the religious system was retained long after other segments of culture were replaced is that since religion deals with powerful, dangerous, feared, uncontrollable or partly uncontrollable forces, the Delawares simply did not dare to give up their beliefs. Should they do so, they felt that they would be punished by the tremendous wrath that supernatural beings could unleash. It is true, of course, that insofar as material items are endowed or sanctioned by supernatural forces, they too are that much more resistant to replacement by superior, competitive analogues. The same reasoning applies to nonmaterial institutions. A case in point is the retention of the phratry system by the Delawares; since it functioned primarily in a religious context, it was retained long after such institutions as the clan had disappeared.

I do not intend to imply that religious customs or ceremonies were completely static while other parts of the culture were undergoing revolutionary change. First, there was a synthesis of rites which produced the tribal Big House Ceremony, which is associated with the appearance and consolidation of the tribe. Secondly, a number of elements from Christianity were adopted and integrated into Delaware belief at various times. In general, however, religious beliefs and customs from the Period of Consolidation to the twentieth century were remarkably impervious to serious alteration.

With the collapse of most parts of Delaware culture in the late nineteenth and early twentieth century, a stage of acculturation was reached which I have termed assimilation. Technologically, economically, socially, and to some extent religiously, the Delawares had approximated the dominant culture. Replacement of many Delaware traits, however, was by institutions that are properly referred to as Indian rather than as American. The old religious system, for example, was replaced in part by peyotism. The principal reason for the replacement of culture traits by Indian rather than by Anglo-American traits is probably to be found in the fact that traits which are familiar and which easily fit in with the old culture have a competitive advantage over foreign traits. Other things being equal, when two culture traits, or complexes of traits, are in competition with each other, the one or ones which are more easily integrated and more easily understood and appreciated in terms of the cultural background will be chosen.

From my point of view Pan-Indianism may be regarded as one of the final stages of acculturation, just prior to completed assimilation. Pan-Indianism has been made possible by the fact that through acculturation Indians of very diverse backgrounds have come to share a common language and to participate in the same economy. This means that they have been able to share, or perhaps to find out that they shared, a common core of tradition and a commonality of situation and purpose. Pan-Indianism may also be explained as an attempt, perhaps largely unconscious, by a minority group composed of many different tribal remnants to find unity and strength in common customs. In a sense, it is a final attempt to preserve a distinctiveness of being which a dominant civilization has tried to destroy. But in another sense it may be regarded as an effort to glorify or enhance a minority group status which the dominant majority has insisted be preserved.

APPENDIX: THE SOURCE MATERIALS

The accuracy of the reconstruction of Delaware culture and the description of its change depend largely upon the trustworthiness of the source materials. The quantity and quality of the documents relating to the Delawares are relatively satisfactory. In the seventeenth century alone eleven individuals of four nationalities were eyewitness reporters of various aspects of native life. The extent to which these accounts agree with one another is reassuring. Most disagreements may be reconciled either as real differences present among the diverse Delawaran peoples, or as honest differences of opinion about customs observed.

Peter Lindestrom, Daniel Denton, and William Penn were the most important of the seventeenth-century sources in the quantity of ethnographic data their accounts contained. Lindestrom, a Swedish engineer and mathematician, came to New Sweden in 1653 and remained in the New World for two years. As an engineer and clerk of the court, he traveled extensively and had ample opportunity to observe and learn about native life, as is shown by his *Geographia Americae,* which was not published until 1691. He had, however, made notes or kept a journal while in the New World. His description of native life is, so far as I can judge, completely trustworthy.

Daniel Denton was among the first settlers in the township of Jamaica in 1656. His observations about the natives seem to be confined to inhabitants of western Long Island. It is possible that these Indians may have been Montauk rather than a Unami division, but if this is so they were culturally indistinguishable from the natives described by Lindestrom, Penn, and others. I have utilized Denton's *A Brief Description of New York* fully; it is not as complete an ethnography as Lindestrom's, but its quality is high, and Denton seems to have abided by his statement: "I. . . have writ nothing but what I have been an eyewitness to. . . ."[1]

William Penn's relatively complete description of Delawaran peoples dates from 1682 or 1683. His letter to the "Committee of the Free Society of Traders" was written after an extensive tour of his lands during which time he had many discussions with the natives about land matters. Some of Penn's statements were probably not derived from firsthand information, but his account agrees tolerably well with others of the late seventeenth century.

The descriptions of Delawaran peoples by Robert Juet and Isaack de Rasieres are the earliest of which I have knowledge. Juet was an officer aboard Henry Hudson's "Half-Moon." Juet's "The Third Voyage of Master Henry Hudson" was written before he sailed on Hudson's fourth voyage in 1610. His knowledge of the natives was superficial, but the very early date of his observations provides useful knowledge of early contacts with Europeans. Isaack de Rasieres' letter was written before the third

[1]Denton, 1845, Preface.

decade of the century; unfortunately for Delaware ethnography, sixteen crucial pages are missing. Despite this lack, De Rasieres shows surprising familiarity with marriage customs and government. When he depended upon secondhand information, however, his account is far less creditable. Johan de Laet's material dealing with the Delawares also dated from the first quarter of the seventeenth century. De Laet never visited America, but I used his data because he explicitly attempted to accurately describe native life and because he quoted extracts from the lost journal of Henry Hudson. He was also the first European to set down a vocabulary of the Delaware and Munsi languages. The fourth native of the Netherlands to write of the Delawares was David Pietersz De Vries. His observations were made in 1632 and 1633, and upon his return to Europe he published a book written from his journal. Myers has said that "he writes in a plain but vivid style and his book both internally and externally has well stood the tests of trustworthiness."[2] He was sympathetic towards the natives and has provided much valuable information. Adriaen Van der Donck, another native of Holland, wrote of the natives of New Netherland about the middle of the century. His description of the people is good, but the usable material is brief. Jaspar Dankers (or Danckaerts) and Peter Sluyter, in their journal kept between 1679 and 1680, contributed a small amount of information, chiefly about the religion and folklore of the natives.

The only German among the seventeenth-century writers was Francis Daniel Pastorius, a lawyer and scholar. His knowledge of the natives was limited, but what he did say about them I have found to be of value. His observations dated from 1683 to the close of the century. Gabriel Thomas, a Quaker by birth, was with the first group of Penn's emigrants. His account of Pennsylvania and "West New-Jersey" was published in 1698, but records events of almost two decades earlier. Myers said that Thomas had "a tendency to exaggerate in some of the passages; these lapses, however, are easily discernible. Where he writes what he himself knows he is in general reliable . . . ."[3] His observations upon native life fit in fairly well with other accounts, although he had the unfortunate habit of lumping all Indians together as far as their customs were concerned. Other information about the early seventeenth-century Delawares was obtained from the reliable data found in Thomas Campanius Holm's *A Short Description of the Province of New Sweden,* and also in Amandus Johnson's summary of the information given by other Swedish writers about the Delawares.

In the first part of the eighteenth century David Brainerd, a religious zealot, provided some insights into religious customs, but little more. Peter Kalm, the great Swedish scientist, was in North America between 1748 and 1751 and has given a little information about the Delawares, chiefly ethnobotanical. By far the most important sources of information about them in the eighteenth century were David Zeisberger and

[2]Myers, 1912, p. 5.
[3]*Ibid.*, p. 311.

John Heckewelder, both Moravian missionaries to the Delawares. They lived with the Delawares many years (in Zeisberger's case for more than fifty) and learned their language. Zeisberger was perhaps more ethnocentric and biased in his attitudes about the Delawares, although he viewed them more realistically than did Heckewelder. Heckewelder was more sympathetic towards them, but had a somewhat more romanticized conception of them than did Zeisberger. Neither man gave much information on religion, but in other respects they seem to have understood and written about the Delawares in a relatively thorough manner, considering the time and their occupations. Since they lived among the Delawares at a time when the culture was changing rapidly, their journals are valuable both for their ethnographic content and for the information they provide on culture change. A number of other sources of information concerning the eighteenth-century Delawares were used, but they were mostly minor, and are not discussed here.

Three nineteenth-century sources of information which I have used extensively deserve some comment: the diary of Abraham Luckenbach, another Moravian missionary, the journal of Lewis Henry Morgan, and the manuscript by Charles C. Trowbridge. Luckenbach maintained a mission to the Delawares on the White River in Indiana between 1801 and 1806. He was the best ethnographer of all the Moravians in terms of his interest in the native culture. He was also, as far as I can determine, the only white person ever to view and describe the Big House Ceremony.

Dr. Leslie A. White very kindly loaned me a copy of the unpublished "Journal of a Visit to Kansas and Nebraska in May and June, 1859, Number IV," by Lewis Henry Morgan. This journal contains many interesting insights into the condition of Delaware culture in 1859. Comments are unnecessary on the utility and validity of this journal and upon the other information supplied by the father of American ethnography.

Charles C. Trowbridge was employed by Lewis Cass, Governor of Michigan Territory, to obtain answers to a pamphlet he had prepared entitled "Inquiries respecting the History, Traditions, Languages, Manners, Customs, Religion, Etc. of the Indians, Living within the United States." Trowbridge wrote a thirty-seven page manuscript, two copies of which with different titles are in the Michigan Historical Collections. Trowbridge gained the information for this work in 1824 on the White River. I have used this account fully, and have utilized Kinietz's passages relating to other manuscripts fostered by Cass.[4]

[4]Kinietz, 1946, pp. 15-18.

LITERATURE CITED

Abbott, C. C.
1875 The Stone Age in New Jersey. Smithsonian Ann. Rep. of 1875, pp. 246-380.

Acrelius, Israel
1876 A History of New Sweden; or, the Settlements on the River Delaware. Trans. from the Swedish with an introduction and notes by W. M. Reynolds. Mem. Hist. Soc. Penn., Vol. II.

Adams, R. C.
1905 Legends of the Delaware Indians and Picture Writing. Washington.
1906 A Brief History of the Delaware Indians. Washington. Senate Document No. 501, 59th Congress, 1st Session.

Annual Reports of the Commissioners of Indian Affairs. 1824-1848, published
1824-1875 with the reports of the War Department; 1849-1875, usually published as part of the Report of the Secretary of Interior. Washington.

Beatty, Charles
1798 The Journal of a Two-Months Tour: with a View of Promoting Religion among the Frontier Inhabitants. Edinburgh.

Benedict, R. F.
1923 The Concept of the Guardian Spirit in North America. Amer. Anthropol. Assoc. Mem., No. 29.

Berlin, A. F.
1887 Mode of Fishing by the Delaware Indians. Amer. Antiquarian and Orient. Journ., 9:167-69.

Bloomfield, Leonard
1946 Algonquian. *In* Linquistic Structures in Native America, by Harry Hoijer and others. Viking Fund Publ. in Anthropol., No. 6. New York. Pp. 85-129.

Bolton, R. P.
1920 New York City in Indian Possession. Indian Notes and Monographs. Mus. Amer. Indian, Heye Found.,2, No. 7:223-395.

Brainerd, Jonathan
1884 Memoirs of Reverend David Brainerd, Based on the Life of Brainerd, Prepared by Jonathan Edwards, D.D., and Afterwards Revised and Enlarged by S. E. Dwight. New York.

Brant, C. S.
1950 Peyotism among the Kiowa-Apache and Neighboring Tribes. Southwest. Journ. of Anthropol., 6, No. 2:212-22.

Brickell, John
1842 Narrative of John Brickell's Captivity Among the Delaware. Amer. Pioneer, ed. by John S. Williams. Cincinnati. 1:43-56.

Brinton, D. G.
1885 The Lenape and Their Legends, with the Complete Text and Symbols of the Walam Olum. Philadelphia.

1890 Folk-Lore of the Modern Lenape. Essays of an Americanist. Philadelphia. Pp. 181-92.

Browne, W. H. (ed.)
1896 Archives of Maryland. Maryland Hist. Soc. Baltimore.

Burggraf, J. D.
1938 Some Notes on the Manufacture of Wampum Prior to 1654. Amer. Antiq., 4:53-58.

Butler, Mary
1947 Two Lenape Rock Shelters Near Philadelphia. Amer. Antiq., 12:246-55.

Butterfield, C. W.
1882 Washington-Irvine Correspondence. The official letters which passed between Washington and Brig. Gen. William Irvine and between Irvine and others concerning military affairs in the West from 1781 to 1783. Madison.

Cross, Dorothy
1941 Archaeology of New Jersey. Archeol. Soc. New Jersey and the New Jersey State Mus., Vol. 1.
1953 Delaware and Related Horizons in New Jersey. Bull. Archeol. Soc. New Jersey, 6:7-13. Trenton.

Dankers, Jaspar, and Peter Sluyter
1867 Journal of a Voyage to New York and a Tour in Several of the American Colonies in 1679-80. Trans. from the original MS in Dutch for the Long Island Hist. Soc., ed. by H. C. Murphy. Mem. Long Island Hist. Soc. Brooklyn. Vol. I.

De Laet, Johan
1909 New World. *In* Narratives of New Netherland, ed. by J. F. Jameson. New York. Pp. 45-58.

Denton, Daniel
1845 A Brief Description of New York Formerly Called New Netherlands. London 1670. Ed. by John Pennington. Proc. Hist. Soc. Penn., Vol. 1, No. 1.

De Rasieres, Isaack
1909 Letter of Isaack de Rasieres to Samuel Blommaert, 1628 (?). *In* Narratives of New Netherland, ed. by J. F. Jameson. New York. Pp. 102-15.

De Smet, P. J.
1859 Western Missions and Missionaries: a Series of Letters. New York.

Devereux, George
1951 Reality and Dream: Psychotherapy of a Plains Indian. New York.

DeVoto, Bernard
1947 Across the Wide Missouri. Boston.

De Vries, D. P.
1857 Collections of the New York Historical Society. 2d. ser. New York. Vol. 3.
1909 From the Korte Historiael ende Journaels Aenteyckeninge, 1633-1643, (1655). *In* Narratives of New Netherland, ed. by J. F. Jameson. New York. Pp. 186-234.
1912 From the Korte Historiael ende Journaels Aenteycheninge, by David

Pietersz de Vries, 1630-1633, 1644 (1655). *In* Narratives of Early Pennsylvania, West New Jersey and Delaware, ed. by A. C. Myers. New York. Pp. 1-29.

Downes, R. C.
1940 Council Fires on the Upper Ohio. Pittsburgh.

Fenton, William N.
1942 Fish Drives among the Cornplanter Seneca. Penn. Archaeologist, 12:48-52.

Fisher, M. W.
1946 The Mythology of the Northern and Northeastern Algonkians in Reference to Algonkian Mythology as a Whole. *In* Man in Northeastern North America, ed. by Frederick Johnson. Papers of the Robert S. Peabody Found. for Archaeol., 3:226-62.

Flannery, Regina
1939 An Analysis of Coastal Algonquian Culture. Catholic Univ. of America, Anthropol. Ser., 7:1-219.

Foreman, C. G.
1946 Black Beaver. The Chronicles of Oklahoma, 24, No. 3:269-92.

Foreman, Grant (ed.)
1937 Adventure on Red River. Report on the Exploration of the Headwaters of the Red River by Captain Randolph B. Marcy and Captain G. B. McClellan. Norman, Oklahoma.
1946 The Last Trek of the Indians. Chicago.

Franklin, Benjamin
1939 Indian Treaties Printed by Benjamin Franklin, 1736-1762. With an Introduction by Carl Van Doren and Historical and Biographical Notes by Julian P. Boyd. Philadelphia.

Griffin, J. B.
1944 The Iroquois in American Prehistory. Papers Mich. Acad. Science, Arts, and Letters, 29:299-303.
1955 Review of: Walam Olum or Red Score: The Migration Legend of the Lenni Lenape or Delaware Indians. 1954. By Eli Lilly, *et al.* Indiana Mag. of Hist., LI, No. 1:59-66.

Gunther, Erna
1950 The Westward Movement of Some Plains Traits. Amer. Anthropologist, 52, No. 2:174-79.

Harrington, M. R.
1908 Vestiges of Material Culture Among the Canadian Delawares. Amer. Anthropologist, 10:408-18.
1913 A Preliminary Sketch of Lenape Culture. *Ibid.*, 15:208-235.
1921 Religion and Ceremonies of the Lenape. Indian Notes and Monographs, Mus. Amer. Indian, Heye Found., Vol. 19.

Hayes, John
1954 John Hayes' Diary and Journal of 1760, ed. by William A. Hunter. Penn. Archaeol., 24, No. 2:63-84. Milton.

Heckewelder, John
1799 Letter to Benjamin Smith Barton, Containing an Account of the Animal Called the Big Naked Bear. Trans. Amer. Philosoph. Soc., O.S., 4:260-62.

Heckewelder, John (Cont.)
1881 History, Manners, and Customs of the Indian Nations Who Once Inhabited Pennsylvania and the Neighboring States. New and rev. ed. Mem. Hist. Soc. Penn., Vol. 12.

Herman, M. W.
1950 A Reconstruction of Aboriginal Delaware Culture from Contemporary Sources. Kroeber Anthropol. Soc. Papers. Berkeley. No. 1:45-77.

Heye, G. G., and G. H. Pepper
1915 Exploration of a Munsee Cemetery near Montague, New Jersey. Contrib. Mus. Amer. Indian, Heye Found., Vol. 2, No. 1.

Hodge, F. W. (ed.)
1907 Handbook of the American Indians North of Mexico. Bur. Amer. Ethnol., Bull. 30, Pts. 1 and 2. Washington.

Holm, T. C.
1834 A Short Description of the Province of New Sweden, ed. by P. S. DuPonceau. Mem. Hist. Soc. Penn., Vol. 3, Pt. 1.

Howard, James H.
1955 Pan-Indian Culture of Oklahoma. Sci. Monthly, 81, No. 5:215-20.

Hrdlička, Alex
1902 The Crania of Trenton, New Jersey, and their Bearing upon the Antiquity of Man in the Region. Bull. Amer. Mus. Nat. His., Vol. 16, Art. III.

Hunt, G. T.
1939 The Wars of the Iroquois, A Study in Intertribal Trade Relations. Madison.

Hunter, William A.
1951 Provincial Negotiations with the Western Indians, 1754-58. Penn. Hist. Harrisburg. 18, No. 3:213-19.
1954 The Ohio, the Indian's Land. *Ibid.*, 21, No. 4:338-50.

Jameson, J. F. (ed.)
1909 Narratives of New Netherland, 1609-1664. New York.

Jemison, Mary
1918 A Narrative of the Life of Mary Jemison. Rev. by Charles D. Vail. 20th ed. New York

Johnson, Amandus
1917 The Indians and Their Culture as Described in Swedish and Dutch Records. Proc. Internat. Congress of Americanists. Washington. 19:277-82.

Juet, Robert
1909 *From* The Third Voyage of Master Henry Hudson. 1610. *In* Narratives of New Netherland, ed. by J. F. Jameson. New York. Pp. 16-28.

Kalm, Peter
1937 Peter Kalm's Travels in North America. The English Version of 1770, rev. from the original Swedish and ed. by A. B. Benson. New York. 2 vols.

Kenny, James
1913 Journal of James Kenny. Penn. Mag. Hist. and Biog, ed. by J. W. Jordan. 37:1-47, 152-210.

Ketchum, William
1865. An Authentic History of Buffalo, New York. Buffalo. 2 Vols.

Kinietz, Vernon
1940 European Civilization as a Determinant of Native Indian Customs. Amer. Anthropologist, 42, No. 1:116-21.
1946 Delaware Culture Chronology. Prehist. Res. Ser., Indiana Hist. Soc., 3, No. 1.

Kroeber, A. L.
1947 Cultural and Natural Areas of Native North America. Berkeley.
1948 Anthropology. New ed., rev. New York.

LaBarre, Weston
1938 The Peyote Cult. Yale Univ. Publ. in Anthropol., No. 19.

LaBarre, Weston, David P. McAllester, J. S. Slotkin, Omer C. Stewart, Sol Tax
1951 Statement on Peyote. Science, 114:582-83.

Lilly, Eli
1944 Tentative Speculations on the Chronology of the Walam Olum and the Migration Route of the Lenape. Proc. Indiana Acad. Sci., 54:33-40.

Lilly, Eli, C. F. Voegelin, Erminie W. Voegelin, Joe E. Pierce, Paul Weer, Glenn A. Black, and Georg K. Neumann.
1954 Walam Olum or Red Score: The Migration Legend of the Lenni Lenape or Delaware Indians. Indianapolis. Pp. 379.

Lindestrom, Peter
1925 Geographia Americae with an Account of the Delaware Indians Based on Surveys and Notes Made in 1654-1656 by Peter Lindestrom. Trans. and ed. by Amandus Johnson. The Swedish Colonial Soc. Philadelphia.

Linton, Ralph
1940 Acculturation in Seven American Indian Tribes. New York
1943 Nativistic Movements. Amer. Anthropologist, 45:230-40.

Loskiel, G. H.
1794 History of the Mission of the United Brethren Among the Indians of North America. Trans. from the German by Christian Ignatius la Trobe. London.

Loudon, Archibald
1808-11 A Selection of Some of the Most Interesting Narratives of Outrages Committed by the Indians in their Wars with the White People. Carlisle, Pa. 2 Vols.

Lowie, R. H.
1920 Primitive Society. New York.

Luckenbach, Abraham
1938 The Moravian Indian Mission on White River; Diaries and Letters, May 5, 1799, to November 12, 1806, ed. by L. H. Gipson. Indiana Hist. Coll. Indianapolis. Vol. 23.

MacLeod, W. C.
1922 The Family Hunting Territory and Lenape Political Organization. Amer. Anthropologist, 24:448-63.

MacNeish, R. S.
1952 Archeology of the Northeastern United States. *In* Archeology of the Eastern United States, ed. by J. B. Griffin. Chicago. Pp. 46-58.

McClure, David
1899 Diary of David McClure. Written in 1748-1820. Ed. by Franklin Dexter. New York.

Mahr, August C.
1951 Materia Medica and Therapy among the North American Forest Indians. Ohio State Archaeol. and Hist. Quart., 60, No. 4:331-54.
1952 The Conversion of Chief Echpalawehund. Reprint from Archiv für Reformationsgesch. Pp. 212-34. No imprint.
1954 Aboriginal Culture Traits as Reflected in 18th Century Delaware Indian Tree Names. Ohio Journ. Sci., 54, No. 6:380-87.
1955 Semantic Analysis of Eighteenth-Century Delaware Indian Names for Medicinal Plants. Ethnohistory, 2, No. 1:11-28.

Mead, Margaret
1932 Changing Culture of an Indian Tribe. New York.

Michelson, Truman
1912 Preliminary Report on the Linguistic Classification of Algonquian Tribes. 28th Ann. Rep. Bur. Amer. Ethnol. Washington.

Mitchell, S. H.
1895 The Indian Chief, Journeycake. Philadelphia.

Mooney, James
1911 Passing of the Delaware Nation. *In* Proc. Mississippi Valley Hist. Assoc., ed. by B. F. Shambaugh. Cedar Rapids. 3:329-40.
1928 The Aboriginal Population of America North of Mexico, ed. by J. R. Swanton. Smithsonian Misc. Coll., 80, No. 7:1-40.

Morgan, L. H.
1859 Journal of a Visit to Kansas and Nebraska in May and June, 1859. Pt. IV. (Unpublished.)
1871 Systems of Consanguinity and Affinity. Smithsonian Instit. Publ., No. 28.
1877 Ancient Society. Holt ed. New York.

Myers, A. C. (ed.)
1912 Narratives of Early Pennsylvania, West New Jersey and Delaware, 1630-1707. New York.

Murdock, G. P.
1949 Social Structure. New York.

Murphy, H. C. (ed.)
1875 The Voyage of Verrazzano: A Chapter in the Early History of Maritime Discovery in America. New York.

Newcomb, W. W., Jr.
1950 A Re-examination of the Causes of Plains Warfare. Amer. Anthropologist, 52:317-30.
1955 The Walam Olum of the Delaware Indians in Perspective. Texas Journ. Sci., 7:57-63.
1955*b* A Note on Cherokee-Delaware Pan-Indianism. Amer. Anthropologist, 57, No. 5:1041-45.

O'Callaghan, E. B.
1850-51 The Documentary History of the State of New York. Albany. 4 vols.

Parkman, Francis
1893 The Conspiracy of Pontiac and the Indian War, after the Conquest of Canada. Tenth ed., rev., with additions. Boston. 2 vols.

Pastorius, F. D.
1912 Circumstantial Geographical Description of Pennsylvania. (Written in 1700.) *In* Narratives of Early Pennsylvania, West New Jersey and Delaware, ed. by A. C. Myers. New York. Pp. 360-448.

Peckham, H. H.
1947 Pontiac and the Indian Uprising. Princeton.

Penn, William
1882 The Life of William Penn: with Selections from his Correspondence and Autobiography, ed. by S. M. Janney. Sixth ed., rev. Philadelphia.
1912 Letter from William Penn to the Committee of the Free Society of Traders. *In* Narratives of Early Pennsylvania, West New Jersey and Delaware, ed. by A. C. Myers. New York. Pp. 231-35.

Petrullo, Vincenzo
1934 The Diabolic Root, A Study of Peyotism. The New Indian Religion Among the Delawares. Philadelphia.

Philhower, C. A.
1931 South Jersey Indians on the Bay, the Cape and the Coast. Proc. New Jersey Hist. Soc., N.S. 16, No. 1:1-21.
1953 The Historic Minisink Site. Bull. Archeol. Soc. New Jersey, No. 7: 1-9.

Rhodes, Willard
1952 Acculturation in North American Indian Music. *In* Acculturation in the Americas. Proc. and Selected Papers of the XXIXth Internat. Congress of Americanists, ed. by Sol Tax. Chicago. Pp. 127-32.

Ritchie, W. A.
1938 A Perspective of Northeastern Archeology. Amer. Antiq., 4:94-112.
1944 The Pre-Iroquoian Occupations of New York State. Rochester Mus. Arts and Sciences. Mus. Mem., No. 1.
1949 The Bell-Philhower Site, Sussex County New Jersey. Indiana Hist. Soc., Prehist. Res. Ser., Vol. 3, No. 2.
1951 A Current Synthesis of New York Prehistory. Amer. Antiq., 17, No. 2:130-36.

Ruttenber, E. M.
1872 History of the Indian Tribes of Hudson's River, Their Origin, Manners and Customs; Tribal and Sub-Tribal Organizations: Wars, Treaties, etc. Albany.

Schweinitz, E. de (trans.)
1905 The Narrative of Marie Le Roy and Barbara Leinenger, for Three Years Captive Among the Indians. Penn. Mag. Hist. and Biog., 29:407-20.

Sipe, C. H.
1931 The Indian Wars of Pennsylvania. An Account of the Indian Events in Pennsylvania of the French and Indian War, Pontiac's War, Lord Dunmore's War, and Revolutionary War and the Indian Uprising from 1789 to 1795. 2d ed. Harrisburg.

Skinner, Alanson
1909 The Lenape Indians of Staten Island. *In* Indians of Greater New York and the Lower Hudson, ed. by Clark Wissler. Anthropol. Papers Amer. Mus. Nat. Hist., Vol. 3.
1920 Two Lenape Stone Masks from Pennsylvania and New Jersey, Indian Notes and Monographs. Mus. Amer. Indian, Heye Found., pp. 5-7.
1947 The Indians of Manhattan Island and Vicinity. Amer. Mus. Nat. Hist., Science Leaflet, No. 41. Sixth ed.

Smith, C. S.
1950 The Archaeology of Coastal New York. Amer. Mus. Nat. Hist., Anthropol. Papers, Vol. 43, Pt. 2.
1955 Revised Chronology for the Archeology of Coastal New York. Bull. Nassau Archeol. Soc. Sea Cliff, N. Y. I, No. 1:4-5.

Smith, John
1884 Captain John Smith .... Works. 1608-1631, ed. by Edward Arber. Birmingham, England.

Smith, Samuel
1877 History of the Colony of Nova Caesaria or New Jersey. Burlington.

Snyderman, George S.
1948 Behind the Tree of Peace: A Sociological Study of Iroquois Warfare. Penn. Archaeologist, 18, Nos. 3-4. 93 pp.
1955 The Functions of Wampum. Proc. Amer. Philosoph. Soc., 98:469-94.

Speck, F. G.
1915 The Family Hunting Band as the Basis of Algonkian Social Organization. Amer. Anthropologist, 17:289-305.
1919 Functions of Wampum Among the Eastern Algonkian. Mem. Amer. Anthropol. Assoc., Vol. 6, No. 1.
1931 A Study of the Delaware Indian Big House Ceremony. Publ. Penn. Hist. Comm. Harrisburg. Vol. 2.
1937 Oklahoma Delaware Ceremonies, Dances, and Feasts. Mem. Amer. Philosop. Soc. Philadelphia. Vol. 7.
1941 Gourds of the Southeastern Indians. Boston.
1943 The Wapanachki Delawares and the English: Their Past as Viewed by an Ethnologist. Penn. Mag. Hist. and Biog., 67:319-44.
1947 Eastern Algonkian Block-Stamp Decoration. Archeol. Soc. New Jersey, The State Mus., Res. Ser., No. 1.
1948 Critical Comments on "Delaware Culture Chronology." Amer. Anthropologist, 50:723-24.
1950 Iconology and the Masking Complex in Eastern North America. Univ. Penn. Mus. Bull., 15, No. 1:31-47.

Spier, Leslie
1925 The Distribution of Kinship Systems in North America. Univ. Washington Publ. in Anthropol., 1:69-88.

Stuart, Charles
1926 The Captivity of Charles Stuart, 1755-57, ed. by B. W. Bond. Mississippi Valley Hist. Rev., 13:58-81.

Swanton, J. R.
1952 The Indian Tribes of North America. Smithsonian Instit., Bur. Amer. Ethnol. Bull., No. 145.

Tantaquidgeon, Gladys
1942 A Study of Delaware Indian Medicine Practice and Folk Beliefs. Commonwealth of Pennsylvania, Dept. Public Inst. Penn. Hist. Comm. Harrisburg.

Thomas, Gabriel
1912 An Historical and Geographical Account of Pennsylvania and of West New Jersey. Written in 1689. *In* Narratives of Early Pennsylvania, West New Jersey and Delaware, ed. by A. C. Myers. New York. Pp. 313-52.

Thompson, C. N.
1937 Sons of the Wilderness. Indiana Hist. Soc. Indianapolis.

Trowbridge, C. C.
n.d. Account of Some of the Traditions, Manners, and Customs of the Lenee Lenaupaa or Delaware Indians. Mich. Hist. Coll. Unpublished. Ann Arbor.

Van der Donck, Adriaen
1909 Of the Americans or Natives, their Appearance, Occupations, and Means of Support. *From* The Representation of New Netherland, 1650. *In* Narratives of New Netherland, ed. by J. F. Jameson. New York. Pp. 300-303.

Voegelin, C. F.
1946 Delaware, An Eastern Algonquian Language. *In* Linguistic Structures in Native America. Viking Fund Publ. in Anthropol. New York. 6:130-57.

Voegelin, C. F., and E. W. Voegelin
1946 Linguistic Considerations of Northeastern North America. *In* Man in Northeastern North America, ed. by Frederick Johnson. Papers of the R. S. Peabody Found. for Archaeol., 3:178-94.

Voegelin, E. W.
1940 Culture Parallels to the Delaware Walam Olum. Proc. Indiana Acad. Sci., 49:28-31.
1944 Mortuary Customs of the Shawnee and Other Eastern Tribes. Prehist. Res. Ser., Indiana Hist. Soc., II, No. 4:227-444.

Wallace, A. F. C.
1947 Woman, Land, and Society: Three Aspects of Aboriginal Delaware Life. Penn. Archaeologist, 17:1-35.
1949 King of the Delawares: Teedyuscung. 1700-1763. Philadelphia.

Wassenaer, N. Van
1909 *From* the Historisch Verhael, by Nicolaes Van Wassenaer, 1624-1630. *In* Narratives of New Netherland, ed. by J. F. Jameson. New York. Pp. 67-96.

Weslager, C. A.
1943 Delaware's Forgotten Folk, the Story of the Moors and Nanticokes. Philadelphia.
1944 The Delaware Indians as Women. Journ. Washington Acad. Sci., 34:381-88.
1950 Indians of the Eastern Shore of Maryland and Virginia. *In* The Eastern Shore of Maryland and Virginia, ed. by Charles B. Clark. New York. 1:39-69.

White, L. A.
1939 A Problem in Kinship Terminology. Amer. Anthropologist, 41:566-73.
1949 The Science of Culture. New York.

Wirth Louis
1945 The Problem of Minority Groups. *In* Science of Man in the World Crisis, ed. by Ralph Linton. New York. Pp. 347-72.

Wissler, Clark
1917 The American Indian. New York.
1941 Indians of the United States. New York.

Wright, M. H.
1951 A Guide to the Indian Tribes of Oklahoma. Norman.

Zeisberger, David
1776 Essay of a Delaware-Indian and English Spelling-book. Philadelphia. Pp. 113.
1871 The Life and Times of David Zeisberger. *In* The Western Pioneer and Apostle of the Indians, ed. by Edmund De Schweinitz. Philadelphia.
1885 Diary of David Zeisberger, a Moravian Missionary Among the Indians of Ohio. Trans. from the Original German MS by E. F. Bliss. Cincinnati. 2 vols.
1887 Zeisberger's Indian Dictionary, ed. by Eben Norton Horsford. Cambridge. Pp. 236.
1910 David Zeisberger's History of Northern American Indians. Reprinted from Ohio Archaeol. and Hist. Quart., Vol. 19, Nos. 1 and 2, 189 pp.

www.ingramcontent.com/pod-product-compliance
Lightning Source LLC
LaVergne TN
LVHW050022250826
846302LV00008B/57